MW01286038

HOMILETICS
AND
PASTORAL THEOLOGY

WILLIAM G. T. SHEDD

SOLID GROUND CHRISTIAN BOOKS
BIRMINGHAM, ALABAMA

SOLID GROUND CHRISTIAN BOOKS
PO Box 660132, Vestavia Hills, AL 35266
205-443-0311
sgcb@charter.net
http://www.solid-ground-books.com

Homiletics and Pastoral Theology

by William G.T. Shedd (1820-1894)

Taken from the 1965 edition by Banner of Truth Books

Published by Solid Ground Christian Books

Classic Reprints Series

First printing October 2003

ISBN: 1-932474-15-3

Manufactured in the United States of America

PREFATORY NOTE.

MOST of the materials of this treatise were originally composed, in the form of Lectures, in the years 1852 and 1853, when the author held the Professorship of Sacred Rhetoric and Pastoral Theology in Auburn Theological Seminary. Upon entering on other lines of study and instruction, they were thrown aside. Several of them within the last two years have appeared in the *American Theological Review ;* and the interest which they seemed to awaken has led to the revision of the whole series, and to their combination (with two or three other Essays upon kindred topics) into the form of a book. Although constructed in this manner, the author believes that one 'increasing purpose' runs through the volume, and hopes that it may serve to promote, what is now the great need of the Church, a masculine and vigorous Rhetoric, wedded with an earnest and active Pastoral zeal.

CONTENTS.

———

HOMILETICS.

CHAPTER I.

PAGE

RELATION OF SACRED ELOQUENCE TO BIBLICAL EXEGESIS, . . 1

CHAPTER II.

DISTINCTIVE NATURE OF HOMILETICS, AND REASONS FOR ITS CUL-
TIVATION, ... 33

CHAPTER III.

FUNDAMENTAL PROPERTIES OF STYLE, ... 51

CHAPTER IV.

GENERAL MAXIMS FOR SERMONIZING, ... 92

CHAPTER V.

SPECIAL MAXIMS FOR SERMONIZING, ... 111

CHAPTER VI.

THE DIFFERENT SPECIES OF SERMONS, ... 126

CHAPTER VII.

THE NATURE AND CHOICE OF A TEXT, ... 139

CHAPTER VIII.

THE PLAN OF A SERMON, ... 156

CHAPTER IX.

EXTEMPORANEOUS PREACHING, ... 190

CHAPTER X.

THE MATTER, MANNER, AND SPIRIT OF PREACHING, . . . 214

CHAPTER XI.

RECIPROCAL RELATIONS OF PREACHER AND HEARER, . . . 226

CHAPTER XII.

LITURGICAL CULTIVATION OF THE PREACHER, ... 259

PASTORAL THEOLOGY.

CHAPTER I.

DEFINITION OF PASTORAL THEOLOGY, ... 279

CHAPTER II.

RELIGIOUS CHARACTER AND HABITS OF THE CLERGYMAN, . . 282

CHAPTER III.

INTELLECTUAL CHARACTER AND HABITS OF THE CLERGYMAN, . . 302

CHAPTER IV.

SOCIAL AND PROFESSIONAL CHARACTER OF THE CLERGYMAN, . . 325

CHAPTER V.

PASTORAL VISITING, ... 340

CHAPTER VI.

CATECHISING, ... 356

HOMILETICS.

CHAPTER I.

THE sources of Sacred Eloquence, it is evident, must lie deeper than those of secular oratory. That address from the Christian pulpit, which, in its ultimate results, has given origin to all that is best in human civilisation and hopeful in human destiny, must have sprung out of an intuition totally different from that which is the secret of secular and civil oratory. It is conceded by all, that eloquence is the product of ideas ; and therefore, in endeavouring to determine what is the real and solid foundation of pulpit oratory, we must, in the outset, indicate the range of ideas and the class of truths from which it derives both its subject-matter and its inspiration. These we shall find in divine revelation, as distinguished from human literature. The Scriptures of the Christian Church, and not the writings of the great masters of secular letters, are the *fons et origo* of sacred

B

eloquence. It will therefore be the aim of this introductory chapter, in a treatise upon Homiletics, to consider the influence, in *oratorical* respects, upon the preacher, of the thorough exegesis and mastery of the Word of God. And in order to perform this task with most success and convincing power, it will be necessary to make some preliminary observations upon the nature of the written revelation itself, and particularly upon the relation in which the human mind stands to it.

The opening of one of the most sagacious and suggestive of modern treatises in philosophy reads as follows : ' Man, as the minister and interpreter of nature, does and understands as much as his observations on the order of nature, either with regard to matter or to mind, permit him, and neither knows nor is capable of more.' [1] In this dictum of Lord Bacon, which he lays down as the corner-stone of his philosophical system, reflecting and speculating man is represented to be an interpreter. The function of the philosopher is not to originate truth, but to explain it. He is to stand up before a universe of matter and a universe of mind, and his office is to interrogate them, and hear what they say : he is not to attempt an exertion of his own power upon them in order to reconstruct them, and thereby put a meaning into them. He is not to distort them, by injecting into them his own prejudices and preconceptions ; but, simply going up to them with reverence and with freedom, he is to take them just as they are, and to question them just as they stand, until he gets *their* answer. The spirit of a philosopher, then,

[1] Bacon, *Novum Organum*, Aph. 1.

according to this sagacious Englishman, is no other than the spirit of an *interpreter;* if we might employ his own proud phrase, 'Francis Verulam thought' that the great aim and office of philosophy is *hermeneutical.* The result of all speculative inquiry into the world of matter and of mind, according to this wise and substantial thinker, should be an *exegesis, an explanation.* Under the impulse and guidance of this theory, modern science, more particularly in the sphere of material nature, has made progress. That wise and prudent interrogation of nature, which has been so characteristic of the last two centuries, has yielded a clear and loud response. The world of matter has replied to many of the questions that have been put to it. The stone has cried out of the wall, and the beam out of the timber has answered.

But if this is true and fruitful in philosophy, it is still more so in theology. The duty and function of the theologian is most certainly that of an interpreter, and that alone. With yet more positiveness may we adapt the phraseology of the opening sentence of the *Novum Organum,* and say, 'Man, as the minister and interpreter of revelation, does and understands as much as his observations on the order and structure of revelation permit him, and neither knows nor is capable of more.' For revelation is as much the product of the divine intelligence as the worlds are the product of the divine power. Man confessedly did not originate the world, and neither did man originate the Christian Scriptures. The ultimate authorship of each alike carries us back to the Infinite. For though in the propagation of the species, and the sustentation of animal life upon the planet, the creature oftentimes seems to have an agency analogous to that of the Creator himself, yet we well know that all things in the material universe are of God ultimately ; so, likewise, though in the production of those documents which make up the canon of inspiration, many individual men were employed with a freedom and spontaneousness that looks like original authorship, yet it was the infinite and all-knowing intelligence of God which is the head-spring, the *fons fontium* of it all.

The attitude, therefore, of the human mind toward revelation should be precisely the same as toward nature. The naturalist does not attempt to mould the mountains to his patterns; and the theologian must not strive to pre-configure the Scriptures to his private opinions. The mountain is an *object*, positive, fixed, and entirely independent of the eye that looks upon it ; and that mass of truth which is contained in the Christian Scriptures is also an *object*, positive, fixed, and entirely independent of the individual mind that contemplates it. The crystalline humour of the eye is confessedly passive in relation to the mountain mass that looms up before it in majesty and in glory. It receives an impression and experiences a sensation, not mechanically or chemically, indeed, as wax melts before fire, or as an alkali effervesces under an acid, yet inevitably and in accordance with the real and independent nature of the mountain. And the moral mind of man, in relation to the moral truth of God which is set over against it in his revelation, should in like manner be recipient, and take an impression that issues inevitably from the nature and qualities of fixed and eternal truth. Neither in the instance of the eye nor of the mind is the function that of authorship or origination; it is that of living recipiency and acquiescence. In the presence of both nature and revelation, man, as Lord Bacon phrases it, is a minister and interpreter, and not a creator and lord.

The talent, then, which comprehends the revelation of the Eternal Mind, is not creative but exegetical. The etymology of the term exegesis implies a leading forth (ἐξηγέομαι) into the light of a clear perception, of an idea that is shut up in human language. It supposes words— words that are filled with thoughts that require to be conducted from behind the veil which covers them. Exegesis, therefore, implies a _written_ word. It supposes a _written_ revelation. There can be no interpretation unless thought has been vocalized, and fixed in outward symbols. An unwritten revelation, confined to the individual consciousness, never projected into language and never taking a literary form, could not be an object of critical examination, and could not yield the rich fruits of analysis and contemplation. Those theorizers who combat the doctrine of a 'book revelation,' and contend for only an internal and subjective communication from the mind of God to the mind of man, present a theory which, if it were transferred to the sphere of human literature, would bring all intellectual investigation and stimulation to a dead stop. If all the thinking of man were confined to consciousness,—if his ideas were never expressed in language, and written down in a literature that is the outstanding monument of what he has felt and thought,—if, within the sphere of secular thinking, man were limited to his isolated individualism, and were never permitted to fix his eye and mind upon the results to which fellow minds had come,—the most absolute stagnation would reign in the intellectual world. If, for illustration, we could conceive that the intellect of Newton had been able to go through those mathematical processes which are now embodied in his *Principia*, without expressing them in the symbols of mathematics and the propositions of human language,—if we could conceive of the *Principia* as held in his individual consciousness merely, and never presented in an outward form to become a κτῆμα ἰς ἀεί for all generations,—it is plain that the name of Newton would not be, as it now is, one of the intellectual forces and influences of the human race. All that mass of pure science which has been the subject-matter of mathematical exegesis for two centuries, and which has been the living germ out of which, by the method of interpretation, the fine growths of modern mathematics have sprung, would have gone into eternity and invisibility with the spirit of Newton, and 'left not a rack behind.'

I. Biblical Interpretation, therefore, postulates a written word and a sacred literature; and in now proceeding to notice some of the oratorical influences that issue from it, we mention, in the first place, the originality which it imparts to religious thinking and discourse. We shall maintain the position, that the sacred orator is quickened by the analytical study of the sacred volume into a freedom, freshness, and force, that are utterly beyond his reach without it.

Originality is a term often employed, rarely defined, and

very often misunderstood. It is frequently supposed to be equivalent to the creation of truth. An original mind, it is vulgarly imagined, is one that gives expression to ideas and truths that were never heard of before,—ideas and truths 'of which the human mind never had even an intimation or presentiment, and which come into it by a mortal leap, abrupt and startling, without antecedents and without premonitions.' But no such originality as this is possible to a finite intelligence. Such ab-originality as this is the prerogative of the Creator alone, and the results of it are a *revelation*, in the technical and strict sense of the term. Only God can create *de nihilo*, and only God can make a communication of truth that is absolutely new. Originality in man is always relative, and never absolute. Select, for illustration, an original thinker within the province of philosophy,—select the contemplative, the profound, the ever fresh and living Plato. Thoughtfully peruse his weighty and his musical periods, and ask yourself whether all this wisdom is the sheer make of his intellectual energy, or whether it is not rather an emanation and efflux from a mental *constitution* which is as much yours as his. He did not absolutely originate these first truths of ethics, these necessary forms of logic, these fixed principles of physics. They were inlaid in his rational structure by a higher Author, and by an absolute authorship; and his originality consists solely in their exegesis and interpretation. And this is the reason that, on listening to his words, we do not seem to be hearing tones that are wholly unknown and wholly unheard of. We find an answering voice to them in our own mental and moral constitution. In no contemptuous, but in a reverential and firm tone, every thinking person, even in the presence of the great thinkers of the race, may employ the language of Job in reference to self-evident truths and propositions: 'Lo, mine eye hath seen all this, mine ear hath heard and understood it. What ye know, the same do I know also; I am not inferior unto you.' And these great thinkers themselves are the first to acknowledge this. Upon the fact of a community in reason, a partnership in the common ideas of humanity, Plato himself founded his famous argument for the pre-existence of the soul. The very fact that every human creature recognises the first truths of science and of morals as no strange and surprising dogmas, but native and familiar, would imply, in his judgment, an earlier world, a golden time, when their acquaintance was made under brighter skies and under happier omens than here and now.[1]

Originality, then, within the sphere of a creature and in reference to a finite intelligence, consists in the power of interpretation. In its last analysis it is *exegesis*—the pure, genial, and accurate exposition of an idea or a truth already existing, already communicated, already possessed. Plato interprets his own rational intelligence; but he was not the author of that intelligence. He expounds his own mental and moral ideas; but those ideas are the handiwork of God. They are no more his than ours. We find what he found, no more and no less, if he has been a truthful exegete. The process in his instance and that of his reader, is simply that of education and elicitation. There

---

[1] Compare the Author's *Discourses and Essays*, p. 125 sq.

has been no creation, but only a development—no absolute authorship, but only an explication. And yet how fresh and original has been the mental process! The same substantially in Plato and in the thousands of his scholars; and yet in every single instance there has been all the enthusiasm, all the stimulation, all the ebullient flow of life and feeling that attends the discovery of a new continent or a new star.

> 'Then feels he like some watcher of the skies
> When a new planet swims into his ken;
> Or like stout Cortes, when with eagle eyes
> He stared at the Pacific, and all his men
> Looked at each other with a wild surmise,
> Silent, upon a peak in Darien.'

Originality in man, then, is not the power of making a communication of truth, but of apprehending one. Two great communications have been made to him,—the one in the book of nature, and the other in the book of revelation. If the truth has been conveyed through the mental and moral structure,—if it has been wrought by the creative hand into the fabric of human nature,—then he is the most original thinker who is most successful in reading it just as it reads, and expounding it just as it stands. If the truth has been communicated by miracle, by incarnation, and by the Holy Ghost,—if it has been imparted by special inspiration, and lies before him an objective and written revelation,—then he is the original thinker who is most successful in its interpretation,—who is most accurate in analyzing its living elements, and is most genial and cordial in receiving them into his own mental and moral being.

These observations find their enforcement and illustra-

tion the instant we apply them to the Christian Scriptures
and their interpretation. We have already noticed that,
in respect to the problems of religion, man can originate
nothing, but must take what he finds given to him from
the skies. Even if revealed religion be rejected, man does
not escape from the authority of fixed truth, unless he
adopt atheism and an absolute licentiousness of thought
and action. The doctrines of natural religion are a divine
communication, as really as those of revealed.[1] They are
immutable in their nature, and as independent of man's
will and prejudices, as those of Christianity itself. When
we wake up to moral consciousness, and begin to reflect
upon the principles of ethics that are wrought into our
moral constitution, we discover that we are already under
their domination and righteous despotism. We have no
option. Neither can we alter them; we cannot make a
hair of them white or black. We are compelled to take
them exactly as they are given. We must be passive and
submissive to what Cudworth denominates the 'immutable
morality,' which antedates all finite existence, and which
was in the beginning with God. And so likewise, when
we pass from the problems of natural religion to those of
revealed,—when we pass from the question concerning
human duty to the awful question concerning human sal-

---

[1] Hence St. Paul employs the same word (ἀποκαλύπτεται) to denote
the ultimate source of the truths of natural religion that he employs in
reference to the plan of redemption itself. The intuitive perception that
God will punish sin, is, in its last analysis, the product of the Creator
himself in the constitution of the human spirit. The ὀργὴ Θεοῦ, fearfully
apprehended in paganism, and the δικαιοσύνη Θεοῦ, known only in Christendom, are both alike 'revelations,'—the one being unwritten and the other
written.—See Rom. i. 17, 18.

vation,—we discover that the principles upon which this salvation reposes, and the methods by which it is to be accomplished, are settled in the heavens. What is written is written, and man the sinner, like man the moralist, must be recipient and submissive to the communication that is made. For the promises of Christianity are more entirely dependent upon the divine option and volition than are the principles of ethics and natural religion. The Deity is necessitated to punish sin, but is under no necessity of pardoning it. When, therefore, the human mind passes from ethics to evangelism, it is still more closely shut up to the record which God has given. If it must take morality just as it is communicated in reason and conscience, it must most certainly take mercy on the terms upon which it is offered in the written word; because these terms depend solely upon the will and decision of the pardoning power.

In this wise and docile recipiency of that which is fixed and eternal, we find the fountain of perennial youth and freshness for the sacred orator. For by it he is placed in vital relations to all that universe of truth which is contained in the Christian Scriptures. Think for a moment of their contents. Bring to mind the ideas and doctrines which hang like a constellation in these heavens. Think of the revelation made in them concerning the trinal unity of God, that infinite vortex of life, being, and blessedness, to which the meagre and narrow unit of deism presents such a feeble contrast. Think of the incarnation, in which all the plenitude of the divine nature blends and harmonizes with the winning helplessness and finiteness of a creature. Think of the ideas that are involved in the biblical account of the origin of man, his fall into the abyss of moral evil, and his recovery to innocence, to holiness, and to glory. Think of the kingdom of God, an idea wholly foreign to the best of the natural religions of the world, with its indwelling energy of the Divine Spirit, and its continual intercourse with the invisible and the eternal. Contemplate these *new* ideas that have been lodged in the consciousness of the human race by the Scriptures of the Old and New Dispensations; think of their suggestiveness, their logical connections, the new light which they flare upon the nature and destiny of man, the totally different colouring which they throw on the otherwise dark and terrible history of man on the globe; weigh this immense mass of truth and dogma in the scales of a dispassionate intelligence, and say if the mind of the preacher will not be filled with freshness, with force, and with originality, in proportion as it absorbs it.

For, to recur to our definition of originality, the human intellect is stirred into profound and genial action, only as it receives an impression from something greater and grander than itself. If it adopts the egoism of such a theory as that of Fichte, for example, and attempts to create from within itself, its action must be spasmodic and barren. To employ the often repeated comparison of Bacon, it is not the spider, but the bee, that is the truly original insect. Only as the sermonizer and orator, by a critical analysis of the biblical words and their connections, saturates his mind with the biblical elements ($\sigma\tau o\iota\chi\epsilon\tilde{\iota}\alpha$), and feeds upon revelation as the insect feeds upon foliage, until every cell and tissue is coloured with its food, will he discourse with freedom, suggestiveness, and energy.

The influence of such familiarity with revelation is well illustrated by that of the great products of uninspired literature. The effect of a continual and repeated perusal of Homer in animating the mind is well known. It starts the intellect into original action. The Greek fire glows in these poems, and kindles everything it touches. Though the range of ideas in the *Iliad* and *Odyssey* is cabined, cribbed, and confined, compared with that of a Dante or a Shakspeare, whose intuition has been immensely widened by the Christian revelation under which he lived and thought,—though the old epic in which the fall of Troy is sung cannot compare for a moment in breadth, depth, and vastness with the Christian epic in which the fall of man is told,—yet every scholar knows that, just in proportion as he imbibes the ideas and spirit of this single pagan poem, all tameness is banished from his own ideas, and all feebleness from his language. The reader of Gibbon's autobiography will notice in the abstract which the historian gives of his readings, that day after day the appointed task of perusing so many lines of the *Iliad* is recorded as having been faithfully performed. And, moreover, he will observe that the study is done in the light of the Port Royal Greek Grammar,—in the light of a careful investigation and mastery of the Greek verb.[1] Now we venture to affirm, that what there is of energy in the monotonous style of Gibbon, and what there is of originality and freshness in his naturally phlegmatic and heavy understanding,

[1] Gibbon, *Autobiography*, p. 444 *et passim*.

is due in no small degree to familiarity with the old bard
of Chios.   We have cited this as only one example of the
impulse to original action that is started in the mind by
the simple exegesis and interpretation of one truly grand
product of the human intellect.   Think of a similar contact with the Italian Dante or the English Chaucer, and
say whether originality is to be acquired by a dead lift,
or by a genial pressure and influence.

Returning now to the Christian Scriptures, we claim
that they are the great and transcendent source of originality and power for the human intellect.   The examples
which we have cited from the range of uninspired literature
fall far short of the reality, when we pass to the written
revelation of God.   Though grouped together in the most
artless and unambitious manner,—though the work of divers
ages and different minds,—though showing a variety and
inequality that pass through the whole scale of composition, from the mere catalogue in the Book of Chronicles
to the sublime ode in Isaiah or the Apocalypse,—though,
so far as mere artistic form and laboured attempt at impression are concerned, almost careless and indifferent,
—nevertheless the body of literature contained in the
Hebrew and Greek Scriptures has moved upon the mind
of man, in his generations, as the moon has moved upon
the sea.   The influence has been tidal.

'Exegesis,' says Niebuhr, 'is the fruit of *finished* study.'
This is a remark which that great historian makes in his
letter to a young philologist, which deserves to be perused
annually by every student, secular or sacred.   'Do not
read the great authors of classical antiquity,' he remarks,

'in order to make æsthetic reflections upon them, but in order to drink in their spirit, and fill your soul with their thoughts,—in order to gain that by reading which you would have gained by reverently listening to the discourses of great men. This is the philology which does the soul good; and learned investigations, even when we have got so far as to be able to make them, always occupy an inferior place. We must be fully masters of grammar (in the ancient sense); we must acquire every branch of antiquarian knowledge, as far as lies in our power; but even if we can make the most brilliant emendations, and explain the most difficult passages at sight, all this is nothing, and mere sleight-of-hand, if we do not acquire the wisdom and spiritual energy of the great men of antiquity, —think and feel like them.'[1] Precisely this is the aim and influence of biblical philology and exegesis. The theologian and preacher, by his patient study of the written revelation, must gain that by reading which he would have gained by reverently listening to the discourses of the prophets and apostles and the incarnate Son of God. And this is the uniform effect of close linguistic investigation. The power of a grammarian is a *vernacular* power. Turn, for illustration, to the commentaries of some of the Greek Fathers, such as Theodoret and Chrysostom, for example, and observe the close and vivid contact which is brought about between their minds and those of the sacred writers, by reason of their home-bred knowledge of the Greek language. These commentators are not equal to some of the great Latin Fathers

[1] Niebuhr, *Life and Letters,* pp. 426, 428.

in respect to the insight that issues from a profound dogmatical comprehension of Christian truth. So far as interpretation rests upon the analogy of faith and a comprehensive system, Chrysostom is inferior to Augustine. But in regard to everything that depends upon the *callida junctura verborum,*—upon the subtle nexus of verbs, nouns, and particles,—these exegetes, who were 'native and to the manner born,' must ever be the resort and the guide of the biblical student.[1]

Now, such an exegesis as this—an exegesis of the Scriptures that is the result of 'finished' study, and that fills the soul with the very thoughts and spiritual energy of the holy men of old who spake as they were moved by the Holy Ghost—is a well-spring of originality. The influence of it is strikingly illustrated by a comparison of the English pulpit of the sixteenth and seventeenth centuries with that of the eighteenth. The minds of Hooker and Howe, of Taylor and South, of Barrow and Bates, were thoroughly imbued with the substance and spirit of the written revelation. It was an age of belief, of profound religious convictions, of linguistic, reverent, and contemplative study of the Word of God. Secular literature itself was tinctured and tinged with the supernaturalism of the Bible. The plays of Shakspeare, nay, the licentious plays of the old English stage, are full of the awful workings of conscience. If men sinned, they suffered for it; if they committed adultery, they were burned in hell-fire therefor. This was the ethics, and this was the drama, of a period

[1] This remark holds true of that acute Greek commentator of the twelfth century, Euthymius Zigabenus, whom De Wette and Meyer so often quote.

for which God was a living person, the Bible an inspired book, and the future life a solemn reality. The strong sense and healthy genius of England had not yet sophisticated itself into the denial of God's holiness, and God's revelation, and the authority of the human conscience. Men had not learned, as they have since, to rush into sin, and then adjust their creed to their passions. Look now into the sermonizing and eloquence of these English divines, and feel the freshness and freedom that stamp them instantaneously as original minds. They differ much in style. Some exhibit an involved and careless construction; others a pellucid and rhythmical flow; and one of them, according to De Quincey, is the only rhetorician to whom, in company with Sir Thomas Brown (himself a reverent and a biblical mind), ' it has been granted to open the trumpet-stop on the great organ of passion.' But all alike are profound religious thinkers, and all alike are suggestive and original discoursers.

Pass now into the eighteenth century, and read the discourses of Alison and Blair. We have descended from the heights of inspired doctrine towards the level of natural religion; from the incarnation, the apostasy, the redemption, to the truth that virtue is right, and vice is wrong,—that man must be virtuous, and all will be well. How tame and unsuggestive are these smooth commonplaces! How destitute of any enlarging and elevating influence upon a thoughtful mind! How low the general range of ideas! And the secret of the torpor and tameness lies in the fact that these intellects had never worked their way into the deep mines of revelation, and found the ore in

c

the matrix.   It was an age in which biblical exegesis had
declined, and they had experienced only the more general
influences of the written Word.   The living elements themselves, the evangelical dogmas, had never penetrated and
moulded their thinking.

And as we look out into this nineteenth century, we
observe the same fact.   The only originality in the Church
or out of it, in sacred or in secular literature, is founded in
faith.   We are well aware that the age is fertile, and that
a rank growth of belles-lettres has sprung up during the last
twenty-five years, having its root in unbelief.   But it is a
crop of mushrooms.   There is nothing in it all that will
live one hundred years.   Compare this collection of sceptical poems, novels, and essays,—these slender attempts of
the modern naturalism to soar with a feeble wing into the
high heaven of invention,—with the unfaltering, sustained
sweep of Dante, steeped in religion, and that, too, the
religion of an intense supernaturalism ; or of Milton,
whose blood and brain were tinged through and through
with Hebrew ideas and beliefs ;—compare the light flutter
of the current sentimentalism with

> ' the pride and ample pinion
> That the Theban eagle bear,
>   Sailing with supreme dominion
> Through the azure deep of air ; '—

and tell us where wisdom shall be found, and where is the
place of understanding.

II.   We pass from this topic, to consider a second effect of
the exegesis and apprehension of the Christian revelation,
that bears yet more directly upon the office and functions

of the pulpit. The thorough exegesis and comprehension of the written Word of God endow the human mind with *authority.*

'By what authority doest thou these things? and who gave thee this authority to do these things?' was a question which the chief priests and the scribes and the elders put to Jesus Christ. If it was a natural question for them to ask of the Son of God, it is certainly a natural question for the secular, and especially the unbelieving, world to ask of the Christian herald. By what right does a mortal man rise upon the rostrum, and make positive statements concerning the origin of the human race, the dark mysterious beginnings of human history, the purposes and plans of the infinite Mind, and conclude with announcing the alternatives of eternal salvation and eternal damnation? With respect to these dark and difficult problems, all men stand upon a common level, if divine revelation is thrown out of the account. Apart from the light poured upon them by a communication from the Divine Mind, Confucius and Socrates have as much right to speculate and dogmatize as you or I. By what right, then, does that portion of the world which calls itself Christendom undertake to inform that portion of the world which is called heathendom, concerning God and the future life,—concerning the soul, its needs, its sorrows, and its doom? What authority has the Christian man above that of the pagan man in regard to the whole subject of religion, and who gave him this authority? Why does not Christendom, as it peers into the darkness beyond the tomb, look reverently to Mohammedanism for light? Why does Christianity insist that Mohammed shall come to the mountain; and why does the mountain refuse to go to Mohammed? As matter of fact, the entire human race is now receiving its lessons in theology and religion from only a portion of the race. In the outset, this portion which set itself up as the teachers of mankind was only a mere fragment of the sum-total—a mere handful of men in a corner of Palestine. The proportion has indeed greatly altered during the eighteen centuries that have elapsed since the death of Christ, but the vast majority of mankind are still pagan. the pupils still immensely outnumber the teachers. By what title does a mere fraction of the equally rational and equally immortal masses that crowd this planet, arrogate to itself the position of the tutor, and demand that the remaining majority take the attitude of the pupil? And, to narrow the circle, by what title does a small class of men rise up in Christian pulpits, and profess to impart instruction to the large congregations of their fellows and their equals, upon the most momentous and the most mysterious of themes?

Unless Christendom possesses a superior knowledge, it has no right to instruct heathendom; and unless the Christian clergy are endowed with the authority of a special revelation, and can bring credentials therefor, they have no right to speak to their fellow-men upon the subjects of human duty and destiny. The first and indispensable requisite, consequently, in both speculative theology and practical homiletics, is *authority;* and this authority must be found in a direct and special communication from the mind of God, or it can be found nowhere. Throw the

Scriptures out of the account, and the whole human race is upon a dead level. No one portion of it, no one age or generation of it, is entitled to teach another. That clear commanding tone, without which the Christian herald has no right to speak, and without which the world will not erect its ears and hear, cannot issue from ethics and natural religion. It must be the impulse and the vibration of the gospel. 'I am not ashamed,' says St. Paul, ' of the gospel of Christ: for it is the power of God.' Divine revelation, in his definition, is divine *power ;* and power is at the bottom of authority. Power generally is not ashamed, and needs not to be. In an age like this, when force is worshipped, when the hero and the Titan are set up as divinities, it will surely not be disputed that where there is power, there need be no hesitation or timidity ; and that whoever is really possessed of it, is entitled to speak out with a commanding and an authoritative intonation. By virtue, then, and only by virtue of its possession of the living oracles of God, Christendom is entitled to sound a trumpet, and tell the world in all its centuries, and all its grades of civilisation, that he that believeth shall be saved, and he that believeth not shall be damned. By virtue of his intuition and mastery of inspired ideas and doctrines, the Christian herald is entitled to attempt

> ' the height of the great argument,
> And justify the ways of God to men.'

1. In applying this topic more particularly to the position and duties of the sermonizer and preacher, we remark, in the first place, that the close exegetical study of the Scriptures imparts a calm and conscious authority, by

reducing the whole body of Holy Writ to harmony. The influence of doubt in respect to the symmetrical agreement and self-consistence of the Bible, is weakening in the highest degree. No sacred orator can be bold and commanding in his tone, if he believes or if he fears that there are fatal contradictions and irreconcilable inconsistencies in the written revelation. It is for this reason that infidelity is now applying its utmost acuteness and ingenuity to detect intrinsic and absolute contradictions in the sacred records. The four Gospels, in particular, are the field of operations. If it can be shown, if it can be demonstrated, that these biographies of the God-man fatally conflict with each other, then the portraiture of that personage who fills all history as the sun fills the hemisphere, becomes a fancy sketch, and Christianity disappears with its founder.

Now, we are certain and confident that the careful and minute study of the evangelists, in the light of grammar, of philology, and of history, results in the unassailable conviction of their trustworthiness. The process is one of those profound and unconscious ones which bring us to the goal before we are aware. The conviction that the four Gospels are organically connected, and constitute one living and perfect harmony, cannot be violently and quickly forced upon the mind. At first sight, the objections and difficulties fill the foreground ; particularly when protruded and pressed upon the notice by the dexterity of the biassed and hostile critic. But as, when we look upon a grand painting, in which there are a great variety and complexity and apparent contrariety of elements, it requires

some little time for the eye to settle gradually and unconsciously into the point from which the whole shapes itself
into harmony and beauty, so it requires wise delay, and
the slow penetration of scholarship and meditation, to
reach that centre from which all the parts of the evangelical biography arrange themselves harmoniously, and all
contradiction disappears for ever. And when this centre
is once reached, and the intrinsic, natural, *artless* harmony
is once perceived, there is repose, and there is boldness,
and there is authority. He who speaks of Christ out of
this intuition, speaks with freedom, with enthusiasm, with
love, and with power. Objections which at first seemed
acute, now look puerile. The piecemeal criticism which,
like the fly,[1] scans only the edge of a plinth in the great
edifice upon which it crawls, disappears under a criticism
that is all-comprehending and all-surveying.

2. And similar to this, in the second place, is the influence of a clear understanding of the dogmatic matter of
revelation. This results in a self-consistent theological
system, and this endows the mind with authority. Say
what men may, it is doctrine that moves the world. He
who takes no position will not sway the human intellect.
Logical men, dogmatic men, rule the world. Aristotle,
Kant, Augustine, Calvin,—these are names that instantaneously suggest systems; and systems that are exact,
solid, and maintain their place from century to century.
And when the system is not a mere product of the human

---

[1] ' Why has not a man a microscopic eye ?
For this plain reason, man is not a fly.'
Pope, *Essay on Man*, i. 6.

mind, like a scheme of philosophy or a theory of art, but is really the scheme and system of God himself imparted to his creatures, and certified to them by miracle, by incarnation, and by the Holy Ghost,—when the body of doctrine has a celestial origin,—it endows the humble and docile recipient of it with a preternatural authority. That which is finite can never inspire and embolden the human soul like that which is infinite. The human mind is indeed a grand and noble intelligence, and we are the last to disparage or vilify its products. We look with respect and veneration upon the great names in all the literatures. We exclaim, with Hamlet, 'How noble in reason! in apprehension how like a god!' But when we are brought face to face with the problems of religion,—when the unknown issues of this existence press heavily upon the apprehensive soul,—when the vortex of eternity threatens to ingulf the feeble immortal,—how destitute of authority and certainty are all the utterances and communications of these heroes of human literature! When I rise into this plane of thought, and propose this class of questions, I need a voice from the open sky to assure me. I demand an authority that issues from God himself, before I can be certain and assured in my own mind, and still more before I can affirm with positiveness and power to the minds of others.

It is here that we observe the difference between the dogmatism of a philosopher and that of a theologian; between the positiveness of the secular and that of the Christian mind. Compare Immanuel Kant with John Calvin. No human being has been more successful than the sage of Königsberg in giving an exact and transparent expression to what he himself denominates ' pure reason.' The crystal under his chemistry acquires a second crystallization. The rational intelligence of man, as developed and expressed by him, answers to the description of wisdom in the apocryphal book : ' She is more mobile than any motion; she penetrates and passes through all things by reason of her pureness.' [1] But it is finite reason; it is human intelligence only. The questions that are raised, and the answers that are given, pertain to a limited province. Within this province, the philosopher is clear as the sun, positive, and dogmatic of right. He knows whereof he affirms, and speaks with a corresponding authority. But when I pass these limits, and invite him to pass them, I hear another tone. The positiveness and the certainty disappear, and we are both alike left to querying and vague conjecture. What can he tell me with confidence and certainty concerning the interior and absolute essence of God ? Does the trinal unity dawn within the hemisphere of his ' pure reason ?' Does he know the name of the first man ? Can he describe to me the origin of that dark ground of evil which, by his own confession, inheres in every human will ? Can he tell me with authority and certainty, when the decaying body is being lowered to its resting-place in the heart of the earth, that ' all that dust shall rise ?' Does he know that there is pity in those stern and ethical heavens which shut down like brass over a guilty and terrified human conscience ? The authority and dogmatic certainty of the philosopher

[1] Wisdom vii. 24.

stop at the limits of his domain; and it is here that the authority and certainty of the theologian begin. Turn to the *Institutes* of the man of Geneva, and observe the boldness and high certainty of that naturally cautious and careful understanding, upon these very themes which make the man of Königsberg to hesitate and waver. Read those words with which Calvin closes, as with a clarion peal, his great argument for the necessity of the Reformation, and say whence come the sublime confidence and overcoming energy: 'We know, and are verily persuaded, that what we preach is the eternal truth of God. It is our wish, and a very natural one, that our ministry might prove beneficial and salutary to the world; but the measure of success is for God to give, not for us to demand. If this is what we have deserved at the hands of men whom we have struggled to benefit, to be loaded with calumny, and stung with ingratitude, that men should abandon success in despair, and hurry along with the current to utter destruction, then this is my voice (I utter words worthy of the Christian man, and let all who are willing to take their stand by this holy profession subscribe to this response): "Ply your fagots." But we warn you, that even in death we shall become the conquerors; not simply because we shall find, even through the fagots, a sure passage to that upper and better life, but because our blood will germinate like precious seed, and propagate that eternal truth of God which is now so scornfully rejected by the world.'[1] This is the positiveness, this is the high celestial dogmatism, that is necessitated by the reception of divine

[1] Calvin, *Necessity of the Reformation, sub fine.*

revelation. There is no option. There may be natural timidity; there may be the shrinking nature of the weeping prophet; but the instant the mind perceives that the eternal Intelligence has originated and communicated a series of revelations, the instant the ear hears the 'Thus saith the Lord,' a transformation takes place, and human weakness becomes immortal strength.

We have thus considered, in a rapid manner, two oratorical influences and effects of the apprehension of revealed truth. Originality and authority issue from this source as from no other. If Sacred Eloquence is to maintain its past commanding position in human history, and is to exert a paramount influence upon human destiny, it must breathe in and breathe out from every pore and particle the living afflatus of inspiration. By this breath of life it must live. If the utterances of the pulpit are to be fresh, spiritual, and commanding, the sacred orator must be an exegete. Every discourse must be but the elongation of a text.

And certainly there never was greater need of originality and authority within the province of religion than now. The cultivated unbeliever is fast settling down upon the low commonplaces of ethics and natural religion, or else is on his way to the arid sands of atheism, and all the freshness of his mind is being dried up. Rejecting all mystery, which is confessedly the parent and nurse of high thinking and lofty feeling; rejecting all supernaturalism, by which alone God comes into quickening and personal contact with his creatures; throwing out of his creed all those truths upon which Christendom rests, and

without which a Christendom is impossible, and reducing
the whole *credenda* and *agenda* of man to the merest and
most meagre minimum,—what can he do toward the im-
pregnation and fertilizing of the human mind ? Look at
the two or three religious dogmas, starved and hunger-
bitten, which are left to the human intelligence after his
manipulations, and tell us if literature and art and philosophy will be characterized by originality, if his methods
prevail. Tell us if pantheism will produce another Shakspeare, if anti-supernaturalism will produce another Milton, if a nerveless, voluptuous naturalism will produce
another Dante. Unless the coming literature of England
and America shall receive a fresh impulse and inspiration
from the old Christian ideas which penetrated and enlivened it in the days of its glory, the future will witness
the utter decline and decay of one of the noblest literatures of the world. The age of sophistry, the age of
pedants, the age of critics, the age of elegant languor, will
come in, and the Anglo-Norman mind, like the Greek and
Roman before it, will give place to the bolder and more
original intelligence of a more believing and solemn race.

The same remark is even more true, when we pass
from the wide domain of general literature to a particular
province in it, like Sacred Eloquence. The Christian
pulpit in this age is in danger of losing its originality, because it is tempted to leave the written revelation and
betake itself to lower and uninspired sources of thought.
Listen to those who neglect the constituent and organific
ideas of Christianity,—the doctrines of sin and guilt, of
grace and redemption,—and who find their themes in that

range of truths which every student sees scattered over
the pages of Plato and Cicero, of Antoninus and Seneca,
and tell us if they are original and stirring homiletes.
The doctrines of natural religion are differentiated from
those of revealed, by the fact that they will not bear everlasting repetition and constant expansion and illustration.
You cannot preach year after year upon the immortality
of the soul and the nature of virtue, and preserve the
theme ever fresh and new. There is a limit in this direction that cannot be passed with safety. But it is not so
with the distinctively Christian truths. Even the dark,
solemn theme of human corruption, expounded by one
who has been instructed out of the written revelation, and
the thronging, bursting consciousness of his own soul,—
even this sorrowful and abstractly repellent theme, when
enunciated in a genuinely biblical manner, fascinates the
natural man himself like the serpent's eye. Such a
preacher is always felt to be original. Men never charge
him with tameness and feebleness. And still more is this
true of that other and antithetic doctrine of the divine
mercy in the blood of the God-man. This string may be
struck with the plectrum year after year, century after
century, and its vibration is ever resonant and thrilling,
yet sweet and Æolian.

And certainly the age requires in its religious heralds
and teachers that other characteristic of authority. If a
man speak at all, he must speak as the oracles of God; he
must speak oracularly and positively. For the intellectual
world is now an arena of contending ideas and systems.
Think you that all the dogmatism of the time is within

the precincts of theology and the Church ? Think you that scepticism stands meek and hesitating, like the ass which Sterne describes, which seemed to invite abuse, and to say to every passer-by : 'Don't kick me, but if you will, you may ? ' No ! all ideas, the false as well as the true, —all systems, the heretical as well as the orthodox,—are positive and assertory. It is no time, therefore, for Christianity,—the only system that has a right to say to the world, ' Thou shalt,' and ' Thou shalt not,'—the only system that has a right to utter its high and authoritative, ' He that believeth shall be saved, and he that believeth not shall be damned,'—it is no time for that absolute and ultimate religion, in and by which this miserable and ruined race must live or bear no life, to be deprecatory, and ' borrow leave to be.'

If such, then, be the relation existing between Sacred Eloquence and Biblical Exegesis, the Christian ministry ought to lay deep the foundations of its address to the popular mind, in the understanding and interpretation of the Word of God. The proper function of the preacher is to put strictly revealed doctrine into oratorical forms for popular impression, and to imbue all discourse in the sanctuary and upon the Sabbath with a strictly biblical spirit. For, after all, it is the *spirit* of a book, the *spirit* of an author, which is of chief importance. Pascal has left an instructive and quickening fragment upon the ' geometrical spirit.' It is the spirit of demonstration,—that bent and tendency in an intellectual person which spontaneously inclines him to define accurately whatever is capable of definition, and to prove irrefragably whatever

is capable of proof. Whoever possesses this spirit, takes
geometry with him wherever he goes. Of such a human
mind—the mind of a Pascal—it may be said, as Plato
said of the Eternal Mind, it perpetually geometrizes.
And the same is true of the biblical spirit. He who
has imbibed it from the close and penetrating study of
the words, clauses, sentences, paragraphs, sections of the
sacred volume, puts the seal of the Eternal Spirit upon
everything that he writes, and everything that he utters.
The written Word of God is not only filled with a distinctive spirit, but it is also dictated by an Eternal Spirit. It
has a Spirit for its Author, and it has a spirit as its inward
characteristic. It is a wheel within a wheel; it is a sea
within a sea; it is an atmosphere within an atmosphere.
Spiritual in its origin, spiritual in its contents, and spiritual in all its influences and effects, well may it be the
sole great aim of the pulpit orator to reach and acquire
the *spirit* of the Scriptures. There is no danger of mysticism in such a striving; and no false spiritualism will
result from it. Such an endeavour to drink in the pure
essence of a merely human product might result in
dreaminess of thought and feeling. The undue and constant musing of the New Platonists upon the Platonic
speculations finally destroyed all clear thinking and
healthy mental action. The effect was like that of the
forbidden fruit upon Adam and Eve. They

> ' fancy that they feel
> Divinity within them breeding wings,
> Wherewith to scorn the earth.'

But the written revelation is a marvellous combination of

the divine with the human, of the spiritual with the material, of the reason with the understanding, of the heavenly with the earthly. All the antitheses are blended, and counterpoise each other, with wonderful harmony, so that no human mind will ever become exorbitant and exaggerated by an exclusive and absorbing study of it. Like the ocean, while it has its undulations, and an un-fathomed swell which no power can level, it never has the everlasting mountains and valleys; it never exhibits or produces extremes.

He, then, whose public discourse is pervaded with the spirit of revelation, and who speaks as the oracles of God, will be eloquent in the highest style. Truth will impart weight, and sincerity will impart earnestness, and feeling will impart glow, and at times devout enthusiasm will impart colour and beauty to his oratory, and he will verify the affirmation which the most highly educated and the loftiest of English poets puts into the mouth of the Son of God, in his reply to Satan, who pleaded the cause of secular letters against that of inspiration:

> 'Their orators thou then extoll'st as those
> The top of eloquence ;
> But herein to our prophets far beneath,
> As men divinely taught, and better teaching,
> In their majestic, unaffected style,
> Than all the oratory of Greece and Rome.'

CHAPTER II.

HOMILETICS is the term that has been chosen to denote the application of the principles of rhetoric to preaching. It is synonymous, consequently, with Sacred Rhetoric. The derivation of the word from the Greek verb ὁμιλεῖν shows that the primary purpose of the homily or sermon was *instruction*. The first sermons were undoubtedly much more didactic than rhetorical in their form and substance. This must have been so for several reasons. In the first place, the assemblies to which the sermon was first addressed were more private and social in their character than the modern congregation. Christianity was in its infancy, and had not become an acknowledged and public religion; and hence its ordinances and instructions were isolated from those of society at large. It was one of the principal charges brought against Christianity by its first opponents, that it was unsocial, exclusive, and sectarian. The Roman complained that the Christian, so far as religion was concerned, was not an integral part of the State, but was a morose, solitary, and unpatriotic man.[1]

---

[1] Tacitus, *Annalium*, xv. 44 : Christianorum multitudo ingens haud perinde in crimine incendii quam *odio humani generis* convicti sunt.

D

The first Christian congregation being thus small, thus isolated, and private, it was natural that the style of address upon the part of the preacher should be more familiar than it can be before a large audience, and upon a strictly public occasion. Hence the sermon in the early history of the Church was much more homiletical—that is, *conversational*—than rhetorical in its character. Like those free and familiar lectures which the modern preacher delivers to a limited audience on the evening of a secular day, the first sermons possessed fewer of those oratorical elements which enter so largely into the discourses that are now prepared for the great congregation in the house of public worship, and on the Sabbath, the great public day of Christendom.

In the second place, the first sermons were naturally and properly more didactic than rhetorical, because the principal work to which the first preachers of Christianity were summoned was instruction. The cardinal doctrines of Christianity were not, as they are now, matters of general knowledge. The public mind was pre-occupied with the views and notions of polytheism, and with altogether false conceptions of the nature and principles of the Christian religion; and hence there was unusual need, during the first centuries of the Church, to *indoctrinate* the Greek and Roman world. Expository instruction was consequently the first great business of the Christian herald, coupled with an effort to disabuse the human mind of those errors to which it was enslaved by a false religious system. Christianity at first was compelled to address itself to the understandings of men, in order to prepare the way for an address to their hearts and wills; and hence its first discourses were rather didactic than oratorical. And the same remark holds true of missionary preaching in the modern world. The missionary repeats the process of the primitive preacher. His audiences are not public, but private. His addresses are more conversational than oratorical,—more for purposes of instruction than of persuasion. From these two causes, the sermon was originally an instructive conversation (ὁμιλία) rather than an oration.

But although the relations of the modern preacher are considerably different from those of the ancient; although the Christian preacher is much more a public man than he was at first, because Christianity is the public religion of the modern world, and the Christian Sabbath is its public holy day, and the Christian congregation is its public religious assembly; although Homiletics has necessarily become more strictly rhetorical in its character, because the sermon has become more oratorical in its form and style,—we must recognise and acknowledge the fact that Sacred Rhetoric is in its own nature more didactic than secular. With all the change in the relations of Christianity to society and to the State, and with all the corresponding change in the circumstances and position of the preacher, it is still true that one very important part of his duty is that of exegetical instruction. Though the modern world is, generally speaking, speculatively acquainted with the Christian system, and does not need that minute instruction and that deliverance from the errors of polytheism which the pagan world requires, still the natural man everywhere and in all ages needs indoctrination. The sermon must be a preceptive discourse, and the information of the mind must be one of the chief ends of Sacred Eloquence.

This brings us to the principal difference between Secular and Sacred Rhetoric. The latter is more didactic than the former. We are speaking comparatively, it will be remembered. We would not be understood as granting the position of some writers upon Homiletics, that there is a distinction in *kind* between Secular and Sacred Rhetoric, —that the didactic element enters so largely into the sermon that the properly rhetorical elements are expelled from it, and it thus loses the oratorical character altogether. The sermon is not an essay or a treatise. It is an address to an audience, like a secular oration. Its purpose, like that of the secular oration, is to influence the will and conduct of the auditor. Like the secular oration, it is a product of *all* the powers of the human mind in the unity of their action, and not of the imagination alone, or of the understanding alone; and, like the secular oration, it addresses *all* the faculties of the hearer, ending with a movement of his will. The distinction between Secular and Sacred Rhetoric is not one of kind, but of degree. In the sermon, there is less of the purely oratorical element than in secular orations, because of the greater need of exposition and instruction. The sermon calls for more argumentation, more narration, more doctrinal information, than secular discourses contain; and hence, speaking comparatively, Secular Rhetoric is more purely and highly rhetorical than Homiletics.

Hence, as matter of fact, the sermon is more solid and

weighty in its contents, more serious and earnest in its tone, and more sober in its colouring, than the deliberative, or judicial, or panegyrical oration of Secular Eloquence. It is a graver production, less dazzling in its hues, less striking in its style, less oratorical in its general character. Recurring to the distinction between the formal and the real sciences, we might say that Secular Eloquence partakes more of the former, and Sacred Eloquence more of the latter.[1]

With this brief elucidation of the distinctive nature of Homiletics, we proceed now to consider a few reasons for its cultivation.

1. The first reason is derived from the intrinsic dignity and importance of the sermon as a species of literature. For if we have regard to the subject-matter and the end in view, the sacred oration is the most grave and weighty of all intellectual productions. The eternal salvation of the human soul, through the presentation of divine truth, is the end of preaching. The created mind is never employed so loftily and so worthily, as when it is bending all its powers, and co-working with God himself, to the attainment of this great purpose. A discourse that accomplishes this aim is second to no species of authorship in intrinsic dignity and importance. Other species of literature may decline in interest and value as the redemption of the human race advances, but this species will speedily tend to its culmination. As the human intellect shall come more and more under the influence of those great ideas which relate to God and eternity, public religious dis-

---

[1] Theremin's *Rhetoric* (Introductory Essay, p. 35 sq.).

course will gain in power and impressiveness, because of the immortal ends which it has in view. Like the Christian grace of charity, which will outlive prophecies and tongues and knowledge, Sacred Eloquence will outlive, or rather transform into its own likeness, all other forms of literature.

Not that philosophy and poetry and history will cease to exist as departments of intellectual effort so long as the human race continues in this mode of being, but they will take on a more solemn character, and assume a more serious and lofty end, whereby they will approximate more and more, in spirit and influence, to the literature proper of the Christian Church,—to the parables of our Lord, the epistles of his apostles, the sermons of his ministers. 'For it is written, I will destroy the wisdom of the wise, and will bring to nothing the understanding of the prudent.' In this way, the superior dignity and importance of the sermon will appear, inasmuch as, through the influence which it will have exerted upon the thinking of the race, the literature of the world will have become spiritualized and sanctified. Through the preaching of the Gospel, and the leavening of the mind with divine truth, we may expect to see the same great end—the glory of God in the eternal well-being of man—set up as the goal of universal letters. Whether, then, there be poetry, it may fail; whether there be philosophy, it may cease; whether there be literature, it may vanish away; but the Word of God liveth and abideth for ever. There will be an ever-enduring dignity and value in that species of intellectual productions whose great end is the indoctrination of the human mind in the truths of divine revelation.

We find, therefore, in the gravity and importance of the sacred oration, a strong reason why the homiletic art should be most assiduously cultivated. The philosopher is urged on to deep and laborious study by the weight and solidity of his department. He feels that it is worthy of his best intellectual efforts, and he is willing to dedicate his whole life to it. The poet adores his art for its intrinsic nobleness and beauty, and, like Milton, is ambitious to glorify it by some product that shall be the most 'consummate act of its author's fidelity and ripeness,—the result of all his considerate diligence, all his midnight watchings, and expense of palladian oil.' The historian spends long years in building up, from the solid foundation to the light and airy pinnacle, a structure that shall render his own name historic, and associate it with the dignity of history. And shall the sacred orator be less influenced than these intellectual workmen, by the nobleness and worth of his vocation? Ought he not, like the greatest of the apostolic preachers, to magnify his vocation, and feel all the importance of the department in which he has been called to labour with his brain and with his heart?

2. A second reason for cultivating Homiletics is derived from the intrinsic difficulty of producing an excellent sermon. In the first place, there is the difficulty which pertains to the department of rhetoric generally, arising from the fact that, in order to the production of eloquence, all the faculties of the mind must be in operation together, and concurring to an outward practical end. In the production of a work of art, the imagination, as a single

faculty, is allowed to do its perfect work unembarrassed by other faculties. The idea of the beautiful is not confused or obscured by a reference to other ideas, such as the true, the useful, and the good. The productive agency in this case is single, uncomplex, and exerted in one straight unhindered course. In the production of a purely logical or speculative product, again, the theoretic reason, as a single faculty, is allowed to do its rigorous work unembarrassed by either the imagination or the moral sense. The philosophic essay is a product which contains but one element, and that the speculative; and hence is far easier to originate than one in which many dissimilar elements —speculative and practical, imaginative and moral—are mingled, and which must, moreover, be made to amalgamate with each other.

The oration, on the other hand, whether secular or sacred, has a far more difficult origin than either of the above-mentioned productions. All the faculties of understanding, imagination, and feeling must be in exercise together ; while above, and beneath, and around, and through them all, must be the agency of that highest and most important of all the human faculties—the will, the character, the moral force of the man. In the origination of the oration, there must be not only the co-agency of all the cognitive, imaginative, and pathetic powers, but the presence and the presidency, in and through them all, of that deepest and most central power in which, as the seat of personality and of character, they are all rooted and grounded. The oration, in this view, is not so much a product of the man as it is the man himself,—an *embodi-*

ment of all his faculties and all his processes.[1] From the general character of the department of rhetoric, then, and the general nature of its products, the origination of an excellent sacred oration is exceedingly difficult; and hence the need of a profound and philosophic study of Homiletics, or the art of Sermonizing.

In the second place, the production of the sermon is a difficult work, because of the nature and extent of the influence which it aims to exert. The sermon is designed to produce an effect upon human character; and this, not upon its mere superficies, but its inmost principles. Unlike secular discourse, the sacred oration is not content with influencing men in regard to some particular or particulars of conduct, but aims at the whole nature of the man. The political orator is content, if by his effort he secures an individual vote for a single measure. The judicial orator is content if he can obtain a favourable verdict respecting the case in hand. The sacred orator, on the other hand, aims at the formation of an entire character—at laying a foundation for an innumerable series of particular actions; or else he endeavours to mould and develope from the centre a character which is already in existence, as when he addresses the Church in distinction from the congregation. If we have regard to the renewal of human nature, the formation within the human soul of entirely new principles of action, it is plain that the construction of a discourse adapted to produce this great effect involves many and great difficulties. It is true that the first and efficient cause of this effect must be sought in

[1] 'Le style, c'est l'homme.'—BUFFON.

the special and direct operation upon the individual soul
of a higher Being than man. Yet it is equally true that
the secondary instrumental cause of this renewal is divine
truth presented by the preacher. There must, therefore,
be an *adaptation* between the cause and the effect, in this
case as much as in any other. Second causes must be
adapted to the effect as much as first causes. There is a
mode of presenting divine truth which is suited to produce conversion, and there is a mode which is not suited
to this end. There is a method of sermonizing which is
adapted to develope the Christian character, and there is a
method which is not at all adapted to this. Now, to produce a discourse which, in all its parts and properties,
shall fall in with the operations of the Holy Spirit, and of
the human spirit when under divine influence,—which
shall not blind the mind, nor impede the flow of the feelings, but shall concur with all that higher influence which
is bearing upon the sinner in the work of regeneration, or
upon the Christian in the hour and process of sanctification,—to produce a discourse of this kind is one of the most
arduous attempts of the human intellect. To assert that
the attempt can be a successful one without study and
training upon the part of the preacher, is to deal differ-
ently with the department of Sacred Rhetoric, from what
we do with other departments of intellectual effort. It is
to treat the higher and eternal interests of men with more
thoughtlessness and indifference than we do their lower
and secular interests. None—unless it be those half-
educated persons who do not recognise the distinction
between science and practice, between a profession and a

trade, and who would annihilate all professional study and training—none, unless it be such as these, deny the importance of a thorough discipline on the part of the jurist and the civilian. It is acknowledged, generally, that learning and culture are requisite to the production of successful pleading in court, and successful debating in the senate. And no one who seriously considers the depth and comprehensiveness of the aim of a sermon, and takes into account that sermonizing is not an intermittent effort, but a steady, uniform process, week after week, and year after year, will be disposed to disparage or undervalue homiletic discipline or the homiletic art. Says one of the earliest and pithiest English writers upon Homiletics : ' Preachers have enough to do, and it will take up their whole time to do it well. This is not an art that is soon learnt, this is not an accomplishment that is easily gained. He that thinks otherwise, is as weak and foolish as the man that married Tully's widow (saith Dio) to be master of his eloquence.' [1]

The difficulty, in the third place, of constructing an excellent sermon is clearly apparent, when we consider the nature of the impression which is sought to be made. Without taking into account such characteristics as distinctness and depth of impression, and many others that would suggest themselves, let us seize upon a single one, —namely, *permanence* of impression,— and by a close examination perceive the need of understanding, both theoretically and practically, the art of Sermonizing.

The test of excellence in a sermon is continuance of

[1] John Edwards, *The Preacher*, Part i. p. 274.

influence. By this, it is not meant that an excellent sermon produces no more impression at the time of its first
delivery than afterwards. Often the vividness of a discourse is most apparent at the time of its origin, because
it was partly the fruit of temporary circumstances, and
derived something of its force from time and place. Yet,
after this is said, it is still true that no sermon is truly
excellent which does not contain something of permanent
value for the human head and heart. It must have such
an idea or proposition at the bottom of it, and be arranged
on such a method, and be filled up with such reflections,
and inspired with such a spirit, as will make it an object
of interest for any thoughtful mind in all time. It is
true that, tried by this test, many sermons would be
found wanting,—and far more of such sermons as draw
miscellaneous crowds, and are fit only to be printed in
a newspaper, than of such as are preached to attentive
audiences, and are unknown save by the solid Christian
character which they help to originate, or to cultivate.
It is true that, tried by the test of permanency of impression, the sacred as well as the secular oration would
often be found defective; and yet every such discourse
ought to be subjected to it. One of the first questions
to be asked, for purposes of criticism, is this question:
Are there in this discourse a solidity and thoughtfulness
which give it more or less of permanent value for the
human mind ?

Now, it is impossible that this weighty intellectual
character, conjoined as it must be in the oration with a
lively and rhetorical tone, should be attained without a

very thorough discipline on the part of the preacher. The union of such sterling, and yet opposite, qualities as thoughtfulness and energy, is the fruit of no superficial education, the result of no mere desultory efforts. The sacred orator needs not only a general culture, but a special culture in his own art. It is not enough that he be acquainted with those leading departments in which every educated, and especially every professional, man is interested; he must also be master of that specific art and department upon which the clerical profession is more immediately founded. He must be well versed in the principles and practice of Homiletics; otherwise, his sermonizing will be destitute of both a present and a permanent interest. If he be a man of learning and of reflective habits, but of no rhetorical spirit, although his discourses may be weighty in matter, and, as theological disquisitions, very meritorious, they will not produce the proper immediate effects of Sacred Eloquence, and neither will they exert the permanent influence of theological treatises. They will fail altogether as intellectual productions. The studious, thoughtful mind especially needs the influence of homiletical discipline, in order to prepare it for the work of addressing and influencing the popular audience. There is a method of so organizing the materials in the mind, of so arranging and expanding and illustrating truth, as to exert the immediate impression of rhetoric, united with the permanent impression of logic and philosophy. This method can be acquired only by the study and the practice of the art of Sermonizing.

3. A third reason for cultivating Homiletics is found

in the increasingly higher demands made by the popular mind upon its public religious teachers.

It is more difficult to make a permanent popular impression now than it was fifty years ago. The public mind is more distracted than it was then. It is addressed more frequently, and by a greater variety, both of subjects and of speakers. It is more critical and fastidious than formerly. It is possessed, we will not say of a more thorough and useful knowledge on a few subjects, but of a more extensive and various information on many subjects. The man of the present day knows more of men and things in general than his forefathers did, though probably not more of man and of some things in particular.

There is more call, consequently, in the present age, for a sermonizing that shall cover the whole field of human nature and human acquirements, that shall contain a greater variety and exhibit a greater compass, and that shall be adapted to more grades and capacities. The preacher of the present day needs to be a man of wider culture than his predecessor, because the boundaries of human knowledge have been greatly enlarged, and because his auditors have come to be acquainted, some of them thoroughly, and some of them superficially, but all of them in some degree, with this new and constantly widening field. Consider a single section of rhetoric like that of metaphor and illustration, and see how much greater is the stock of materials now, than it was previous to the modern discoveries in natural science, and how even the popular mind has become possessed of sufficient knowledge in these departments, not merely to understand the orator's allusions and representations, but to demand them of him. A modern audience, though it may not possess a very exact knowledge of what has been accomplished in modern science, is yet possessed of sufficient information to detect any such ignorance in a public speaker, and especially in the preacher, as shows him to be inferior to the educated class to which he belongs, and behind the present condition of human culture and knowledge. It was urged not many years since by the classes of a teacher who had been distinguished in his day, and whose instructions still exhibited a solid and real excellence that ought to have overruled the objection in this instance, that he had not kept up with the literary and scientific movement of the modern mind; that his style of presenting, establishing, and illustrating truth had become obsolete, although the truth itself which he taught was unobjectionable. In proof of this, it was affirmed that certain illustrations which were taken from the astronomy that existed a century ago, but which had been rendered not only incorrect but absurd by more recent discoveries, were still allowed to stand. It was complained that rhetoric, in this instance, had been vitiated by the telescope. The popular mind, also, is nice and fastidious, and will immediately detect any appearance of deficiency in literary and scientific culture in the preacher, especially if it affects his style and diction, and will give it far more weight than it is really entitled to.

But, to take a more important part of Sacred Rhetoric than style, or diction, or illustration, consider for a moment the *method* and *arrangement* of a sermon, and see what a difficult task the popular mind of the present day imposes upon its public religious teachers.

The greatest difference between the men of the present day and their forefathers consists in the greater distinctness and rapidity of their mental processes. They are not more serious and thoughtful than their ancestors, but they are more vivid, animated, and direct in their thinking than they were. They are more impatient of prolixity, of a loose method of arrangement, and of a heavy dragging movement in the exhibition of truth. Audiences a century ago would patiently listen to discourses of two hours in length, and would follow the sermonizer through a series of divisions and subdivisions that would be intolerable to a modern hearer. The human intellect seems to have shared in that increased rapidity of motion which has been imparted to matter by the modern improvements in machinery. The human body is now carried through space at the rate of a mile a minute, and the human mind seems to have learned to keep pace with this increase of speed. Mental operations are on straight lines, like the railroad and telegraph, and are far more rapid than they once were. The public audience now craves a short method, a distinct, sharp statement, and a rapid and accelerating movement, upon the part of its teachers.

Now, the preacher can meet this demand successfully, only by and through a strong methodizing power. He cannot meet it by mere brevity. The popular mind still needs and craves instruction, and, impatient as it is of dulness, will listen with more pleasure to a discourse that possesses solid excellence, though it be tedious in its

method and somewhat dull in style, than to a discourse
which has no merit but that of shortness. The task, therefore, which the sacred orator of the present day has to
perform, is to compress the greatest possible amount of
matter into the smallest possible form, and in the most
energetic possible manner. *Multum in parvo* is now the
popular maxim. *Plurimum in minimo* must now be the
preacher's maxim. Hence he must possess the power of
seizing instantaneously the strong points of a subject, of
fixing them immoveably in a rigorous logical order, and of
filling them up into a full rhetorical form, by such subordinate thoughts and trains of reflection as will carry
the hearer along with the greatest possible rapidity, together with the greatest possible impression.[1] This power
of organizing, united with the other principal power of
the orator—that of amplifying to the due extent—is imperatively demanded of the preacher, by the active, clear,
driving mind of the present age ; and whoever shall acquire
it will wield an influence over the public, either for good
or for evil, greater probably than could be exerted by an
individual in an age characterized by slower mental processes.

But is such an ability as this a thing of spontaneous
origin ? Will it be likely to be possessed by an indolent
or an uneducated mind ? Any one who will reflect a

---

[1] 'Reason and argument must be made use of by the preacher, and the
more of these the better. *But the closer this powder is rammed, the
greater execution it will do.* The sum of this head is this : that a preacher
is to take care that he always speak good sense, and argue *closely*. Nothing
that comes from him is to be raw and indigested, but all must be well
ripened by judgment.'—JOHN EDWARDS, *The Preacher*, Part i. p. 127.

E

moment, will perceive that even a fine poetic or artistic talent would be far more likely 'to come by nature,' and without culture, than this fundamental ability of the orator. In these first instances, much depends upon the impulses and gifts of genius. There is much of spontaneity in the poetic and artistic processes. But a powerful methodizing ability implies severe tasking of the intellect, a severe exercise of its faculties, whereby it acquires the power of seizing the main points of a subject with the certainty of an instinct, and then of holding them with the strength of a vice,—and all this, too, while the feelings and the imagination, the rhetorical powers of the soul, are filling out and clothing the structure with the vitality and warmth and beauty of a living thing. This power of quickly and densely methodizing can be attained only by diligent and persevering discipline; and hence it should be kept constantly before the eye of the preacher as an aim, from the beginning to the end of his educational and professional career. He cannot meet the demands which the public will make upon him as its religious teacher, unless he acquires something of this talent; and he may be certain that, in proportion as he does acquire and employ it, he will be able to convey the greatest possible amount of instruction in the shortest possible space, and, what is of equal importance for the orator's purpose, he will be able to produce the strongest possible impression in the shortest possible amount of time.

CHAPTER III.

THE fundamental properties of good discourse are as distinct and distinguishable as those of matter. Many secondary qualities enter into it, but its primary and indispensable characteristics are reducible to three: viz. *plainness, force,* and *beauty.* We propose, in this chapter, to define and illustrate these essential properties of style; and while the analysis will be founded in the general principles of rhetoric and oratory, it will also have a special reference to Sacred Eloquence and the wants of the pulpit.

1. It is agreed among all writers upon rhetoric, that the first property in style is that by virtue of which it is intelligible. The understanding is the avenue to the man. No one is affected by truth who does not apprehend it. Discourse must therefore, first of all, be *plain.* This property was termed *perspicuitas* by the Latin rhetoricians. It is transparency in discourse, as the etymology denotes. The word ἐνάργεια, which the Greek rhetoricians employed to mark this same characteristic, signifies distinctness of outline. The adjective ἐναργής is applied by Homer to the gods, when actually appearing to human vision in their own bright forms, when, like Apollo, they broke through the dim ether that ordinarily veiled them from mortal

eyes, and stood out on the edge of the horizon distinctly defined, radiant, and splendid.[1] *Vividness* seems to have been the ruling conception for the Greek in this property of style, and *transparency* for the Latin. The English and French rhetoricians have transferred the Latin *perspicuitas* to designate this quality of intelligibility in discourse. The Germans have not transferred the Latin word, because the remarkable flexibility of their language relieves them from the necessity of transferring words from other languages; but they have coined one (Durchsichtigkeit) in their own mint, which agrees in signification precisely with the Latin *perspicuitas.* These facts evince that the modern mind is inclined with the Latin to compare the property of intelligibility in style to a clear, pellucid medium—to crystal or glass, that permits the rays of light to go through, and thus permits the human eye to see through.

While, however, the attention is fixed upon this conception of transparency, and the property under consideration is denominated perspicuity in the rhetorical nomenclature, it is important not to lose sight of that other conception of distinctness or vividness which was the leading one for the Greek mind. Style is not only a medium; it is also a form. It is not only translucent and transparent, like the undefined and all-pervading atmosphere; it also has definite outlines, like a single object. Style is not only clear like the light; it is rotund like the sun. While, therefore, the conception of perspicuity of

---

[1] Αιεὶ γὰρ τὸ πάρος γε θεοί φαίνονται ἐναργεῖς
'Ημῖν εὖτ' ἔρδωμεν ἀγακλειτὰς ἑκατόμβας.
—*Odys.* vii. 201, 202.

medium is retained, there should also be combined with it the conception of fulness of outline and vividness of impression, so as to secure a comprehensive and all-including idea of that first fundamental property of style which renders it intelligible.

Inasmuch as modern writers upon rhetoric have generally followed the Latin rhetoricians, and have discussed the subject almost exclusively under the conception of transparency and the title of perspicuity, there is special reason for solicitude lest the Greek conception of fulness of form and definiteness of outline be lost out of sight. Moreover, close reflection upon the nature of the case will show that the Greek mind in this, as in most other instances, was more philosophical than the Latin. It seized upon a very profound and essential characteristic. It is not enough that thoughts be seen through a clear medium ; they must be seen in a distinct shape. It is not enough that truth be visible in a clear, pure air ; it must also stand out in that air, a single, well-defined object. The atmosphere must not only be crystalline and sparkling, but the things in it must be bounded and defined by sharply-cut lines. There may be perspicuity without distinctness; especially, without that *vivid* distinctness which is implied in the Greek ἐνάργεια. A style may be as transparent as water, and yet the thoughts be destitute of boldness and individuality. Such a style cannot be charged with obscurity, and yet it does not set truth before the mind of the reader or hearer in a striking and impressive manner. Mere isolated perspicuity is a negative quality ; it furnishes a good medium of vision but it does not present any distinct object of vision. Distinctness of outline, on the other hand, is a positive quality. It implies a vigorous action of the mind upon the truth whereby it is moulded and shaped; whereby it is cut and chiselled like a statue; whereby it is made to assume a substantial and well-defined form which smites upon the eye, and which the eye can take in.

Without discussing these two conceptions further,—a discussion which, we would remark in passing, is most interesting, leading as it does to a consideration of the differences between the mental constitution of different nations, as displayed in their languages,—we proceed to a more particular examination of that fundamental property in style which renders it intelligible. We denominate it *plainness.* A thing is plain (*planus*), when it is laid out open and smooth upon a level surface. An object is in plain sight, when the form and shape of it are distinctly visible. Chaucer, in his *Canterbury Tales,* makes the franklin, the English freeholder of his day, to say, when called upon for his story:

> ' I lerned never rhetorike certeine.
> Thinge that I speke, it most be bare and pleine.'

This quotation shows that in Chaucer's time rhetoric was the opposite of a lucid and distinct presentation of truth. In his age, it had become excessively artificial in its principles, and altogether mechanical in its applications. Hence the plain, clear-headed Englishman, whose story turns out to be told with a simplicity and perspicuity and raciness that renders it truly eloquent, supposed that it must necessarily be faulty in style, because his own good sense and keen eye made it impossible for him to discourse in the affected and false rhetoric of the schools of that day. For this plainness of style is the product of sagacity and keenness. A sagacious understanding always speaks in plain terms. A keen vision describes like an eye-witness.

There is no characteristic more important to the preacher than this, and none which ought to be more earnestly coveted by him. Sermons should be plain. The thoughts which the religious teacher presents to the common mind should go straight to the understanding. Everything that covers up and envelopes the truth should be stripped off from it, so that the bare reality may be seen. There is prodigious power in this plainness of presentation. It is the power of actual contact. A plain writer or speaker makes the truth and the mind impinge upon each other. When the style is plain, the mind of the hearer experiences the sensation of being touched; and this sensation is always impressive, for a man starts when he is touched.

Fine examples of this property are found in the style of John Locke and Thomas Hobbes. We mention these writers, because plainness is their dominant characteristic. They were both of them philosophers of the senses, rather than of the reason and the spirit. Hence their excellences, and hence their defects. They are not to be especially recommended for those other properties of style which spring out of a more profound and spiritual way of thinking, such as living energy and ingrained beauty; but for pure perspicuous address to the understanding, they have never been excelled. Trying to find everything in the senses, to convert all the mental processes ultimately into sensation, it is not surprising that whatever is exhibited by them stands out palpable and tangible. Thought seems to have become material, and to strike upon the understanding like matter itself. 'You Scotchmen,' said Edward Irving to Chalmers, 'would handle an idea as a butcher handles an ox.'[1] Whether this is true of the Scotch mind we will not affirm, but it is certainly true of writers like Locke and Hobbes. Their thoughts can be seen, handled, and felt.

The writings of Archdeacon Paley also furnish fine examples of the property we are considering. His was one of the most sagacious minds in English literary history,—eminently characterized by what Locke denominates 'large roundabout sense.' There was no mysticism in his intellectual character. Indeed, his affinities for the spiritual, in either philosophy or religion, were not so strong as they ought to have been. The defects in his ethical and theological systems are traceable to this. Still, upon subjects that did not call for a highly profound and spiritual mode of contemplation, upon subjects that fall properly within the range of the senses and the understanding, he was perfectly at home, and always discourses with a significant plainness that renders him a model for the preacher, so far as this characteristic is concerned.

Consider the following paragraph, from his *Natural Theology*, in which he disposes of the theory of creation by development, as a specimen of pure plainness in

[1] Hanna, *Life of Chalmers,* iii. 168.

presenting thoughts: 'Another system which has lately been brought forward, and with much ingenuity, is that of *appetencies*. The principle and the short account of the theory is this: Pieces of soft, ductile matter, being endued with propensities or appetencies for particular actions, would, by continual endeavours carried on through a long series of generations, work themselves gradually into suitable forms; and at length acquire, though perhaps by obscure and almost imperceptible improvements, an organization fitted to the action which their respective propensities led them to exert. A piece of animated matter, for example, that was endued with a propensity to *fly*, though ever so shapeless, though no other, we will suppose, than a round ball to begin with, would, in a course of ages, if not in a million of years, perhaps in a hundred million of years (for our theorists, having eternity to dispose of, are never sparing in time), acquire *wings*. The same tendency to locomotion in an aquatic animal or rather in an animated lump, which might happen to be surrounded by water, would end in the production of *fins;* in a living substance confined to the solid earth, would put out *legs* and *feet;* or, if it took a different turn, would break the body into ringlets, and conclude by *crawling* upon the ground.'[1] What plainness and pertinency in style and phraseology are here! How easy of comprehension are the thoughts, and yet with what directness and effect do they strike the understanding! The truth comes into actual contact with the mind. The statement of the false theory is so thorough, and

[1] Paley, *Natural Theology*, ch. xxiii.

so plain because it is thorough, that it becomes the refutation. The mind that reads or hears such discourse, is affected with the sensation of weight, density, and solidity; as we have said before, it is *impinged* upon.

The preacher should toil after this property of style, as he would toil after virtue itself. He should constantly strive, first of all, to exhibit his thoughts plainly. Whether he shall add force to plainness, and beauty to force, are matters to be considered afterwards. Let him, in the first place, begin at the beginning, and do the first thing. Endeavours after force, elegance, and beauty will be likely to succeed, provided this first fundamental in discourse is attained; and they will be sure to fail if it is not.

The preacher at the present time is liable to temptation in respect to the property of style under consideration, because it is not a showy property. The public is too eager after striking externals, for its own good. It demands brilliancy before plainness, without sufficient regard for that basis of strong sense which must ever support this quality, in order that it may have true value. The preacher is consequently tempted to yield to this false taste of the ill educated, and to become like the public. The form soon outruns the substance. He pays more and more attention to the expression, and less and less to the thought, and degenerates into a pretentious and glittering declaimer.

Now, there is nothing that will prevent a preacher from falling into this false manner, but a *determination* to be plain,—a determination, whether he does anything else or not, to bring the truth into contact with the human understanding. In the midst of all this clamour for fine writing and florid style, the preacher should be a resolute man, and dare to be a plain writer. It is ,the doctrine of one of the best theorizers upon rhetoric, that eloquence is a virtue.[1] the theory is corroborated by the subject under discussion; for it is easy to see that, in respect to that fundamental property of style which renders it intelligible, a very strong *will*—a very high *character*—is needed in the pulpit orator, in order to practise this self-denial, and also to bring the popular mind up to it.

Again, the preacher must make this property of style a matter of theory and a matter of conscience. He must distinctly perceive and acknowledge to his own mind, that plainness is the *foundation* of style; that the true theory of eloquence imposes this property upon the orator, as the very first one to be acquired. He must feel that he cannot conscientiously pass by or neglect this characteristic; that the interests of truth and of the human soul imperatively require of him that he be plain-spoken, even if he is nothing more. Under the pressure of these two—a correct theory of eloquence and a sober conscience—the preacher will be likely to determine to be plain. This determination will affect his whole sermonizing. It will appear in the structure of the plan, casting out of it everything that does not belong to a clear and clean method. It will appear in the composition and manner, in a stripping, flaying hatred of circumlocutions, and of all unnecessary ornament. The preacher whose head is right, and whose conscience is right, will soon come to possess a love

[1] Theremin, *Eloquence a Virtue.*

for this plainness. He will not be able to read authors who do not understand themselves. He will be impatient with a public speaker who does not distinctly know what he is saying. He will be interested in any book and in any discourse which sets forth plain truth.

Still another means of acquiring this property of style is found in the cultivation of what is termed, in common parlance, common sense. Common sense is that innate sagacity of the understanding which detects truth by a sort of instinct, and which, for this very reason, is dissatisfied with anything short of the truth. An instinct of any kind cannot be deceived, and it cannot be put off with appearances and pretences. It is discontented and restless until it meets its correlative object. The young swan is uneasy until it finds the element it has never yet seen; then

> 'with arched neck,
> Between her white wings mantling proudly, rows
> Her state with oary feet.'

Through all nature and all mind, the existence of an instinctive intelligence presupposes a corresponding object, in respect to which the instinct cannot be deceived, and without which it is unsatisfied.

Now, this common sense of mankind is an instinctive appetency for truth, and it cannot be met with anything short of the pure reality. Even a sophisticated mind is caught by plain utterances. The man who has spoiled his tastes and sympathies by an artificial and showy cultivation, is nevertheless struck by the vigour and raciness of plain sense. In the phrase of Horace, though he has driven nature out of his understanding with a fork, she yet returns when truth appears. And this is the hold which a plain speaker has upon an audience of false tastes and false refinement. There is an instinctive sagacity in man which needs this plainness of presentation, and which craves it, and is satisfied with it. It is by the cultivation of this common sense, this native sagaciousness of the human understanding, that the preacher is to acquire the property in style that corresponds to it. Let him always seek, first of all, an open and transparent view of a subject. Let him pass by all superficial qualities, and aim at the substance. Let him gratify and cultivate his common sense, by a knowledge that is *thorough* as far as it goes. Let him content himself with no dim and obscure apprehensions.

A fourth aid in the acquisition of a plain style of discourse, is subtlety of mind. It is important to distinguish subtlety from mere acuteness. A subtle mind perceives the interior connection or contradiction, while a merely acute mind perceives the exterior only. Hence acuteness by itself leads to hair-splitting; than which nothing is more abhorrent to the common sense of mankind. Subtlety is a profound talent which takes its distinctions in the very heart of a subject, and sees into its inner structure and fibre. Subtlety, therefore, is an ally to sagacity, and contributes greatly to that distinctness and plainness in thought which results in plainness and vividness in language. This talent aids in separating the non-essentials from the essentials of truth, so that only the leading and impressive characteristics of a subject may be exhibited to the common mind.

In instancing Locke, Hobbes, and Paley as examples of
plainness in style, we directed attention to the philosophic
ground of the property. We found it in the disposition
to found all knowledge upon sensation, in distinction from
conception. A mind which strongly desires to know
everything by the mode of sensation is one whose statements are always perspicuous. A writer or speaker,
therefore, who incessantly strives to impart a *conscious*
knowledge to his hearers or readers, must of necessity be
lucid, because consciousness is internal sensation. And
the property thus originating will contain both of the
characteristics to which we alluded in the opening of this
chapter. It will combine the Latin *perspicuitas* with the
Greek *ἐνάργεια*. It will not only be transparent, but vivid.

This quality in style, we have remarked, requires force
of character in the orator. He must be determined to be
so intelligible, that the mind of the hearer cannot fail to
understand him. He must *compel* the hearer to understand. He must force his way into consciousness by the
most significant, the most direct, the very plainest address
to his cognitive powers. The title of one of .the philosophical tracts of Fichte reads thus: 'An account, clear as
the sun, of the Real Nature of my Philosophy; or, an
Attempt to compel the Reader to Understand.'[1] The title
corresponds to the contents; for the tract is one of the
plainest productions of one of the clearest heads that ever
lived. This is the temper for the orator, as well as for the

---

[1] 'Sonnenklarer Bericht an das gröszere Publikum über das eigentliche
Wesen der neuesten Philosophie, ein Versuch, die Leser zum Verstehen
zu zwingen.'

philosopher. Let the preacher, whether he is master of any other properties of style, and before troubling himself about them, be clear as the sun in his presentation of truth, and then he will compel men to understand.

2. The second property of style which should receive attention is *force.* This characteristic in discourse renders it penetrative. Plainness is more external in its relations to the mind; force is more internal. The former is of the nature of an exhibition; the latter is of the nature of an inspiration and a permeation. While, however, this is the general distinction between the two, it would not be proper to call plainness a superficial property, and neither should we confine force to the depths. No man is plain unless he sees the truth, and no man sees the truth who does not look beyond its exterior; neither is any man forcible whose contemplation never comes up to the surface, but who contents himself with a mystical intuition. Force is power *manifested,*—power streaming out in all directions, and from every pore of the mind.

And this brings us to the first source and essential characteristic of true force in style. It originates in truth itself, and partakes of its nature; it does not spring ultimately from the energy of the human mind, but from the power of ideas and principles. We shall consider this fact, first, in its more general aspects as pertaining to philosophy, and then in reference to the rhetorical topics under consideration.

Speaking generally, then, power in the finite mind is derived, not from the mind itself, but from the objective world of truths and facts to which it is correlated. For the finite mind is a created thing, and all created things are dependent. It is the prerogative of the Infinite alone, to derive its energy from the depths of his own being. God has power, as He has life in himself, and therefore He does not sustain the relation of a dependent individual to an objective universe. He is self-sufficient, and independent of all objects. Man's power, on the contrary, is conditioned upon the relation which he sustains to that which is other than himself, greater than himself, and higher than himself. He cannot draw upon his own isolated being, as the ultimate source of power, because his own being is not self-sufficient. His power lies, therefore, in that *objective* world of truth and of being, over against which he stands as a finite and dependent subject. In simple and common phraseology, which so often, however, contains the highest philosophic truth, man's strength is in God, and the mind's strength is in truth.

The fact here stated, and the principle upon which it is based, are of general application; and the worst errors in theory and practice have resulted from its being denied or forgotten. The efficient power of the human intellect results, not from spinning out its own notions and figments, but from contemplating those objective and eternal ideas to which it is pre-conformed by its rational structure. If the human mind, by a hard, convulsive effort, analogous to the dead-lift in mechanics, attempts to *create* thought and feeling without any contemplation; if it attempts to think and to feel, without beholding the proper objects of thought and feeling, it fails of necessity. The mind cannot think successfully without an object of thought, and

the heart cannot feel strongly and truly without an object
of feeling. There can be no manifestation of power, therefore, and no force in the finite mind, except as it has been
nourished, stimulated, and strengthened by an object other
than itself.

The history of philosophical speculation teaches no
truth more plain and important than this—namely, that
insulation, isolation, and *subjective* processes generally are
destructive of all energy and vitality in the created mind,
while communion with real and solid verities promotes
both. Take, for example, the systems of idealism in philosophy. These proceed upon the hypothesis that the truth
lies ultimately in the subject, and not in the object; that
in reality there is no object, except what the mind makes
for itself; that we reach truth by isolating the intellect
from all external realities, and simply creating from within.
The mental processes, upon this theory, become speculative
instead of contemplative. The mental products, upon this
theory, are pure figments, the manufactures of the human
mind, and have no more absolute reality than a brain
image. All such thinking is destitute of true force and
vitality, because it is exercised by the mind in insulation
and isolation, from the world of outward truth and being.
There is mental action enough, but no intuition. The
mind sees nothing, but images everything. The intellect
spins with great intensity upon its own axis, but it makes
no other movement. There is incessant motion, but no
progress.

This abstract discussion might be prolonged, but sufficient has been said to justify and show the grounds of the

F

position with which we started—namely, that the power of the human mind issues ultimately from the truth and reality which it contemplates, and that no finite mind can be energetic in its manifestations that does not first behold objective truth. All attempts to be forceful by mere speculation, by an intellectual activity that falls short of a direct intuition of an objective reality, must fail. And this, because the human mind is rather a capacity than a self-sufficient fulness. It was made to receive truth into itself and not to originate it out of itself. The human mind is recipient in its nature, and not creative; it beholds truth, but it does not make it.

What, now, is the application of these principles to Sacred Eloquence? What connection has this philosophic theory with the matter of style in the preacher? We shall be able to answer this question by considering the fact, that the written revelation stands in the same relation to the sacred orator that the world of nature does to the philosopher. The Bible is something *objective* to the human mind, and not a mass of subjective thinking which human reason has originated. Revelation is not a particular phase or development of the finite intellect, like the origination of a new form of government, or a new school of philosophy. It is not one fold of the varied unfolding of the human mind, and of the same piece with it. On the contrary, it is divine wisdom given to man, out and out, to be received by him, and taken up into his mental structure, for purposes of religious renovation and growth. Human reason, therefore, is the subject, or the knowing agent and the Scriptures are the object, or the thing to be known.

All true power, consequently, in the sacred orator springs from this body of objective variety. It is not by a speculative, but by a *biblical* process, that he is to make a powerful impression upon the popular mind. The neglect of revelation, and an endeavour to spin out matter from his own brain, by processes of ratiocination, must result in feeble discourse. The oratorical power of the preacher depends upon his recipiency; upon his contemplation of those ideas and doctrines which the Supreme Mind has communicated to the created and dependent spirit; upon his clearly beholding them, and receiving through this intuition a fund of knowledge and of force of which he is naturally destitute.

Hence the preacher's first duty, in respect to the property of style under consideration, is to render himself a biblical student. The term is not employed here in its narrower signification to denote one who is learned in the literary externals of the Bible, and nothing more. A genuine biblical student is both an exegete and a dogmatic theologian. He is one whose mind is continually receiving the whole body of Holy Writ into itself in a living and genial way, and who, for this reason, is becoming more and more energetic in his methods of contemplation, and more and more forcible in his modes of presentation. A truly mighty sacred orator is 'mighty in the *Scriptures*.' By this, it is not meant that a preacher whose memory is tenacious, and holds a great number of texts which he can repeat readily, is necessarily a powerful orator. Excessive quotation of Scripture is as injurious to the true living force in a sermon, as pertinent and

choice quotation is conducive to it. Scripture should not
lie in the preacher's mind in the form of congregated
atoms, but of living, salient energies. True biblical
knowledge is dynamic, and not atomic. There is no
better word to denote its nature than the word *imbue.*
The mind, by long-continued contemplation of revelation,
is steeped in divine wisdom, and saturated with it.

Now, such a knowledge of the Scriptures as this, imparts
power to the sacred orator, which manifests itself in force
of style, for the following reasons:—In the first place,
revealed truth is not speculative, but intuitional and
contemplative. There is not a single abstraction in the
Scriptures. The Bible is a revelation of actual facts and
practical doctrines. When, consequently, the action of the
preacher's mind is that of simply beholding facts and
simply contemplating doctrines, it strengthens instead of
exhausting itself. If the sermonizing process were purely
speculative, if the preacher were called upon, as he is on
the rationalistic theory, to make a revelation instead of
proclaiming one, the inherent insufficiency of the finite
intellect would soon appear. Rationalism, therefore—the
theory that all revelation must be subjective, the production of the human reason—is the worst of all theories for
the sacred orator. It forces him to seek his materials
where they cannot be found. More .tyrannical than the
Egyptian taskmaster, it compels him to make bricks, not
only without straw, but without clay. The command of
God is otherwise: 'Preach the preaching that I bid thee;
behold these facts and these truths, which have an existence and reality independent of the individual mind; look

at them steadily and long, until their meaning is seen and their power felt; and then simply proclaim them, simply preach them.' The preacher is a *herald*, and his function is proclamation. In this way, the ideas which he presents to his fellow-men augment, instead of diminishing his strength. He gives no faster than he receives. He simply suffers divine truth, which is never feeble, and never fails, to pass through his mind, as a medium of communication, to the minds of his fellow-men.

In the second place, this knowledge and reception of the Bible as an objective revelation imparts power to the preacher's mind and force to his style, because biblical truth is more living and energetic than any other species. A full discussion of this position would carry us over an immense expanse. The field, moreover, has been of late so much ploughed and worked, that its fertility is somewhat impaired. During the last ten years, the ministry itself has been too much occupied with eulogizing the Scriptures. All mere panegyrics, as Swift has said, contain an infusion of poppy. It would be better, for a while at least, to cease these attempts to render the sun luminous. It would be better if the ministry would so imbue themselves with the Bible itself, and would so reproduce it in their preaching, that the endeavour to prove it to be a powerful book would be a palpable and tedious superfluity.

While, however, there is little need of the preacher's proving to the popular mind that revealed truth is highly energizing in its nature and influence, there is perhaps all the more need that he prove it to his own mind. Even while he is formally establishing this position to his audience, he may be the greatest unbeliever of them all. Indeed, that preacher is most liable to degenerate into a mere eulogist of the Bible, who finds little interest for his mind and his heart in its distinguishing doctrines. The man whose whole soul is intensely biblical, the man into whose intellectual and moral texture the substance of revelation has been woven, the man in whom the written Word has become incarnate,—this man is not the one to hyperbolize and elocutionize about the Scriptures. It is the preacher who harps most upon this string who most needs to understand the note he is sounding.

While, therefore, he says little about it, the sacred orator should really know and feel that revealed truth is the most profoundly energizing influence which his mind can come under. He should find the hiding place of power in the revealed ideas of God's personality and mercy, and man's responsibility and guilt. In proportion as his mind becomes biblical in its conceptions upon these two subjects, will he be an intense preacher, and a living preacher, and a powerful preacher. But if, instead of contemplating the view presented in the written Word of the character of God and man, he attempts to reach the truth upon these themes by a merely speculative process, he will fall either into pantheism or deism. And neither of these schemes is compatible with any vital and powerful address to men upon religious subjects. Saying nothing of the influence of pantheistic and rationalizing methods upon moral and religious character, it is indisputable that they are the death of eloquence. Neither naturalism nor rationalism has ever thrilled the common mind from the rostrum. There cannot be, and as matter of fact there never has been, any vivid and electrical discourse in the Christian pulpit, when the preacher has denied or doubted the truth of the revealed representations of God's nature and man's character. On the contrary, all the high and commanding eloquence of the Christian Church has sprung out of an intuition like that of Paul and Luther,—a mode of conceiving and speaking of God and man, and their mutual relations, that resulted entirely from the study of the Hebrew and Greek Scriptures.

Having directed attention to that theory of realism in philosophy which leads to the contemplation of an actual object, and is opposed to all merely speculative and idealizing methods, and after showing that, in the instance of the sacred orator, all his power and eloquence must take its origin in an objective revelation, and not in the operations of the unassisted and isolated human intellect, it will be appropriate to consider, very briefly, some characteristics of that property of style which we are discussing. At the same time, however, it should be observed, that in pointing out where power lies, and what is the true method of coming into possession of it, we have to some extent exhibited its essential nature. Force, generally, cannot be disconnected from its sources, and cannot easily be described. The orator can be directed to that sort of self-discipline, and that method of thinking, and those objects of thought, from which power springs of itself, but the living energy itself cannot be so pictured out to him that he will be able to attain it from the mere description. No drawing has yet been made of the force of gravitation.

The best and only true definition of life is to show signs of life; and the best and only definition of power is a manifestation of it.

The principal quality in a forcible style, and that which first strikes our attention, is *penetration.* While listening to a speaker of whom this property is a characteristic, our minds seemed to be pricked as with needles, and pierced as with javelins. His thoughts cut through the more dull and apathetic parts into the quick, and produce a keen sensation. Force is electrical; it permeates and thrills. A speaker destitute of energy never produces such a peculiar sensation as this. He may please by the even flow of his descriptions and narrations, and by the elegance of his general method and style, but our feeling is merely that of complacency. We are conscious of a quiet satisfaction as we listen, and of a soft and tranquil mental pleasure as he closes, but of nothing more. He has not cut sharply into the heart of his subject, and consequently he has not cut sharply into the heart of his hearer.

The principal, perhaps the sole, cause of the success of the radical orator of the present day with his audience, is his force. He is a man of one lone idea; and if this happens to be a great and fundamental one, as it sometimes does, it is apprehended upon one of its sides only. As a consequence, he is an intense man—a forcible man. His utterances penetrate. It is true that there are among this class some of less earnest spirit and less energetic temper,—amateur reformers, who wish to make an impression upon the public mind from motives of mere vanity. Such men are exceedingly feeble, and soon desist from their undertaking. For, while the common mind is ever ready, too ready, to listen to a really earnest and forcible man, even though his force proceeds from a wrong source and sets in in an altogether wrong direction, it yet loathes a lukewarm earnestness, a counterfeited enthusiasm. One of the most telling characters in one of the most brilliant English comedies, is Forcible Feeble. Take away from the man who goes now by the name of Reformer,—the half-educated man who sees the truth, but not the *whole* truth,—take away from him his force, and you take away his muscular system. He instantaneously collapses into a flabby pulp.

It is this penetrating quality, then, which renders discourse effective. And the preacher is the man, above all men, who should be characterized by it, if the theory which we have laid down respecting the origin of power is the true one. The preacher who studies and ponders the Bible as a whole, will not be a half-educated man. He will not see great ideas on one side, but on all sides, because they are so exhibited in the Scriptures. Whatever power he derives from the contemplation of inspired truth will be legitimate, and it will be regulated. His force will not be lawless and without an aim, like that of the man whose thoughts are mere speculations. His power will be like power in material nature. The forces of nature are denominated, indifferently, forces or laws; and the power of the biblical mind is one with eternal law and eternal truth.

A striking writer of the present age furnishes an example which, in the way of contrast, throws light upon the particular aspect of the subject we are considering. We allude to Thomas Carlyle. Force, intense penetration, and incisive keenness, is the secret of his influence over the younger class of educated men. Take these away from his thoughts, and there is not enough of depth, comprehensiveness, and originality in them, to account for the impression which he has made, as an author, upon his generation. But this force in Carlyle is, after all, wholly subjective, and therefore spasmodic. It does not originate from a living reception into his mind of the great body of objective and revealed truth. Suppose that that intellect were truly contemplative,—suppose that it had brooded over those two single ideas of the divine personality and human apostasy, with their immense implication,—what a difference there would be in the quantity and the quality of its force! How much broader and deeper would be its intuition; how much more practical and influential would be its projects for ameliorating the condition of man; and how much more permanent would be its influence in literary history!

For the energy in this instance is convulsive, and of the nature of a spasm. It is the force of a fury, and not of an angel. The muscle is bravely kept tight drawn by an intense volition, and for a while there is the appearance of self-sufficient power. But the creature is finite, and a slight tremor becomes visible, and the cord finally slackens. The human mind needs to repose upon something greater, deeper, grander than itself; and when, either from a false theory or from human pride, or from both, there is not this recumbency upon objective and eternal truth, its inherent finiteness and feebleness sooner or later appear. The created mind may endeavour to make up for this want of inward power by a stormy and passionate energy; but time is long, and truth is infinite, and sooner or later the overtasked, because unassisted, intellect gives out; and its possessor, weary and broken by its struggles and convulsions, rushes to the other extreme of tired and hopeless scepticism, and cries with Macbeth:

> ' Life's but a walking shadow—a poor player
> That struts and frets his hour upon the stage,
> And then is heard no more : it is a tale
> Told by an idiot, full of sound and fury,
> Signifying nothing.' [1]

The Christian mind is preserved from this fault of unnatural and feeble forcefulness, because it has received into itself a *complete* system of truth and doctrine. Any mind that is biblical is comprehensive and all-surveying. Its power originates from a full view. Its intensity springs from an intuition that is both central and peripheral. And the times demand this quality in the pulpit

---

[1] The defect in this unnatural force displays itself in the rhetoric as well as in the philosophy of the writer in question. His style corresponds to his thought. We do not here allude to the German-English phraseology, which seems now to have become a second nature with Carlyle. This characteristic is unduly magnified by critics, and is by no means the principal fault in his manner. It can be endured in him, though unendurable in his imitators. We allude rather to the exaggeration and spasmodic contortion which appear in his style, especially in his later productions. It is the tug and strain to be forcible without calm inward power. It is the effort to cut and penetrate to the core without really doing so. His style wears the appearance of a desire to be tremendously strong. The aspiration is infinite, but the performance is infinitesimal.

orator. Rapidity is the characteristic of the mental processes of this generation. An age that is itself full of energy craves an eloquence that is powerful; and this power must be pure and sustained. The energy must display itself through every fibre and the whole fabric. The sermon should throb with a robust life. But it will not, until the preacher has inhaled into his own intellect the energy and intensity of revealed ideas, and then has dared to strip away from the matter in which this force is embodied, everything that impedes its working. Powerful writers are plain. The fundamental properties of style are interlinked; and he who has secured plainness will secure force, while a failure to attain the former carries with it the failure to attain the latter.

3. The third fundamental property of style is *beauty*. The best definition that has been given of beauty is that of the Roman school of painting,—namely, *il piu, nell' uno*, multitude in unity. The essential principle of beauty is that by which all the manifoldness and variety in an object is moulded into unity and simplicity. Take a painting, for example. In this object there are a great many particular elements: there is colour of many varieties, and many shades of the same variety; there is the blending and contrast of these colours so as to produce the varieties of light and shade; there is a general harmony of tints, and a pleasing texture in the objects exhibited in the picture. Again, there are in this painting a great many lines as well as colours—curved lines and right lines; indeed all the geometrical elements intermingled, and in every variety of relation to each other.

Again, in this painting a great many different properties of matter are represented. Some of the objects in it are compressed and solid, others are diffuse and airy; some are colossal and firm, others are slender and slight; some are rigid and immoveable, others are mobile and pliant. Again, there are in this painting a variety of more distinctively intellectual elements, such as proportion, symmetry, exactness, neatness, elegance, grace, dignity, sublimity.

Here, then, if we have regard to number alone, is a great sum of separate items or elements in this painting. Each one is distinct from all the rest. But more than this, these items are also diverse from each other. The sensuous elements of colour are different from the geometrical elements of lines; and the more distinctively intellectual elements, such as proportion, exactness, and elegance, are different from both. In short, the more closely we analyse this painting, the more clearly shall we see that it is composed of a great amount and variety of particulars. If we look at its items and elements, we shall perceive that, as an object, it is manifold—it is a 'multitude' of items and elements.

And yet, if it is a beautiful picture, it is a 'unity' also. As we stand before a great painting like the Last Supper of Da Vinci, for example, we are conscious of receiving but one general impression. We do not receive a distinct and separate impression from each one of these items and elements that constitute its manifoldness, but a general and total impression. We do not experience a hundred thousand impressions from a hundred thousand particulars. We see and we feel that the work is a unity. It breathes one spirit, and is pervaded by one tone. It is, according to the definition with which we began, 'multitude in unity;' and hence it is beautiful.

For it is to be observed that, while and so long as we are busy with particulars alone, we perceive no beauty. That analytic process, while it is going on, prevents any æsthetic perception and pleasure. So long as we are counting up the items of this multitude, and before we have come to the intuition of the unity of the whole work, we are unconscious of its beauty. It is not until the analysis stops, and the synthesis begins; it is not until we are aware that all this multitude of particulars has been *moulded*, by the one idea of the artist's imagination, into a single breathing unity, that we feel the beauty that is in the painting. If the mind of the beholder could never get beyond this analysis of particulars, and could never do anything more than enumerate these items, it could never experience the feeling of beauty. If the eye of the beholder were merely a brute's eye, merely receiving the impressions made by the items and elements of the vision, it could never perceive the beautiful. The brute's eye is impressed by the manifoldness of the object or the scene, but never by the unity. As it roves over the landscape spread out before it, the organ of the animal is undoubtedly subject to the same sensuous and particular impressions as those of a Raphael; and perhaps if the brute were capable of analysing and enumerating, it might detect the greater portion of those elements that make up the manifoldness of the picture. But the modifying power is wanting. That unifying principle which can mould these elements into a unity, and bring simplicity into this diffusion and separation of particulars, has not been given to the brute.

We have thus briefly examined this definition of beauty, not merely because it is the most philosophical of any that has been given, but because it is the most useful and safest definition for the purposes of the orator, and particularly of the sacred orator. It is too much the habit to regard beauty as mere *ornamentation,*—as something that is added to other properties, instead of growing out of them. Hence it is too much the habit to cultivate the beautiful in isolation.—to set it up before the mind as an independent quality, and to make every other quality subservient to it. In no department is this more pernicious and fatal to true success than in rhetoric.

This habit is founded, partly at least, upon a wrong conception of beauty. It is not defined in accordance with its essential principle, but rather in accordance with its more superficial characteristics. Beauty, with too many, is that which ornaments, which decks out and sets off, plainness and force, or whatever the other properties may be, with which it happens to be juxtaposed. But if the definition that has been given be the true one, beauty is rather an inevitable accompaniment, than a laboured decoration. It has a spontaneous origin. It springs into existence whenever the mind has succeeded in imparting the properties of unity and simplicity to a multitude of particulars which, taken by themselves, are destitute of these properties. But unity and simplicity

are substantial properties; they have an intrinsic worth.
True beauty, therefore, springs into existence at the very
time that the mind is seeking to impart to the object of
its attention its most sterling and necessary characteristics.
It does not arise when the mind is neglecting essential
and necessary characteristics, and is aiming at an isolated
and an independent decoration.

Take the case of the sacred orator, and see how true
this position is. Suppose that the preacher, in the composition of a sermon, altogether or in part neglects the
necessary property of unity, and endeavours to superinduce
upon a heterogeneous mass of materials, which he has
gathered together, the element and property of beauty.
By the supposition, he has not *moulded* these materials
in the least. There they lie,—a great 'multitude' of items
and particulars ; but the mind of the preacher has pervaded
them with no unifying and no simplifying principle.
There is multitude, manifoldness, variety, but there is no
unity. Now it is not possible for him to compose a
beautiful oration in this manner. He may decorate as
much as he pleases ; he may cull words, and invent
metaphors, and wire-draw metaphors into similes ; he may
toil over his work until he is grey; but he cannot, upon
this method, compose a truly beautiful work. So long as
this sermon is destitute of a moulding and unifying
principle which assimilates and combines this multitude
of particulars into a whole, into a simple and pure unit,
it cannot be made beautiful. So long as this sermon is
destitute of unity, it must be destitute of beauty.

The course which the sermonizer should take in this

case is plain. He should cease this effort to ornament this aggregate of separate items and particulars, and begin to reduce them into unity and simplicity of form. This is no time for him to be thinking about the beauty of his sermon. If he will cease altogether to think about it, and will aim at those necessary and essential properties which his sermon as yet lacks, he will find in the end that a real and true beauty has spontaneously sprung into existence. He who finds beauty shall lose it, but he who loses beauty shall find it. He who is prematurely anxious to secure beauty will fail; but he whose anxiety has respect first to the necessary properties of style, will find beauty following in their train, as the shadow follows the substance.

For it is plain, that just in proportion as the sermon rounds into unity, does it swell into beauty. It pleases the taste and the sense for the beautiful, just in proportion as the unifying and simplifying process goes on. The eye, at first, sees no form or comeliness in the multitude of materials, because they *are* a mere multitude; because they are arranged upon no method, and moulded by no principle of unity. But, gradually, the logic of the preacher's mind penetrates and pervades the mass of particulars; the homogeneous elements are assimilated, and the heterogeneous are sloughed off; the vital currents of a system and a method begin to play through the parts, and the work now takes on a rounded unity and a chaste simplicity. And now, for the first time, beauty begins to appear. The sermon is seen to be a beautiful product because it is one, and simple in its structure and impression.

G

Thus it appears that true beauty is not an ornament washed on from without, but an efflux from within. The effort to be methodical results in beauty; the endeavour after unity results in beauty; the effort to be simple results in beauty. But method, unity, and simplicity are essential properties. True beauty in rhetoric, therefore, is the natural and necessary accompaniment of solid and substantial characteristics, both in the matter and in the form. It is found in every composition that is characterized by 'unity in multitude,' and by simplicity in complexity.

Having thus stated and explained this definition, we proceed to notice some of its excellences and advantages. And, first, it is a *safe* definition for the orator. There is no property in style so liable to be injured and spoiled by excess as beauty. The orator cannot be too plain or too forcible, but he may be too beautiful. The æsthetic nature, unlike the rational or the moral, may be too much developed. The development of the taste and imagination must be a *symmetrical* one, in order to be a just and true one. If the æsthetic processes should exceed their true proportion, and absorb into themselves all the rational and moral processes of the human soul, so that it should become wholly imaginative and merely æsthetic, this would be an illegitimate and false development. The true proportion, in this instance, is a subordination of the imagination and the taste to the purposes and aims of the rational and moral faculties. If, now, it be said in reply to this, that proportion is equally required in the rational and moral processes of the soul, that the reason ought not to absorb the imagination any more than the imagination the reason, we answer that this cannot happen. For in the true and pure development of the rational and moral powers, a proper and subordinate development of the imaginative and æsthetic is necessitated. A true and pure unfolding of the rational and moral nature of man would *inevitably* be a proportionate, and hence a beautiful one. Reason and right are the absolute; and in developing them, all things that rest upon them are developed also. The true and the good are necessarily beautiful.

But although such is the fact, the human mind is too unwilling to trust to the simple and chaste beauty of truth and reason. It lusts after a divorced and an independent beauty. It tends to an excessive, disproportioned, unsubordinated development of the æsthetic sense. The influence of such a tendency upon eloquence and oratory is pernicious in the highest degree; and one great aim of a true and high theory of eloquence is to counteract it. And certainly that definition of beauty which makes it to be more than mere decoration,—which regards it as the result of a unifying principle, moulding into one a great multitude of particulars,—is a safe one for the preacher in the respects of which we are speaking. There is no danger of an excess of unity and method in the sermon. The closer and more compact the materials, the simpler and more symmetrical the plan, the better the sermon. These characteristics never can become exorbitant; and hence that beauty which springs out of them can never become an extravagant and false ornamentation. The same is true of simplicity. This shows itself more in the style and diction of a sermon than in the plan and its parts. But can there ever be too much of chaste and pure simplicity in the language and style ? The more there is of this property, the nearer does the work approach to that most purely beautiful of all the productions of Grecian art—the Ionic column. Compare the Ionic with the Corinthian column, and the difference between pure and excessive beauty is apparent. In the Ionic column, the unity completely pervades and masters the manifoldness. The eye is not distracted by complexity of parts or a multitude of particulars, but rests with a tranquil complacency upon the simple oneness, the chaste pure beauty of the column. In the Corinthian column, there are not this entire pervasion and perfect domination of the manifold by the unity. The variety of parts and particulars somewhat overflows the unity of the whole. There is too much decoration, the æsthetic sense is a little satiated, the appetite is a little palled, and the eye does not experience that entire satisfaction in taking in the column as a whole which it feels on beholding the less decorated Ionic. As a work of art, it is not so clean, so nice, so elegant, so purely and simply beautiful.

The definition which we are considering, then, is a safe one in its influence, because it insists upon the presence and the presidency of the idea of unity. This idea logically precludes over-ornament. It forbids an excess of materials—too much variety, too much manifoldness, in the parts and particulars. And supposing there is no excess in the amount of materials, supposing the manifold elements are in just proportion, then this idea and principle of unity preclude the isolation, the disconnection, the independence of any of them. There can be no *excess* according to this definition. The beauty that results is a pure and a safe embellishment.

In the second place, the definition under consideration is a *useful* one for the sacred orator. It is practically available for the purposes of preaching. For it teaches not only that unity and simplicity are essential to the existence of beauty, but that the effort to obtain them is really an effort to obtain beauty. The definition implies that success in respect to unity—to unity that is thorough and perfusive, and *moulds* the multitudes of materials—is success in respect to beauty.

The sacred orator, consequently, knows exactly what he needs to do in order to secure that property of style which we are considering. And this is of more importance than it might at first seem. For it is more difficult to proceed intelligently in respect to the precept, 'Be beautiful,' than in respect to the precept, 'Be plain,' or 'Be forcible.' Indeed, if that definition of beauty which we are recommending be rejected, it seems to us that the mind of the orator must be perplexed when he is desirous of imparting this property to his work. How shall he begin to render his oration beautiful? and when shall he end the effort? are questions that are answered, not only the most safely, but the most intelligently, by bidding him impart the greatest possible unity to it. Certainly there is no other property or characteristic in beauty so prominent as this of unity, and there is no one that is so distinct and easily apprehensible.

Let the preacher, then, adopt this definition, because it is a working definition; let him see and believe that all true beauty springs naturally from unity and simplicity, and then let him act accordingly. Let him, first of all, strive to make his sermon a unit and a whole, so far as its method is concerned. Just in proportion as he succeeds in so doing will he construct a beautiful plan,—a plan that will satisfy the æsthetic sense at the very time that it satisfies the logical understanding. Let him seek to render this property of unity pervading and perfusive, so far as style and diction are concerned, and his style and diction will be beautiful. For this unifying principle, working thoroughly and clear to the edge, like the principle of life in nature, will display itself in simplicity of style, and chasteness and purity of diction. If style and diction are not essentially simple and pure and chaste, can any possible amount of ornamentation ever make them beautiful ? Is not unity pervading the manifoldness, in this instance as well as in that of the plan, the essence and basis of beauty ?

In the third place, this definition recommends itself to the sacred orator, because it is *comprehensive.* We have seen in the first part of this chapter, that more comprehensive terms are desirable than 'perspicuity' and 'energy;' and hence we have chosen the terms 'plainness' and 'force,' to denote those properties of style which address the powers of cognition and feeling. A wider and more comprehensive term than 'elegance'—the term that is usually associated with 'perspicuity' and 'energy'—is also needed, to denote that property of style which addresses the imagination and æsthetic nature; and hence we have selected the term 'beauty.' This term is sufficiently comprehensive to include a number of particulars, each of which is pleasing to the taste.

First in order among these, is *neatness*. This property in style renders it clean and pure ; as the Latin verb *niteo, nitesco,* from which it comes, denotes. This purity and niceness, as some of the meanings of these Latin verbs indicate, may become a very bright and splendid quality. The sculptor may cut the statue so very cleanly, and impart such a high neatness to it, that it shall actually shine and gleam like silver. This seems to be the explanation of the uses of the Latin root, and shows how a primarily plain property may be heightened into ornament and splendour. The passage from neatness to elegance is very easy and imperceptible; and, like elegance itself, neatness is·a property that is æsthetic, and pleases the taste.

And this conducts to the second particular under the head of beauty—viz. *elegance.* The etymology of this word shows its meaning to be kindred to that of neatness. Elegant is from *e* and *lego.* Elegance is a nice choice The elegant is the elect. The elegant is the select. Out of a multitude of particulars the most fitting is chosen. Under the influence of that principle and idea of unity of which we have spoken, the orator selects the most appropriate word,—the word which promotes the simplicity of the statement; and thus his diction is elegant. Or, under the influence of this same idea of unity, he culls the most suitable metaphor out of a multitude ; and thus his illustration is elegant.

The third particular under the head of beauty is *grace.* This has been defined to be beauty in motion. When we have a still picture, a tranquil repose of beauty, there is no grace. But start this property into motion, and it takes on this aspect. We speak of a beautiful landscape and a graceful figure,—of a beautiful colour, and a graceful curve. The colour is still; the curve is a line; and the line is a point in motion, according to the old geometry, and its curved *motion* is graceful.

Lastly, there is what we must denominate, for want of a better term, *beauty proper,* or *specific beauty.* We cannot here give a full definition of this element in the general conception of the beautiful. We mean by it more than neatness, and more than elegance. Perhaps that which goes under the name of ornament and embellishment in style is nearest to it. It is that flush of colour, and that splendour of light, which are poured over the discourse of a highly imaginative mind,—like that of Jeremy Taylor, for example. Placing neatness as the lowest degree in the scale of general beauty, then specific beauty would be the last and highest degree,—elegance and grace being intermediate. In· this way, the term beauty becomes comprehensive, and sufficient for all purposes of rhetoric. For every orator should exhibit something of this fundamental property of style. Even the least imaginative preacher should discourse in a manner that possesses some of these elements of beauty—that not only does not offend a cultivated taste, but satisfies and pleases it. No writer or speaker should be debarred from the beautiful. It is a legitimate property in style, and should appear, in some of its qualities and degrees, in every man's discourse.

This brings us to the practical application of this discussion of the nature and extent of the beautiful; and what we have to say will be contained in several rules or maxims. First, the preacher should always make beauty of style subservient to plainness and force. This third fundamental property should not overflow and submerge the first two. In all its degrees, from neatness up to beauty in the stricter specific sense, it should contribute to render discourse clear to the understanding, and influential upon the feelings. The moment that this property, in any of its forms, oversteps this limit of subordination and subservience, it becomes a positive fault in style. Excessive beauty is as much a defect as positive deformity. Showy, gaudy over-ornament is as much a fault as downright ugliness. But in following the definition that has been given, beauty will inevitably be subordinated to plainness and force of style. For no more of neatness, of elegance, of grace, and of embellishment will be admitted or employed than the principles of unity and simplicity will permit. The endeavour to impart oneness to the sermon throughout and in every particular, the effort to secure unity in logic, style, and diction, will keep out all extravagant ornamentation. The striving of the preacher after harmony and simplicity, which according to the definition are the inmost essence of beauty, will allow no decoration to characterize his sermon but that which is harmonious and simple. And such embellishment as this is subservient to plainness and force.

Secondly, the degree and amount of beauty in style should accord with the characteristics of the individual. The style of some preachers contains more of the beautiful than that of others, and ought to; for there are differences in the mental structure. Some minds are more imaginative and poetic than others. Yet every mind possesses more or less of imagination. 'Even the dullest wight,' says Coleridge, 'is a Shakspeare in his dreams.' Hence, while the property of beauty, as we have already remarked, belongs to style generally, and should be seen in every man's manner of discourse, it is yet a thing of degree and amount. This degree and amount must be determined by the amount of imagination that has been bestowed upon the individual. Some men are so constituted that neatness is the utmost that is proper in them. If they attempt more than this lowest grade of the beautiful, they injure their style and render it positively offensive to taste. Stopping with neatness, they secure beauty. Others may be elegant, others graceful, others—and these are the few—may be beautiful with the embellishment and ornament of Jeremy Taylor. In each and every instance, the grade of beauty should accord with the individuality. If it does not, it is, in reference to the individual, excessive and isolated beauty, which is offensive to the taste, and therefore really of the nature of the deformed and the ugly. A property overwrought, and carried to excess, turns into its own contrary, just as frost, raised to its utmost intensity, produces the same sensation as fire.

But in what other way can this adjustment of the

amount of beauty in style to the individuality of the preacher be secured than by proceeding from the ideas of unity and simplicity, than by adopting and working upon that definition which makes these the essentials and basis of the beautiful? If the preacher sets up mere decoration as his aim, he will inevitably outrun his capacities. He will attempt to embellish his sermon more than his mental peculiarities will warrant. There will not be a true harmony and accord between the amount of imagination in his soul and the amount of ornament in his sermon. On the other hand, the endeavour to infuse unity, symmetry, and simplicity through the whole sermon, through the matter and the form, will secure a just proportion between the product of the preacher's mind and the characteristics of the preacher's mind. The orator will then exhibit his own grade of beauty in his style,—no more and no less than his mental qualities justify. And this grade is the truly and the highly beautiful, for *him*, and in *him*.

CHAPTER IV.

MAXIMS for the composition of sermons are of two classes, general and special—those, namely, which relate to the fundamental discipline that prepares for the construction of a sermon, and those which are to be followed in the act of composition itself.

Before particular precepts can be given with profit, it is necessary to call attention to some *general* rules, the observance of which greatly facilitates the process of writing a discourse. The sermonizer often loses much time and labour in the season of immediate preparation for the pulpit, because he has made little general preparation for the work. As in mechanics the workman always seeks to increase the efficiency of a force by applying it under all the advantages possible, so the intellectual workman should avail himself of all that can render his direct and immediate efforts more effective and successful. A dead-lift should be avoided by the mind, as well as by the body. Power in both the material and mental worlds should be aided by what the mechanic terms a *purchase*. If the sermonizer goes to the construction of a sermon after he has made preparation of a more general nature, he will be far more successful than if he begins abruptly, and by a violent or perhaps spasmodic application of his powers.

1. The first of these general maxims is this: *Cultivate a homiletic mental habit.* By this is meant, such a habitual training of the mind as will impart a sermonizing tendency to it. The human understanding, by discipline and practice, may be made to work in any given direction, provided it is a legitimate one, with something of the uniformity and precision and rapidity of a machine. It can be so habituated to certain processes, that it shall go through them with very little effort, and yet with very great force. We shall of course not be understood as advocating a material philosophy, or as affirming that the operations of the mind are really mechanical. We are only directing attention to the fact acknowledged by all philosophers, that certain mental operations—such as the logical, the imaginative, for example—may be so *fixed* by exercise and habit, that the mind may perform them with an ease and a readiness that resembles the operations of an instinct or a machine. Compare the activity of an intellect that has been habituated to the process of logic, with one that has had little or no exercise in this direction. With what rapidity and precision does the former speed through the process, and how slowly and uncertainly does the latter drag along! The former has acquired a logical tendency, and needs only to fasten its grasp upon a subject that possesses a logical structure, that has logic in it, to untie it immediately, and untwist it entirely.

Now, in relation to the purposes of his profession and

calling, the preacher ought to acquire and cultivate a homiletical habitude. Preaching is his business. For this he has educated himself, and to this he has consecrated his whole life. It should therefore obtain undisputed possession of his mind and his culture.[1] He ought not to pursue any other intelléctual calling than that of sermonizing. He may therefore properly allow this species of authorship to monopolize all his discipline and acquisitions. It is as fitting that the preacher should be characterized by a homiletical tendency, as that the poet should be characterized by a poetical tendency. If it is proper that the poet should transmute everything that he touches into poetry, it is proper that the preacher should transmute everything that he touches into sermon.

This homiletic habit will appear in a disposition to skeletonize, to construct plans, to examine and criticize discourses with respect to their logical structure. The preacher's mind becomes habitually organific. It is inclined to build. Whenever leading thoughts are brought into the mind, they are straightway disposed and arranged into the unity of a plan, instead of being allowed to lie here and there, like scattered boulders on a field of drift. This homiletic habit will appear, again, in a disposition to render all the argumentative and illustrative materials

[1] 'We are told of a Grecian general who, when he travelled and viewed the country around him, revolved in his mind how an army might be there drawn up to the greatest advantage ; how he could best defend himself, if attacked from such a quarter ; how advance with greatest security ; how retreat with least danger. Something similar to this should be the practice of a public speaker.'—LELAND, *Preface to the Orations of Demosthenes.*

which pour in upon the educated man, from the various fields of science, literature, and art, subservient to the purposes of preaching. The sermonizer is, or should be, a student, and an industrious one, a reader, and a thoughtful one. He will consequently, in the course of his studies, meet with a great variety of information that may be advantageously employed in sermonizing, either as proof or illustration, provided he possesses the proper power to elaborate it and work it up. Now, if he has acquired this homiletic mental habit, this tendency to sermonize, all this material, which would pass through another mind without assimilation, will be instantaneously and constantly taken up, and wrought into the substance and form of sermons.[1]

The possession of such an intellectual habitude as this, greatly facilitates immediate preparation for the pulpit. It is virtually a primary preparation, from which the secondary and more direct preparation derives its precision, thoroughness, rapidity, and effectiveness. Without it, the preacher must be continually forced up to an unwelcome and ungenial task in the preparation of discourses, instead of finding, in this process of composition, a grateful vent for the outflow and overflow of his resources.

2. The second general maxim for the sermonizer is this : *Form a high ideal of a sermon, and constantly aim at its realization.* There is little danger of setting a standard too high, provided the preacher is kept earnestly at work in attempts to reach it. The influence of a very perfect conception of a thing is sometimes injurious upon one whose

---

[1] These materials will readily overflow, in the form of skeletons, metaphors, illustrations, etc., into the preacher's Commonplace Book.

mental processes are somewhat morbid and unhealthy. An artist whose beau-ideal is high, but who has little productive energy and vigour, will dream away his life over his ideal, and accomplish nothing ; or else fill up his career as an artist with a series of disappointed, baffled efforts. Such a one should content himself, in the outset at least, with a somewhat lower idea of perfection, and rouse himself up to more vigour and energy of execution. In this way he would take courage, and would gradually elevate his standard, and carry his power of performance up along with his ideal. But if there be a vigorous willingness to work, and a sincerely good motive at the bottom of mental efforts, there is no danger of aiming too high. Though the perfect idea in the mind will never be realized—for a man's ideal, like his horizon, is constantly receding from him as he advances towards it—yet the grade of excellence actually attained will be far higher, than if but an inferior, or even a moderate standard is assumed in the outset.

The preacher's idea of a sermon must therefore be as full and perfect as possible. He must not be content with an inferior grade of sermonizing, but must aim to make his discourses as excellent in matter and in manner as his powers, natural and acquired, will possibly allow. And especially must he subject his efforts at sermonizing to the criticism and the discipline of a high ideal, while he is in the *preparatory course* of professional education. It is probably safe to say, that in all theological seminaries too many sermons are written, because the conception of a sermon is too inadequate. A higher standard would diminish the quantity and improve the quality in this department of authorship. We are well aware of the frequent demands made by the churches upon the theological student before he has entered the pastoral office. These demands ought to be met, so far as is possible, in view of the lack of preachers in this great and growing country. And yet this very demand calls for great resolution and great carefulness on the part of the professional student. He should not court, but discourage, this premature draft upon his resources, so far as he can consistently with a wise regard to circumstances. He ought to insist upon the full time in which to prepare for a life-long work,—a work that will task the best discipline and the ripest culture to the utmost. He ought to keep his ideal of a sermon high and bright before his eye, and not allow his mind, by the frequency and insufficiency of its preparations, to become accustomed to inferior performances, because this is the next step to becoming satisfied with them.

It is possible, as we have already remarked, that a high model may in some instances discourage efforts, and freeze the genial currents of the soul. But in this age of intense mental action, when all men are thinking and speaking and writing, there is little danger in recommending a high standard to the professional man. Where one mind will be injured by it, a thousand will be benefited. Moreover, if there only be a vigorous and healthy state of mind—a disposition to act, think, and to write —on the part of the clergyman, there is little danger of his becoming unduly fastidious or morbidly nice. Add to this the fact, that as soon as the clergyman has once

H

entered upon the active duties of his profession, necessity
is laid upon him, and he *must* compose, *nolens volens,*
and we have still another reason why a high ideal is not
liable, as it is sometimes in the case of the artist or poet,
to impede and suppress his activity. All disposition to
brood morbidly over performances because they are not
close up to the perfect model in the mind, will be broken up
and driven to the four winds by the consideration, that on
next Lord's day two sermons must be preached, at the call
of the bell, to that expecting and expectant congregation.

We are also aware that it is possible to expend too
much time and labour upon an individual sermon. Some
preachers, and some very celebrated in their day, have
had their 'favourite sermons,' as they are styled,—sermons
upon which an undue amount of pains was expended, to
the neglect and serious injury of the rest of their sermonizing. A certain American preacher is said to have
rewritten one particular discourse more than ninety times !
But this is not the true use of a high ideal. A high
conception ought to show its work and its power in
every sermon. The discourses of a preacher ought uniformly to bear the marks of a lofty aim. Not that one
sermon will be as excellent as another, any more than
one subject will be as fertile as another. But the course
of sermonizing, year after year, ought to show that the
preacher is satisfied with no hasty perfunctory performance of his duties,—that there is constantly floating
before him, and beckoning him on, a noble and high
idea of what a sermon always should be.

There is little danger, however, of excessive elaboration

during the course of professional study. The theological student is more likely to under-estimate the close study of his plans, and the elaborate cultivation of his style and diction, than to over-estimate them. He is apt to shrink from that persistent self-denial of the intellect which confines it to long and laborious efforts upon a single discourse, instead of allowing it to expatiate amid a greater variety of themes. The student, in his best estate, is too little inclined to that thorough elaboration to which the ancient orators accustomed themselves in the production of their master-pieces, and which exhibits itself equally in the compactness and completeness of the organization and in the hard finish of the style. 'The prose of Demosthenes,' savs an excellent critic, 'is, in its kind, as perfect and finished as metrical composition. For example, the greatest attention is bestowed by Demosthenes upon the sequence of long and short syllables, not in order to produce a regularly recurring metre, but in order to express the most diverse emotions of the mind by a suitable and ever-varying rhythm or movement. And as this prose rhythm never passes over into a poetical metre, so the language as to its elements never loses itself in the sphere of poetry, but remains, as the language of oratory ever should, that of ordinary life and cultivated society. And the uncommon charm of this rhetorical prose lies precisely in this, that these simple elements of speech are treated with the same care whibh usually only the poet is wont to devote to words. Demosthenes himself was well aware of this study which he bestowed upon his style, and he required it in the

orator.   It is not enough, said he, that the orator, in order
to prepare for delivery in public, write down his thoughts;
he must, as it were, *sculpture* them in brass.   He must
not content himself with that loose use of language which
characterizes a thoughtless fluency; but his words must
have a precise and exact look, like newly-minted coin,
with sharply-cut edges and devices.   This comparison of
prose composition with sculpture appears to have been a
favourite one with the ancient rhetoricians; as Dionysius
also remarks of Demosthenes, Plato, and Socrates, "their
productions were not so much works of writing, as of
carving and embossing."'[1]

This high ideal, both in matter and style, should therefore float constantly before the eye of the student during
his whole preparatory course.   In this way he will habituate himself to intense and careful efforts in composition, so
that when he goes out into active professional life, he may,
when compelled to do so by the stress of circumstances,
even relax something of this strain and tension of intellect, and yet throw off with rapidity sermons that will be
highly methodical and highly finished, because this style
of sermonizing has become natural to him.   By this severe
discipline of himself in the beginning, he will have acquired
the right to be daring and careless, when compelled to be
by the stress of circumstances; and, what is more, he will
have acquired the ability to be so, without disgrace to his
calling, and with success in it.

3. A third general maxim for the sermonizer is this: *In
immediate preparation for the pulpit, make no use of the*

[1] Theremin, *Demosthenes and Massillon*, p. 142.

immediate preparation of other minds, but rely solely upon personal resources. This maxim forbids the use of the skeletons and sermons of other sermonizers in the process of composition. Such a general preparation as has been described—namely, a homiletic mental habit conjoined with a high ideal—renders this help unnecessary. Such a sermonizer is strong in himself, and needs no supports or crutches ; such a preacher is rich in himself, and does not need to borrow. He prefers to follow the leadings of his own well-disciplined and well-informed mind, rather than to adjust himself to the movements of another, however firm and consecutive they may be.

In this day, when so many aids to sermonizing are being furnished, it is well to form a correct estimate of their real value. These collections of skeletons and plans, more or less filled up, which seem to be multiplying along with the general multiplication of books, ought to be entirely neglected and rejected by both the theological student and the preacher. As matter of fact, they are neglected by all vigorous and effective sermonizers. They are the resort of the indolent and unfaithful alone.

The only plausible reason that can be urged for using them is, that they furnish material for the study of plans —that they are necessary to the acquisition of the art of skeletonizing. But a good collection of sermons is of far more worth for this purpose. There is very little discipline in looking over a plan that has been eliminated from a sermon by another mind. But there is a very great discipline in taking the sermon itself, and eliminating the plan for ourselves. In the first instance the mind is

passive, in the second it is active. The plan of a truly
excellent discourse is so identified with the discourse, is so
thoroughly organic and one with the filling up, that it
requires great judgment and close examination to dissect
it, and separate it from the mass of thought, in which it is
lightly yet strongly embedded. Why, then, lose all the
benefits of this examination and exertion of judgment by
employing the collector of skeletons to do this work for
us ? Why not take the living structure to pieces ourselves,
and derive the same knowledge and skill thereby which
the anatomist acquires from a personal dissection of a subject ? It is only by actual analysis that actual synthesis
becomes possible. It is only by an actual examination of
the parts of an oration, and an actual disentanglement of
them from the matter of the discourse, that we can acquire
the ability of putting parts together, and building up a
methodical structure ourselves. Instead, therefore, of
buying a collection of skeletons, the student and preacher
should buy a collection of sermons, and obtain the discipline which he needs, from a close and careful study of
their logical structure and rhetorical properties ; for in this
way he will acquire both a logical and a rhetorical discipline. If he studies a skeleton merely, logical discipline is
the most he can obtain ; and this, too, as we have seen, in
only an inferior degree. If, on the other hand, he studies
a sermon, while the effort to detect and take out the plan
that is in it will go to impart a fine logical talent, a fine
constructive ability, the attention which will at the same
time be given to the style, illustration, and diction of the
discourse as a whole, will go to impart a fine rhetorical

talent also. The method of criticism will correspond to
the method of production. As the sermon came into existence in a growth-like way,—plan and filling up, skeleton
and flesh, all together,—so it will be examined in the same
natural method. The skeleton will not be contemplated
alone, and isolated from the thoughts which it supports ;
neither will the thoughts be examined in a state of separation from the plan of the whole fabric. The method of
criticism, like the method of authorship, will be the method
of nature.[1]

But when these collections of plans are seriously offered
to the preacher as sources from which to derive the
foundations of his sermons, nothing can be said in their
recommendation, either on the score of literature or
morality. An English treatise upon the art of sermonizing, which is filled up with very full plans of sermons
by various distinguished preachers, contains such remarks
as the following : ' An immense number of examples, in
which passages are laid out in logical order, are to be
found in Burkitt on the New Testament, and more especially in Henry, and these may be often turned to good
account. Some ministers are very cautious of using any
of these plans, because the volumes of Burkitt and Henry
are possessed by many families ; but surely some new
casting might easily be devised that would give the air
of novelty, and please the fastidious, if they be thought
worth the pleasing.' Again he says : ' I do not wish to

---

[1] The careful analysis of such sermons as those of South, Barrow, and
Saurin would be a discipline for the young preacher, more valuable than
to read a hundred treatises upon rhetoric without it.

draw you from your independent study and the resources of your own minds; but if at any time you feel indisposed towards mental labour, or time will not allow you to enter upon it, regard it as perfectly lawful to avail yourselves of the materials furnished by such an author as Henry.' Again he observes: 'As to Burkitt, he is full of both long and short skeletons, that is, skeletons upon long and short passages, which a little pains would so modernize, that when our knowing people saw their old friend with a new face, they certainly would not recognise him again. This is, I suppose, what we wish, when we find ourselves out of condition for close study, or have not time for it.' The author then goes on to say, with an innocent simplicity that is quite charming, that 'it is necessary to obtain a knowledge of Burkitt's key-words,—his "Observe," his "Note," his "Learn." When he says "Observe," he is about to give you a head or division of the passage in an expository view,' etc. etc.[1]

---

[1] Sturtevant, *Manuel*, pp. 57–59.—The views in the English Church are very indulgent in reference to preparations for the pulpit. Archdeacon Paley, in a sermon to the young clergy of Carlisle, addresses them as follows : 'There is another resource by which your time may be occupied, which you have forgot, in urging that your time will hang heavy upon you. I mean the composition of sermons. I am far from refusing you the benefit of other men's labours ; I only require that they be called in, not to flatter laziness, but to assist industry. You find yourself unable to furnish a sermon every week ; try to compose one every month.' The *English Churchman* contains the following announcement : 'A clergyman of experience and moderate views, who distinguished himself during his University course in Divinity and English Composition, will furnish original sermons, in strict accordance with the Church of England, in a legible hand, at 5s. 6d. each. Only one copy will be given in any diocese. A specimen will be sent, if wished for. Sermons made to order, on any required subject, on reasonable terms. For further particulars apply,' etc.

Now, such recommendations as these are both illiterate and immoral. No scholar, no preacher who has even a becoming regard for the literary character, to say nothing of the edifying character, of his sermonizing, could possibly subject his intellect to such copying. A proper estimate of the sermon as a piece of authorship, if nothing more, would lead the sacred orator to despise such servile artifices, from which nothing but an artificial product could result. Upon such a method as this, the whole department of Sacred Eloquence would lose all its freshness and originality, and would die out. 'Dull as a sermon' would be a phrase more true and more significant than it is now.

But upon the score of morality, this act of stealing sermons is utterly indefensible. A preacher ought to be an honest man throughout. Sincerity, godly sincerity, should characterize him intellectually as well as morally. His plans ought to be the genuine work of his own brain. Not that he may not, at times, present a plan and train of thought similar to those of other minds; but he ought not to know of it at the time. Such coincidences ought to be undesigned,—the result of two minds working upon a similar or the same subject, each in an independent way, and with no intercommunication. Then the product belongs to both alike; and the coincidence results from the common nature of truth and the common structure of the human mind, and not from a servile copying of one mind by another.

Beside this critical study of the best sermonizers, in the several languages with which the preacher may be acquainted, he should be a diligent student of the standard theological treatises in them. There are, in each of the leading literatures of the modern world, and also in the patristic Greek and Latin, a few treatises which are so thoroughly scriptural in their matter and so systematic in their structure, that they cannot be outgrown by either the theologian or the sermonizer. Upon these, in connection with a faithful study of the Scriptures themselves, the preacher ought to bestow his time. This method of preparing for the process of composition, unlike that indolent method of having recourse to the plans and sermons of others, strengthens and enriches the intellect. The preacher daily becomes a more discriminating exegete, a more profound theologian, a more natural rhetorician; and the end of his ministerial career finds him as thoughtful and as fertile a sermonizer as ever.

The union of a close critical study of the Scriptures themselves, with a thorough and continuous study of those sterling theological treatises which, because they have grown up out of the Scriptures, partake most of their root and fatness, cannot be too earnestly recommended to the sermonizer, as the best general preparation for direct and particular preparation for the pulpit. The time and ability of the preacher, in this age of innumerable small books upon innumerable small subjects, is too often expended upon inferior productions. Let him dare to be ignorant of this transitory literature, whether sacred or secular, that he may become acquainted with the Bible itself, and those master-works of master-minds which contain the methodized substance of the Bible, and breathe its warmest, deepest inspiration.

Intimately connected with this study of the Bible, and of theological systems and treatises, is the study of philosophy. This point merits a fuller treatment than is possible within our limits. We would only briefly remark that the study of philosophy, rightly pursued, is a great aid to the theologian and the preacher. If the department of philosophy be employed rather as a means of disciplining the mind, and of furnishing a good *method* of developing and presenting truth, than as a source whence the truth itself is to be taken, it becomes the handmaid of theology and religion. If, on the contrary, it is regarded as the *source* of truth, and the theologian and preacher seeks his subject-matter from the finite reason of man instead of from the Supreme Reason as it has revealed itself in the Scriptures, then the influence of philosophical studies is most injurious. But this is not the true idea of philosophy. Bacon called his philosophical system the 'novum organum,'—the new organ or instrument by means of which truth was to be developed, established, and applied. He did not style it a new *revelation* of truth, but a new *medium* of truth.

If, now, the theologian and preacher adopts this true and rational view of the nature of philosophy, if he regards it as a means whereby his mind obtains the best method of developing and not of originating truth, if he views it as a simple key to unlock the casket which contains the treasure, and not as the treasure itself, or even the casket,—if the theologian and preacher adopts this sober and rational view of the nature and uses of philosophy, he will find it of great assistance. All that part of rhetoric which treats of plan and invention, all the *organizing* part of rhetoric, is most intimately connected with philosophy. Moreover, a correct knowledge of the laws of the human mind, a correct idea of the relation of truth to the human mind, and a correct method of enucleating and establishing truth, cannot be acquired without the discipline that results from philosophical studies; and without such knowledge, the preacher can neither think profoundly and consecutively, nor discourse clearly and forcibly.[1]

4. The fourth general direction for the sermonizer is this: *Maintain a spiritual mind.* This direction is a practical one, and, while it includes all that is implied in the common injunction for all Christians to cultivate personal piety, it is more specific in reference to the necessities of the preacher. By a spiritual mind in this connection, is meant that solemn and serious mental frame which is naturally and constantly occupied with eternal realities. Some Christians seem to be much more at home in the invisible realm of religion than others. They are characterized by a uniformly earnest and unearthly temper, as if their eye were fixed upon something beyond the horizon of this world, as if they saw more, and saw farther, than thoughtless and unspiritual

---

[1] Says John Edwards in his work on *Preaching :* ' As for metaphysics, it cannot be denied that they are useful to the helping us to a clear and distinct apprehension of things, and to the enlarging of our minds, and the cultivating of our thoughts. Whence it is that unthinking persons, and those that never study for accuracy of conceptions, hate this sort of learning as much as a deist doth creeds and catechisms.'—Preface to Part i.

men about them. Their eye *is* fixed upon something beyond time and sense, and they *do* see more, far more of 'the things unseen and eternal,' than the average of Christians.

Now, this mental temper is of great worth to the preacher. Aside from the fact that one who possesses it is always *in the vein* for writing or speaking upon religious themes, such a one discourses with an earnest sincerity that is always impressive and effective. He speaks seriously, because he understands the nature of his subject. He speaks clearly and distinctly, because this spiritual-mindedness makes him substantially an eye-witness of eternal realities. He speaks convincingly, because he knows what he says, and whereof he affirms.

Let the preacher, then, maintain a spiritual mind,—a mind that is not dazzled with the glare of earth, that is too solemn to be impressed by the vanities of time, and made habitually serious by seeing Him who is invisible. Dwelling among the things that are unseen and eternal, such an orator, when he comes forth to address volatile and wordly men, will speak with a depth and seriousness of view, and an energy and pungency of statement, that will leave them thoughtful and anxious. Without this abiding sense of the reality and awfulness of eternal things, though the preacher may send men away entertained and dazzled, he cannot send them away thinking upon themselves and upon their prospects for eternity. And of what worth is a sermon that does not do this? The principal lack in the current preaching is not so much in the matter as in the *manner*. There is truth sufficient to save the soul in most of the sermons that are delivered; but it is not so fused with the speaker's personal convictions, and presented in such living contact with the hearer's fears, hopes, and needs, as to make the impression of stern reality. The pulpit must become more intense in manner, or the 'form of sound words' will lose its power.

CHAPTER V.

HAVING, in the preceding chapter, laid down some rules for the general preparation for sermonizing, we proceed to give some maxims for the *immediate* preparation of sermons. If the preacher has fitted himself for the direct composition of discourses, by acquiring a homiletic mental habit, by forming a high ideal of a sermon, by training himself to self-reliance, and by uniformly maintaining a serious and spiritual mind, he is ready to compose sermons always and everywhere. He is a workman that has learned his craft, and is in possession of a constructive talent which he can use whenever he is called upon. But these general maxims need to be supplemented by some particular rules relating to the process of composition itself, and these we now proceed to specify.

1. Before beginning the composition of a sermon, *bring both the intellect and the heart into a fervid and awakened condition.* Although this general preparation for sermonizing of which we have spoken will naturally keep the mind and heart more or less active, still there will be need of more than this ordinary wakefulness, in order that the preacher may do his best work. Such a general preparation, it is true, will prevent the sermonizer from being a

dull and lethargic man, but he will need some more immediate stimulation than this, in order that he may compose with the utmost energy and vigour possible. As, in the chemical process of crystallization, a smart stroke upon the vessel in which the solution has been slowly preparing for the magical change from a dull fluid to a bright and sparkling solid will accelerate the movement, and render the process seemingly an instantaneous one, so a sort of shock given to the mind, filled as it is with rich stores, and possessed as it is by a homiletic habit, will contribute greatly to the rapid and vigorous construction of a sermon.

Some agitation and concussion is requisite in order to the most efficient exercise of the understanding. The mental powers need to be in an aroused condition—so to speak, in a state of exaltation—in order to work with thoroughness and energy. Hence, some very distinguished literary men have been wont to resort to the stimulus of drugs or of alcohol to produce that inward excitement which is needed in order to the original and powerful action of the intellect. Poets and orators, in particular, feel the need of this intellectual fermentation ; and hence the instances of such artificial stimulation of the intellectual powers are most common among these. The preacher is precluded by Christian principle from the use of such means of rousing and kindling his mind, even if the lower prudential motives should not prevail with him. For the mind, like the body, is fearfully injured by artificial and unnatural stimulation. Minds which have been accustomed to it, and have been forced up in this unnatural way to unnatural efforts, show the effects of such treatment in premature debility, and commonly in final insanity or idiocy.

The true and proper stimulant for the intellect is *truth.* There is no sin in being excited by truth. There is no mental injury in such excitement. The more thoroughly the intellect is roused and kindled by a living verity, the more intensely it is affected and energized by it, the better is it for the intellect and the man. In order, therefore, that the sermonizer may produce within his mind that excitement which is needed in order to original and vigorous composition, let him possess it with some single truth adapted to this purpose. And this, from the nature of the case, should be that leading idea which he proposes to embody in his discourse. Every sermon ought to be characterized by unity,—a unity arising from the presence and the presidency within it of some one leading thought. The *theme,* or *proposition,* of the sermon should, therefore, be that particular truth by which the sacred orator should excite his intellect, and awaken his powers to an intenser activity. If the preacher is not able to set his mind into a glow and fervour by his subject, let him not seek other means of excitement, but let him ponder the fact of his apathy, until he is filled with shame and sorrow. Let him remember, that if he is not interested in the truth, if divine truth has no power to quicken and rouse his intellectual faculties, he lacks the first qualification for sermonizing.

But the sermonizer who has made that great general preparation for his work of which we have spoken, will find all the stimulation he needs in his theme. It will be

I

taken from the circle of truths in which he has become most interested, both by the habits of his mind, and by his general culture. It will be suggested to him by his own spiritual wants and those of his audience. It will have direct reference to the supply of these wants. Let the preacher, then, so far as intellectual excitement is concerned, so fill his mind with the particular idea of the discourse which he is about to prepare, that all inaction and lethargy shall be banished at once. Let him, before beginning the construction of a sermon, set all his mental powers into a living play by the single leading truth he would embody in it.

But, besides this intellectual awakening, some more than ordinary enlivenment of the *feelings* and *affections* is needed in order to vigorous and eloquent composition. And this is especially true of the composition of sermons, one main purpose of which is to reach the affections and feelings of the human soul. Without that warm glow which comes from a warm heart, the purely intellectual excitement of which we have spoken will fail to influence the hearer in the way of emotion and action. A purely intellectual force and energy may arrest and interest an audience; but, taken by itself, it cannot persuade their wills or melt their hearts. The best sermons of a preacher are generally composed under the impulse of a lively state of religious feeling. If preachers should be called to testify, they would state that those discourses which were written when they were in their best mood as Christians constitute the best portion of their authorship.

The sermonizer, therefore, should seek for a more

than ordinary quickening of his emotions and affections, as he begins the work of immediate preparation for the pulpit. It is difficult to lay down rules for the attainment of this state of feeling that will be suited to every one. Each individual Christian is apt to know the best means of rousing his own mind and heart, and hence it is better to leave the person himself to make a choice out of the variety that are at his command. Generally speaking, however, anything that contributes to awaken in the soul a livelier sense of the excellence of divine things, anything that tends to stir and quicken the Christian affections, will furnish the preacher what he needs in order to vigorous composition. Probably, therefore, no better advice can be given to the sacred orator, in the respect of which we are speaking, than that very same advice which he gives to the common Christian when he asks for the best means and methods of quickening his religious affections. It has been said by one of the most profound and devout minds in English literature, that 'an hour of solitude passed in sincere and earnest prayer, or the conflict with and conquest over a single passion or subtle bosom sin, will teach us more of thought, will more effectually awaken the faculty and form the habit of reflection, than a year's study in the schools without them.' If prayer and Christian self-discipline do this for the habits of thought, most certainly will they do the same for the habits of feeling. If an hour of serious self-examination and self-mortification, or an hour of devout meditation and earnest prayer, does not set the affections of the preacher into a glow, probably nothing in the way of means can. The greatest

preachers have, consequently, been in the habit of preparing for composition by a season of prayer and meditation. The maxim of Luther, *Bene orasse est bene studuisse,*
is familiar to all. Augustine says, 'Let our Christian
orator, who would be understood and heard with pleasure,
pray before he speak. Let him lift up his thirsty soul to
God before he pronounce anything.' Erasmus, a man in
whom the intellectual was more prominent than the spiritual and devotional, yet observes, that 'it is incredible
how much light, how much vigour, how much force and
vitality are imparted to the clergyman by deep earnest supplication.' And the pagan Pericles, according to Plutarch,
'was accustomed, whenever he was to speak in public,
previously to entreat the gods that he might not utter
against his will any word that should not belong to his
subject.'

By filling his mind with his theme, and awakening his
religious affections by prayer and devout meditation, the
sacred orator will bring his whole inner being into that
awakened and exalted condition which prepares for direct
and rapid composition. He will become a *roused* man, and
will find all his faculties of cognition and feeling in free
and living action.

2. And this brings us to the second maxim for facilitat-
ing the process of composition, which is, *Compose continuously.* When the preacher has made all the preparation,
general and particular, of which we have spoken, and his
mind and heart are ready to work, he should proceed in
the composition of a sermon without intermission. The
intellect works with far the greatest intensity and energy

when it works continuously. It acquires strength by motion, and hence a stop in its action diminishes its force. When, therefore, a full preparation for its agency has been made, it ought to be allowed, or, if need be, compelled to work as hard and as long as is compatible with the physical structure of the individual. Some men are capable of much more protracted mental efforts than others; though, in this case, the mental processes themselves are apt to be much slower. When the mind moves with rapidity, it is unable to continue in motion so long as when its movements are more dull and heavy. Each man should know himself in these respects, and understand how much his mind and body can endure without injury. Having this knowledge, he ought then to subject himself to as intense and as long-continued composition as is possible. Having seated himself at his writing-desk, he ought not to lay down his pen until he has tired himself by the process of original composition. Then let him unbend in good earnest, and allow his mind and his body a real genuine relaxation.

Too many sermons are composed during an intermittent activity of the mind, which does not draw upon its deepest resources and its best power. The sermon is the product of a series of isolated efforts, instead of one long, strong application. It wears, consequently, a fragmentary character and appearance, as if it were written one sentence at a time, or each paragraph by itself. Even if there is a connection of the parts, there is no *fusion* of them. Even if the discourse has method, it has no glow.

'Write with fury and correct with phlegm,' is admirable advice for the sermonizer. But it is impossible to rouse this fury of the mind, except by a continuous application of its energies. If the composer stops for a season, his intellect begins to cool again, and much of the energy of his succeeding effort is absorbed in bringing it up to the same degree of ardour at which it stood at the close of the preceding effort. It is as if the smith should every moment withdraw his iron from the fire, instead of letting it stay until it has acquired a white heat. The same amount of mental application, condensed into a single continuous effort, will accomplish far more than if it is scattered in portions over a long space of time. 'Divide up the thunder,' says Schiller, 'into separate notes, and it becomes a lullaby for children; but pour it forth in one continuous peal, and its royal sound shall shake the heavens.'

One principal reason why the pulpit ministrations of the clergy do not, as they should, exhibit their utmost possibility of effort, lies in the fact that too many sermons are composed scatteringly all along through the week. They are the products of the desultory efforts of the clergyman. He allows himself to be interrupted during the season of composition, or else he has no fixed and stated season. The consequence is, that the sermon, instead of being produced by one uninterrupted gush of soul, or at least by a few gushes and outpourings that form a true connection with each other, and so are virtually a single continuous effort, is the patched and fragmentary collection of odd hours, and of ungenial moods. The discourse, in this way, drags its slow length along through the whole week, and the entire mental labour expended upon it, though apparently so much, is not equal in true productive force, in real originant and influential power, to five hours of continuous glowing composition.

Let the sermonizer, then, proceed upon the maxim of writing continuously, when he writes at all. Let him have his set season for composition. Let him fix the time of writing and the length of effort in accordance with his physical strength, and then let him go through with the process of composition with all the abstraction, absorption, and devotedness of prayer itself. In this way the very best power of the man, the theologian, and the Christian will be evolved, and will appear in a discourse that will be fresh, energetic, and impressive. In this way the sermon would become a more uniformly vivid production, and a more generally vital species of authorship, than it now is.

It must be remembered, however, that this injunction to write continuously and furiously, is a maxim only for one who has obeyed the other maxims, general and special, that have been laid down for sermonizing. It is no maxim for one who has not. It is one of a series, and presupposes obedience to what precedes, and also to what succeeds. If the preacher has formed a homiletic habit of mind, if his ideal of a sermon is high, if he has trained himself to self-reliance, if he has acquired a spiritual way of thinking, and if he has roused his mind by his subject, and his heart by prayer—if he has done all this, then what he does in the hour of composition, let him do quickly and continuously.

3. The third maxim to be followed by the sermonizer in actual composition is this, *Avoid prolixity.* By pro-

lixity is meant a tiresome length which arises from an excessive treatment of a subject,—as excessive explanation, or excessive illustration, or excessive argumentation. Theremin, in his treatise upon Rhetoric,[1] enunciates the important distinction between the philosophical and the rhetorical presentation of truth. The former is that exhaustive and detailed development of a subject which is proper in the scientific treatise. The latter is that rapid and condensed, yet methodical, exhibition of thought which is required of the orator by the circumstances in which he is placed. Recurring to this distinction, the maxim, 'Avoid prolixity,' is equivalent to the rule, 'Exhibit truth rhetorically,' in distinction from exhibiting it philosophically or poetically.

The orator, of all men, should know when he is through, and should stop when he is through. The preacher should perceive when he has subjected a subject, or a portion of a subject, to a treatment that is sufficient for the purposes of oratory, and should act accordingly. As soon as his presentation has reached the due limits of rhetoric, he should bring it to an end instantaneously, lest it pass over into a mode of representation that is foreign to the orator, and is inimical to all the aims of an orator. Prolixity, or excessive treatment, arises when the sermonizer continues to dwell upon any part of his discourse after he has already sufficiently developed it. A plan is prolix, when it is filled up with subdivisions which are so evidently contained in the principal divisions that the mind of the auditor feels itself undervalued by their formal enunciation. An

[1] Book i. ch. 10, 11 ; Book ii. ch. 4.

argument is prolix, when, from the employment of the philosophical instead of the rhetorical mode of demonstration, it is made tedious by syllogisms instead of enthymemes, and by trains of ratiocination instead of bold and direct appeals to consciousness. An illustration is prolix, when the short and rapid metaphor is converted into the long and detailed simile or allegory.[1]

Without, however, entering upon these particulars of plan, proof, and illustration, we would briefly call attention to that prolixity, or excessive and tedious treatment of a subject, which arises from an imperfect mastery of it. Suppose that the sermonizer has not made that general and special preparation for composition which we have described, and yet attempts the production of a sermon. In the first place, his manner of presentation will inevitably be confused; in the second place, it will inevitably be prolix because it is confused; and, in the third place, it will inevitably be tedious, because it is prolix and confused. Instead of handling his theme with that strong yet easy grasp which is natural to a mind that is master of itself and of the truth, he handles it irresolutely, hesitat-

---

[1] Figures are now the chief source of false rhetoric. The preacher talks trope, instead of talking truth and sense. Aristotle was not an orator, but he held the key to eloquence, by virtue of his sagacious insight and scientific analysis. One of his pregnant remarks is, that 'the *metaphor* is the orator's figure, and the simile is the poet's.' The metaphor is swift and glancing, flashing its light instantaneously, and not impeding the flow of thought and truth ; the simile is the metaphor wire-drawn, detailed, and expanded, so as to fill the whole foreground of the discourse with pictorial elements, in which both speaker and hearer lose sight of the subject. If this dictum of the Stagyrite were heeded, there would be less of prolix poetical fustian, and more of genuine eloquence, in the discourses of a certain class of preachers.

ingly, and awkwardly. Instead of a clear, downright
statement, because he *knows* whereof he affirms, he expresses himself obscurely and doubtfully, because he does
not certainly and positively know. Statement follows statement, and yet there is little or no progress towards a
final statement. Conscious. that he has not done justice
to the topic, he dares not let it drop and take up another.
Conscious that he has not lodged the truth fairly and
surely in the mind of the auditor, he does not leave it, but
continues to hover about it, and work at it, in hope of
better success in the end. The result is, that instead of
crowding the greatest possible amount of matter into
the smallest possible form, the preacher spreads the least
possible amount of truth over the widest possible surface.
He hammers out his lead very thin. For, in this process,
the truth itself suffers. Instead of appearing in the
sermon as it is in its own nature, bright, dense, and gem-
like, under the manipulations of such a workman it
becomes dull and porous. The sacred oration, instead of
being a swift, brief, and strong movement of thought,
becomes a slow, long, and feeble one.

But prolixity may arise also from another cause besides
ignorance of the subject. There may be prolixity from
too much information. The preacher may have stored his
memory with a multifarious knowledge, and not having
acquired that thoroughly organizing habit of mind which,
like life in nature, sloughs off all that is not needed, this
knowledge inundates the sermon. It comes pouring in
upon him by a merely passive effort of the memory, while
the judgment is unawakened and unemployed, and, borne

along upon this general deluge of materials, the preacher becomes the most prolix and tedious of mortals. Long after the topic under consideration has been sufficiently explained to the understanding, he continues to explain. Long after the topic has been sufficiently illustrated to the imagination, he continues to illustrate. Copiousness of information, unless it is under the regulation and guidance of a strongly methodizing ability and true rhetorical talent, leads to prolixity as inevitably as sheer ignorance.

While the preacher is on his guard against this fault, he is at the same time to remember that he is dealing with the common mind, and must not be so brief as to be obscure. A certain degree of repetition even is required in the sermon, especially if it is highly doctrinal, in order to convey the truth completely. This trait should be managed with great care, however ; for even the common mind is less offended at a nakedness of statement which leaves it something to do, even if it is in the way of supplying ellipses and deficiencies, than it is at an excessive repetition, which tires and tantalizes it. It is impossible to lay down a general rule for the length of a sermon. It will not do to say that it should be thirty minutes in length, or forty-five minutes, or one hour. The length of a discourse will vary with the nature of the theme, and the peculiarities of time and place. And no stiff rule is needed, provided the sermonizer possesses that good judgment, that tact which discerns when the subject, as a whole, or in its parts, has received a sufficient treatment. It is, in reality, a sort of instinctive feeling which comes in the course of a good rhetorical training and practice, rather than any outward rule, that must decide when the development of truth has reached that point where it must stop. Hence the remark so often made in praise of a skilful orator, ' He knows when he is done.' In fact, it is not the item of length, but the item of prolixity which wearies an audience. An auditory will listen with increasing interest to a sermon of an hour's length, provided their attention is kept upon the stretch by a sermonizer who says just enough and no more upon each point, and who passes from topic to topic with rapidity, and yet with a due treatment and exhaustion of each ; while they will go to sleep under a sermon of a half-hour's length, in which there is none of the excitement that comes from a skilful management of the heads, and none of the exhilaration of a forward motion. There is less fatigue and weariness in shooting through two hundred miles of space in a rail-car, than in lumbering over ten miles of space in a slow coach.

The importance of avoiding prolixity is very apparent, when we consider the relation of the sermon to the feelings and affections of the hearer. The feelings of the human soul are often very shy, and apparently capricious. The preacher sometimes succeeds in awakening a very deep feeling, say that of conviction of sin ; but he is not satisfied with having said just enough, or perhaps he is destitute of that tact of which we have spoken, and does not *know* that he has, and continues to enlarge and amplify. The feeling of conviction in the hearer, which ought to have been left to itself, begins to be weakened by the unnecessary repetition or prolixity of the discourse, and perhaps is ultimately dissipated by it. If the preacher had stopped when he was really through, and had left the mind of the auditor to its own workings and those of the Holy Spirit in it, a work would have been done in the soul, which all this labour of supererogation on his part only serves to hinder and suppress.

Let the preacher acquire this nice discernment, by acquiring a good rhetorical discipline, by making all the general and special preparation for sermonizing, and by studying the capacities of his congregation, and then he will instinctively avoid all prolixity in the discussion of truth. Then his sermons, whether they are longer or shorter, will all of them exhibit that just proportion, that roundness of form and absence of all superfluity which we see in the works of nature, and which appears in the productions of every wise and cunning workman who imitates nature.

CHAPTER VI.

THE DIFFERENT SPECIES OF SERMONS.

IN classifying sermons, it is well to follow the example of the scientific man, and employ as generic distinctions as possible. It is never desirable to distinguish a great many particulars, and elevate them into an undue prominence, by converting them into generals. That classification, therefore, which would regard the 'applicatory' sermon, the 'observational' sermon, and such-like, as distinct classes, only contributes to the confusion and embarrassment of the enquirer. The three most generic species of sermons are the *topical*, the *textual*, and the *expository*.

1. The Topical Sermon is one in which there is but a single leading idea. This idea sometimes finds a formal expression in a proposition, and sometimes it pervades the discourse as a whole, without being distinctly pre-announced. Topical sermons are occupied with one definite subject, which can be accurately and fully stated in a brief title. South preaches a discourse of this kind, from Numbers xxxii. 23: 'Be sure your sin will find you out.' The proposition of the sermon is this: 'Concealment of sin is no security to the sinner.' The leading idea of the discourse is the *concealment* of sin; and the particular idea in the hearer, to which this idea in the sermon is referred,

is the idea of *happiness*.[1] The concealment of sin is affirmed to be incompatible with the soul's peace and enjoyment; and the positions by which the idea or proposition of the sermon is led back to this fundamental idea, in the mental constitution of the hearer, are these: 1. The sinner's very confidence of secrecy is the cause of his detection. 2. There is sometimes a providential concurrence of unexpected events, which leads to his detection. 3. One sin is sometimes the means of discovering another. 4. The sinner may unwittingly discover himself, through frenzy and distraction. 5. The sinner may be forced to discover himself by his own conscience. 6. The sinner may be suddenly smitten by some notable judgment that discloses his guilt. Or, 7, His guilt will follow him into another world, if he should chance to escape in this.

The topical sermon is more properly an oration than either of the other species. It is occupied with a single definite theme, that can be completely enunciated in a brief statement. All of its parts are subservient to the theoretical establishment of but one idea or proposition in the mind of the hearer, and to the practical realization of it in his conduct. In the case of the textual sermon, as we shall see when we come to examine it, there is less certainty of unity in the subject, and, consequently, in the structure of the discourse. And the expository sermon partakes least of any of the characteristics of oratory and eloquence.

Inasmuch as the topical sermon approaches nearest to the unity, and symmetry, and convergence to a single point, of the oration proper, it is the model species for

[1] Theremin, *Rhetoric*, pp. 72-75.

the preacher. By this is meant that the sermon, ideally, should contain one leading thought rather than several. It should be the embodiment of a single proposition, rather than a collection of several propositions. It should announce but one single doctrine, in its isolation and independence, instead of exhibiting several doctrines in their interconnection and mutual dependence. The sermon must preserve an oratorical character. It should never allow either the philosophical or the poetical element to predominate over the rhetorical. The sermon should be eloquence, and not poetry or philosophy. It should be a discourse that exhibits singleness of aim, and a converging progress towards an outward practical end.

It is for this reason, therefore, that we lay down the position, that the topical sermon is the model species for the sermonizer. If he constructs a textual sermon, he ought to make it as topical as is possible.[1] He must aim to pervade it with but one leading idea, to embody in it but one doctrine, and to make it teach but one lesson. In constructing an expository sermon, also, the preacher should make the same endeavour; and although he must in this instance be less successful, he may facilitate his aim by selecting for exposition only such passages of Scripture as have but one general drift, and convey but one general sentiment.

The importance of this maxim may be best seen by

---

[1] This is not to be attained by making the plan a mixture of topical and textual,—by stating a proposition, and following with a purely textual division. The plan should be textual, but the style and movement of the discourse should be distinguished, so far as possible, by unity, simplicity, and progressiveness,—that is, by oratorical or topical qualities.

considering the fact, that sermons are more defective in respect to unity of structure, and a constant progress towards a single end, than in any other respect. But these are strictly oratorical qualities, and can be secured only by attending to the nature and laws of eloquence,— to the rhetorical, as distinguished from the philosophical presentation of truth. Too many sermons contain matter enough for two or three orations, and consequently are not themselves orations. This is true of the elder English sermonizers, in whom the matter is generally superior to the form. Take the following plan of a sermon of South (in oratorical respects the best of the earlier English preachers) on Jer. vi. 15: 'Were they ashamed when they had committed abomination? Nay, they were not at all ashamed, neither could they blush; therefore they shall fall among them that fall: at the time that I visit them they shall be cast down, saith the Lord.' It is a topical discourse. The theme or proposition is, 'Shamelessness in sin is the certain forerunner of destruction.' The sermon contains sixteen pages, of which only four and a half are filled with matter that, upon strictly rhetorical principles, goes to establish the proposition. The first three-quarters of the sermon are occupied with an analysis of the *nature* of 'shamelessness in sin.' The discourse is shaped too disproportionately by the category of truth,— a category that is subordinate, and should not be allowed so much influence in the structure and moulding of an oration.[1] The consequence is, that this sermon possesses less of that oratorical fire and force so generally character-

[1] Theremin, *Rhetoric*, Book i. ch. x.

K

istic of South. It is not throughout pervaded by its own
fundamental proposition. It does not gather momentum
as it proceeds. There is no greater energy of style and
diction at the end than at the beginning. It is clear, it
is instructive, it has many and great excellences; but it
lacks the excellence of being a true oration—a rounded
and symmetrical discourse, pervaded by one idea, breathing but one spirit, rushing forward with a uniformly
accelerating motion, and ending with an overpowering
impression and influence upon the will. This discourse
would be more truly topical, and thus more truly oratorical, if the proportions had been just the reverse of
what they now are; if but one-fourth of it had been
moulded by the metaphysical category of truth, and the
remaining three-fourths by the practical idea of happiness;
if the discussion of the *nature* of shamelessness in sin had
filled four pages, and the *effects*, or reasons why it brings
down destruction or unhappiness upon the sinner, had filled
the remaining twelve.

2. The Textual Sermon is one in which the passage of
Scripture is broken up, and either its leading words or its
leading clauses become the heads of the discourse. For
example, Rom. xiv. 12, 'So then every one of us shall give
account of himself to God,' might be the foundation of a
discourse upon human accountability. The divisions are
formed by emphasizing the leading words, and thereby
converting them into the divisions of the sermon, as follows: 1. An *account* is to be rendered. 2. This account
is to be rendered to *God*. 3. *Every one* is to render this
account—mankind generally. 4. Every one of *us* is to

render this account—men as individuals. 5. Every one of us is to render an account of *himself.*

It is not necessary that the words of the text should be employed, as in the example given above. The substance of the separate clauses may be made the divisions, and the sermon still be textual. Barrow has a sermon founded on Eph. v. 20: 'Giving thanks always, for all things, unto God.' The plan is as follows: 1. The duty itself—giving thanks. 2. The object to whom thanks are to be directed —to God. 3. The time of performing the duty—always. 4. The matter and extent of the duty—for all things.

What are sometimes termed 'observational' sermons, are also textual. The following, taken from a plan of a sermon by Beddome, upon Acts ix. 4, 'Saul, Saul, why persecutest thou me?' will illustrate this. The observations upon this text are suggested either by the text as a whole, or by some of its· parts. 1. It is the general character of unconverted men to be of a persecuting spirit. This observation is suggested by the text as a whole. 2. Christ has his eye upon persecutors. This observation is also suggested by the text as a whole. 3. The injury done to Christ's people, Christ considers as done to himself. This observation is suggested by a part of the text—by an emphasized word in it—'why persecutest thou *me?*' 4. The calls of Christ are particular. This observation is suggested by a part of the text—'*Saul, Saul.*'

There are two things requisite to the production of a good textual sermon—viz. a significant text, and a talent to discover its significance. The text must contain distinct and emphatic conceptions, to serve as the parts of the

division. In the text given above, Rom. xiv. 12, 'So
then every one of us shall give account of himself to
God,' there are these distinct and emphatic ideas: an
account; a judge; humanity generally; the individual in
particular; personal confession.   These fertile conceptions
are full of matter, and the skill of the sermonizer is seen
in the thoroughness and brevity with which he exhausts
them and their contents.   Upon the number, variety, and
richness of such distinct and emphatic ideas in a passage,
depends its fitness for textual discourse.

Again, the text, in case it does not contain a number of
such conceptions, must contain a number of distinct positions or affirmations, to serve as parts of the division.
There may be no single conceptions in a text suitable to
constitute the plan of a sermon, while there are several
statements in it direct or implied.   Take, for example,
Ps. xc. 10: 'The days of our years are threescore years
and ten: and if by reason of strength they be fourscore
years, yet is their strength labour and sorrow: for it is
soon cut off, and we fly away.'   The single conceptions in
this text are not weighty enough to constitute heads in a
discourse, but the affirmations, the positions, and the statements implied in it are.   This text, treated in this way,
would furnish the following divisions of a textual sermon:
1. Human life, however lengthened out, must come to
an end.   2. Human life, at longest, is very short.   3. That
which is added to the ordinary duration of human life is,
after all, but little to be desired.

The second requisite, in order to the production of a
good textual sermon, is a talent to detect these emphatic

conceptions, or these direct or indirect positions, in a passage of Scripture. A preacher destitute of this talent will
pass by many texts that really are full of the materials of
textual sermonizing. He has no eye to discover the rich
veins that lie concealed just under the dull and uninteresting surface. If a text is so plain that he needs only to
cull out the leading words,—if the formation of the plan is
merely a *verbalizing* process,—he can, perhaps, succeed in
constructing a textual discourse that will probably be commonplace, because its structure is so very evident and easy.
But the number of such texts is small, and the range of
such a sermonizer must be narrow. A tact is needed in
the preacher to discover the hidden skeleton. This tact
will be acquired gradually and surely by every one who
carefully cultivates himself in all homiletic respects. Like
all nice discernment, it comes imperceptibly in the course
of training and discipline, and, therefore, no single and
particular rule for its acquisition can be laid down. It
must be acquired, however, or the fundamental talent for
textual sermonizing will be wanting. Moreover, this tact
should be judicious. It is possible to find more meaning
in a text than it really contains. The Rabbinic notion,
that mountains of sense are contained in every letter of
the inspired volume, may be adopted to such an extent, at
least, as to lead the preacher into a fanciful method that is
destructive of all impressive and effective discourse. This
talent for detecting the significance of Scripture must be
confined to the gist of it,—to the evident and complete
substance of it.

3. The Expository Sermon, as its name indicates, is an

explanatory discourse. The purpose of it is to unfold the meaning of a connected paragraph, or section of Scripture, in a more detailed manner than is consistent with the structure of either the topical or the textual sermon. Some writers upon Homiletics would deny it a place among sermons, and contend that' it cannot legitimately contain enough of the oratorical structure and character to justify its being employed for purposes of persuasion. They affirm that the expository discourse is purely and entirely didactic, and can no more be classified with the connected and symmetrical productions of oratory and eloquence, than the commentary or the paraphrase can be.

But while it is undoubtedly true that the expository sermon is the farthest removed from the oration, both in its structure and in its movement, it is not necessary that it should be as totally unoratorical as commentary or paraphrase. An expository discourse should have a logical structure, and be pervaded by a leading sentiment, as really as a topical sermon. And, certainly, it ought to be free from the dilution of a mere paraphrase. It should have a beginning, middle, and end, and thus be more than a piece of commentary. In short, we lay down the same rule in relation to the expository sermon that we did in relation to the textual—viz. that it be assimilated to the topical model as closely as the nature of the species permits. But in order to this assimilation, it is necessary to select for exposition a passage or paragraph of Scripture that is somewhat complete in itself. The distinction between expository preaching and commentary originates in the selection, in the former instance, of a rounded and self-included portion of inspiration, as the foundation of discourse; while in the latter instance, the mind is allowed to run on indefinitely, to the conclusion of the Gospel or the Epistle. The excellence of an expository sermon, consequently, depends primarily upon the choice of such a portion of Scripture as will not lead the preacher on and on, without allowing him to arrive at a proper termination. Unless a passage is taken that finally comes round in a full circle, containing one leading sentiment, and teaching one grand lesson—like a parable of our Lord,—the expository sermon must either be commentary or paraphrase. And if it be either of these, it cannot be classed among sermons, because the utmost it can accomplish is information. Persuasion, the proper function and distinguishing characteristic of eloquence, forms no part of its effects upon an audience.

Even when a suitable passage has been selected, the sermonizer will need to employ his strongest logical talent, and his best rhetorical ability, to impart sufficient of the oratorical form and spirit to the expository sermon. He will need to watch his mind and his plan with great care, lest the discourse overflow its banks and spread out in all directions, losing the current and deep strong volume of eloquence. This species of sermonizing is very liable to be a dilution of divine truth, instead of an exposition. Perhaps, among modern preachers, Chalmers exhibits the best example of the expository sermon. The oratorical structure and spirit of his mind enabled him to create a current in almost every species of discourse which he undertook, and through his Lectures on Romans we find a strong, unifying stream of eloquence constantly setting in, with an increasing and surging force, from the beginning to the end. The expository preaching of this distinguished sacred orator is well worth studying in the respect of which we are speaking.

Having thus briefly sketched the characteristics of the three species of sermons, the question naturally arises, To what extent is each to be employed by the preacher ?

The first general answer to this question is, that *all* the species should be employed by every sermonizer, without exception. No matter what the turn or temper of his mind may be, he should build upon each and every one of these patterns. If he is highly oratorical in his bent and spirit, let him by no means neglect the expository sermon. If his mental temperament is phlegmatic, and his mental processes naturally cool and unimpassioned, let him by no means neglect the topical sermon. It is too generally the case that the preacher follows his tendency, and preaches uniformly one kind of sermons. A more severe dealing with his own powers, and a wiser regard for the wants of his audience, would lead to more variety in sermonizing. At times the mind of the congregation needs the more stirring and impressive influence of a topical discourse, to urge it up to action. At others, it requires the instruction and indoctrination of the less rhetorical and more didactic expositions of Scripture.

And this leads to the further remark, as a definite reply to the question above raised, that the preacher should employ all three of the species, in the order in which they have been discussed. Speaking generally, it is safe to say that the plurality of sermons should be topical, pervaded by a single idea, or containing a single proposition, and converging by a constant progress to a single point. For this is the model species, as we have seen. The textual and the expository sermon must be as closely assimilated to this species as is possible, by being founded upon a single portion of Scripture that is complete in itself, and by teaching one general lesson. Moreover, textual and expository sermons will not be likely to possess this oratorical structure, and to breathe this eloquent spirit, unless the preacher is in the habit of constructing proper orations; unless he understands the essential distinction between eloquence and philosophy, and makes his audience feel the difference between the sacred essay and the sacred oration.

Next in order follows the textual sermon; and this species is next in value for the purposes of persuasion. Easy and natural in its structure—its parts being either the repetition of Scripture phraseology, or else suggestions from it,—the textual sermon should be frequently employed by the preacher.

And, lastly, the expository sermon should be occasionally employed. There is somewhat less call for this variety than there was before the establishment of Sabbath schools and Bible classes. Were it not that these have taken the exposition of Scripture into their own charge, one very considerable part of the modern preacher's duty, as it was of the Christian Fathers and the Reformers, would be to expound the Bible. Under the present arrangements of the Christian Church, however, the ministry is relieved from this duty to a considerable extent. But it is not wholly relieved from it. It is the duty of the preacher, occasionally, to lay out his best strength in the production of an elaborate expository sermon, which shall not only do the ordinary work of a sermon,—which shall not only instruct, awaken, and move,—but which shall also serve as a sort of guide and model for the teacher of the Sabbath school and the Bible class. Such sermonizing becomes an aid to the instructor in getting at the substance of revelation, and in bringing it out before the minds of the young. Probably the preacher can take no course so well adapted to elevate the standard of Sabbath-school and Bible-class instruction in his congregation, as occasionally to deliver a well-constructed and carefully elaborated expository discourse.

By employing, in this manner, all three of the species in their relative and proper proportions, the preacher will accomplish more for his people, and for his own mind, than by confining himself to one species only. As the years of his ministry roll on, he will bring the whole Bible into contact with the hearts and consciences of his audience. Divine Revelation, in this way, will become all that it is capable of becoming for the mind of man, because all its elements will be wrought into the mass of society. The preacher himself will perform all his functions, and not a portion only. He will instruct and awaken, he will indoctrinate and enkindle, he will inform and move, he will rebuke, reprove, and exhort. In short, he will in this way minister to the greatest variety of wants, and build up the greatest variety and breadth of Christian character in the Church.

CHAPTER VII.

THE sermon is always founded upon a passage of Scripture, which is denominated a *text*. This term is derived from the Latin *textum*, which signifies woven. The text, therefore, etymologically denotes either a portion of inspiration that is woven into the whole web of Holy Writ, and which, therefore, must be interpreted in its connection and relations, or else a portion of inspiration that is woven into the whole fabric of the sermon. We need not confine ourselves to either meaning exclusively, but may combine both significations. A text, then. is a passage of inspiration which is woven, primarily, into the web of Holy Writ, and, secondarily, into the web of a discourse. By uniting both of the etymological meanings of the word, we are led to observe the two important facts, that the subject of a sermon is an organic part of Scripture, and therefore must not be torn away, alive and bleeding, from the body of which it is a vital part; and, secondly, that the subject or text of a sermon should pervade the whole structure which it serves to originate and organize. If this definition of the text be kept in mind, and practically acted upon, it will prevent the sermonizer from treating it out of its connection with the context and the general tenor of revelation, and will lead him to regard it as the formative principle and power of his sermon, and to make it such. The text, then, will not be tortured to teach a doctrine contrary to the general teachings of inspiration, and it will be something more than a motto for a series of observations drawn from a merely human source—the preacher's own mind.

The custom of founding religious discourse upon a text, has prevailed ever since there has been a body of inspiration from which to take a text. In the patriarchal age, religious teachers spoke as they were moved by the Holy Ghost, without a passage from the Canon of inspiration, because the Canon was not yet formed. Noah was a 'preacher of righteousness,' and probably reasoned of righteousness, temperance, and judgment to come, much as Paul did before Felix, without any formal proposition derived from a body of Holy Writ. As early as the time of Ezra, however, we find the Sacred Canon, which during the Captivity had fallen into neglect, made the basis of religious instruction. Ezra, accompanied by the Levites, in a public congregation 'read in the law of God distinctly, and gave the sense, and caused them to understand the reading.' [1] Our Saviour, as his custom was (conforming, undoubtedly, to the general Jewish custom), went into the synagogue on the Sabbath-day, and 'stood up for to read' the Old Testament. He selected the first and part of the second verse of the sixty-first chapter of Isaiah for his text, and preached a sermon upon it, which fastened the eyes of every man in the synagogue upon Him in the very beginning, and which, notwithstanding its gracious words, finally

[1] Neh. viii. 6-8.

developed their latent malignity, and filled them with wrath, so that they led Him to the brow of the precipice on which their city was built, that they might cast Him down headlong.[1] The apostles also frequently discoursed from passages of Scripture. Peter, soon after the return of the disciples from the Mount of Ascension, preached a discourse from Psalm cix. 8, the object of which was to induce the Church to choose an apostle in the place of Judas.[2] And again, on the day of Pentecost, this same apostle preached a discourse, founded upon Joel ii. 28–32, which was instrumental in the conversion of three thousand souls.[3] Sometimes, again, the discourse, instead of being more properly homiletic, was an abstract of sacred history. The discourse of Stephen, when arraigned before the high priest, was of this kind.[4] The dense and mighty oration of Paul on Mars Hill, if examined, will be found to be made up, in no small degree, of statements and phrases that imply a thorough acquaintance with the Old Testament. They are all fused and amalgamated, it is true, with the thoughts that came fresh and new from Paul's own inspiration, and yet they are part and parcel of the earlier inspiration under the Jewish economy.

The homilies of the early Christian Church in the post-apostolic age were imitations of these discourses in the Jewish synagogue, and of these sermons of the apostles. They became more elaborate and rhetorical in proportion as audiences became more cultivated; and, on the other hand, they became less excellent, both in matter and in

---

[1] Luke iv. 16–29.   [2] Acts i. 15 sq.
[3] Acts ii. 14–36.   [4] Acts vii. 2–53.

form, in proportion as the Church became ignorant and superstitious. But during all the changes which the sermon underwent, it continued to be founded upon a passage of Scripture, and to contain more or less of Scripture matter and phraseology. Melancthon does indeed mention, as one of the inconsistencies and errors of Popery, that the Ethics of Aristotle were read in church, and that texts were taken from his writings. Still, as a general thing, the ministry, whether scriptural or unscriptural in its character, has in all ages, since there has been a collected Sacred Canon, gone to it for the foundation of its public discourse. That at this time there is less likelihood than ever before of this custom becoming antiquated, is one of the strongest grounds for believing that Christianity is to prevail throughout the earth. We have now the best reason for thinking that to the end of time, wherever there shall be the sermon, there will be the Bible; and that wherever there shall be homiletic discourse, there will be a scriptural basis for it.

The following reasons may be assigned for selecting a passage of Scripture as the foundation of the sermon: 1. First, the selection puts honour upon Revelation. It is a tacit and very impressive acknowledgment that the Scriptures are the great source of religious knowledge. Every sermon that is preached throughout Christendom, in its very beginning, and also through its whole structure, points significantly to the Divine Revelation, and in this way its paramount authority over all other literature is affirmed. No sermonizer could now take his text from a human production, even though it should contain the very substance, and breathe the very spirit of the Bible, without shocking the taste and the religious sensibilities of his audience. This fact shows that the practice of which we are speaking fosters reverence for the Word of God, and that it is consequently a good one. 2. Secondly, the practice of selecting a text results in the extended exposition of the Scriptures to the general mind. Sermonizing, while it is truly oratorical, in this way becomes truly expository. The sermon is a regularly constructed discourse; and yet, when it is founded upon a text, and is pervaded by it, it contains more or less of commentary. In this way the general mind is made acquainted with the contents of Revelation. 3. Thirdly, the sermon, when based upon a text, is more likely to possess unity and a methodical structure. If the preacher should give no one general direction to his mind by a passage of inspiration, the sermon would degenerate into a series of remarks that would have little use or apparent connection with each other. Like the observations of a person when called upon, without any premeditation, to speak in a public meeting, the sermon, though religious in its matter, would be more or less rambling in its manner. Without a text, the preacher would be likely to say what came uppermost, provided only it had some reference to religion. And the ill effects of this course would not stop here. The sermon would become more and more rambling, and less and less religious in its character, until, owing to this neglect of the Scriptures, it would eventually become dissevered from them, and the sacred oration would thus become secular. 4. Fourthly, the selection of a text aids the memory of the hearer. It furnishes him with a brief statement which contains the whole substance of the sermon, and is a clue to lead him through its several parts. We all know that the hearer betakes himself to the text first of all, when called upon to give an account of a discourse. If he re-members the text, he is generally able to mention the proposition, and more or less of the trains of thought. 5. Fifthly, the text imparts authority to the preacher's words. The sermon, when it is really founded upon a passage of inspiration, and is truly pervaded by it, pos-sesses a sort of semi-inspiration itself. It is more than a merely human and secular product. The Holy Spirit acknowledges it as such by employing it for purposes of conviction and conversion. A merely and wholly human production, properly secular eloquence, is not one of those things which the Holy Ghost 'takes and shows unto the soul.' A truly scriptural discourse, provided we do not strain the phraseology too far, has much of the authority of Scripture itself.

The following are some of the rules that should guide in the choice of a text: 1. First, a passage of Scripture should be selected, towards which the mind at the time sponta-neously moves. Choose a text that attracts and strikes the mind. The best sermons are written upon such passages, because the preacher enters into them with vigour and heartiness. Yet such texts are not always to be found. They do not present themselves at the very moment they are wanted. Hence the sermonizer must aid nature by art, must cultivate spontaneity by prudence and forethought. He should keep a book of texts, in which he habitually and carefully writes down *every* text that strikes him, *together with* all of the skeleton that presents itself to him at the time. Let him by no means omit this last particular. In this way the spontaneous movements of his mind will be on record. The fresh and genial texts that occur, together with the original and genial plans which they suggest, will all be within reach. A sermonizer who thus aids nature by art, will never be at a loss for subjects. He will be embarrassed more by his riches than his poverty.

2. Secondly, a text should be complete in itself. By this it is not meant that it should be short. No rule can be given for the length of a text. The most that is required is, that the passage of Scripture selected as the foundation of the sacred oration should, like the oration itself, be single, full, and unsuperfluous in its character. It should be single, containing only one general theme. It should be full, not a meagre and partial statement of this theme. It should be unsuperfluous, not redundant in matter that would lead the sermonizer into trains of discussion and reflection foreign to the one definite end of an oration. Texts must vary in length, from the necessity of the case. As a general rule, however, they should be as brief as is compatible with completeness. Short texts are more easily remembered. They are more likely to result in concise and effective sermons,—in sermons that are free from prolixity, and that converge constantly to a single end. Sermonizers like Latimer and South, who are distinguished for a rapid, driving method, affect short pithy texts like the following: 'Lying lips are an abomination to the Lord.' 'He that walketh uprightly, walketh surely.'

L

' The wisdom of this world is foolishness with God.'   ' So
that they are without excuse.'   ' Be sure your sin will find
you out.'   Again, preachers like Alison and Blair, who are
distinguished not so much for vigour and effectiveness, as
for a clean, neat, and elegant method, select brief texts,
like these: ' Thou art the same ; and thy years shall not
fail.'   ' In your patience possess ye your souls.'   ' Can ye
not discern the signs of the times ? '   ' Thou hast made
summer and winter.'   ' That I would, I do not.'   ' Un-
stable as water, thou shalt not excel.'   It will be found
to be true generally, that in proportion as a preacher's
mind is vivid and energetic, and the public mind is awake
and active, texts become brief, and sermons become direct
and convergent.   The texts of the sermons preached by
the German and English Reformers are short and pregnant.
Besides being easily remembered, a short text allows of
emphatic repetition.   Some sermons become very effective
by the reiteration of the inspired declaration at the conclusion of each head.   In this instance the text becomes a
clincher.   The affirmations of the preacher are *nailed*, to
use a phrase of Burns, with Scripture.[1]

3. Thirdly, a text should be chosen from which the
proposition of the sermon is derived plainly and naturally.
Sometimes a preacher desires to present a certain subject
which he has revolved in his mind, and upon which his
trains of thought are full and consecutive, and merely pre-

---

[1] ' Even ministers, they ha'e been kenned,
        In holy rapture,
    A rousing whid at times to vend,
        And nail't wi' Scripture.'

faces his sermon with a passage of Scripture which has
only a remote connection with his theme. In this case
the relation of the sermon to the text is that of adjustment rather than that of development. Having made
selection of a passage from which his proposition and trains
of thought do not naturally flow, he is compelled to torture
the text into an apparent unity with the discourse. Rather
than take this course, it would be better to make the text
a mere motto or title, and not pretend to an unfolding of
a Scripture passage. But there is no need of this. The
Bible is rich in texts for all legitimate sermons, for all
propositions and trains of thought that properly arise
within the province of sacred, as distinguished from secular eloquence. Let the preacher take pains, and find the
very passage he needs, and not content himself with one
that has only an apparent connection with his subject. But
when the passage selected is a true text,—that is, a portion
of Scripture out of which the proposition, trains of thought,
and whole substance of the discourse are *woven*,—let the
preacher see to it that he derives from it nothing that is
not in it. His business is not to involve into the text
something that is extrinsic, but to evolve out of it something that is intrinsic. Hence a text should be of such a
character as *evidently* to furnish one plain and significant
proposition, and to allow of a straightforward, easy, and
real development of it.

4. Fourthly, oddity and eccentricity should be avoided
in selecting a text. There is more need of this rule now
than formerly. The public mind is more ludicrous in its
associations, and more fastidious in its taste, than two

centuries ago. In the older sermonizers, applications of Scripture are very frequent that involuntarily provoke a smile in a modern reader, but which in their day were listened to with the utmost gravity by sober-minded men and women. The doctrine of a double sense, together with a strong allegorizing tendency in both preacher and hearer, contributed to this use of Scripture which seems to us fanciful and oftentimes ludicrous.

Illustrations of this trait are without number. Dr. Eachard, whose volume gives a very lively picture of the condition of the English clergy at the close of the seventeenth and the beginning of the eighteenth century, furnishes some curious examples of this eccentric spirit both in the choice of texts and in drawing out doctrine from them. He tells us of a preacher who selected Acts xvi. 30, 'Sirs, what must I do to be saved?' and preached upon the divine right of Episcopacy. 'For Paul and Silas are called "Sirs," and "Sirs" being in the Greek κύριοι, and this in strict translation meaning "Lords," it is perfectly plain that at that time Episcopacy was not only the acknowledged government, but that bishops were peers of the realm, and so ought to sit in the House of Lords.' Another preacher in the time of Charles II., he says, selected for his text the words, 'Seek ye first the kingdom of God,' and drew from them the proposition that kingly government is most in accordance with the will of God. 'For it is not said, seek the *parliament* of God, the *army* of God, or the *committee of safety* of God, but it is, seek the *kingdom* of God.' Another preacher took Matthew i. 2, 'Abraham begat Isaac;' and argued against pluralists and

non-residency in the ministry: 'For had Abraham not
resided with Sarah his wife, he could not have begot
Isaac.' Another sermonizer selected Isaiah xli. 14, 15,
'Fear not, thou worm Jacob, . . . thou shalt thresh the
mountains,' and drew the inference that the worm Jacob
was a threshing worm. In the same vein another
preacher takes for his text Isaiah lviii. 5, 'Is it such a
fast that I have chosen? a day for a man to afflict his
soul? Is it to bow down his head as a bulrush?' and
deduces the proposition that 'repentance for an hour or
a day is not worth a bulrush.' Still another preacher
selected his text from Psalm xciv. 19, 'In the multitude
of my thoughts within me, thy comforts delight my soul,'
and preached upon election and reprobation, deducing the
proposition, 'that amongst the multitude of thoughts there
was a great thought of election and reprobation.'[1] Similar examples of eccentricity in the choice and treatment of
a text have been handed down from other sources. An
aged New England minister, during the colonial period,
once preached before a very unpopular deputy governor
from Job xx. 6, 7, 'Though his *Excellency* mount up to
the heavens, and his head reach unto the clouds; yet he
shall perish for ever like his own dung.' Another preached
to the newly-married couples of his congregation upon a
part of Psalm lxxii. 7, 'And abundance of peace so long
as the *moon* endureth.' Dean Swift is reported to have
preached the annual sermon to the Associated Tailors
of Dublin upon the text, 'A *remnant* shall be saved.'
Among his printed sermons there is one upon Acts xx. 9,

[1] Eachard, *Works*, p. 66, *et al.*

'And there sat in a window a certain young man named Eutychus, having fallen into a deep sleep: and as Paul was long preaching, he sunk down with sleep, and fell down from the third loft, and was taken up dead,' which thus begins, 'I have chosen these words with design, if possible, to disturb some part in this audience of half an hour's sleep, for the convenience and exercise whereof this place, at this season of the day, is very much celebrated.'[1]

Such instances as these, however, are very different from that quaint humour of preachers like Hugh Latimer and Matthew Henry, which is so mingled with devout and holy sentiment as to lose all triviality, and to make only a serious impression. The following from the commentary of Henry, while it raises a smile, only deepens the sense of the truth conveyed. Remarking upon the requirement of the Mosaic law that the green ears of corn offered as a meat-offering must be dried by the fire, so that the corn might be beaten out, Henry observes, that 'if those who are young do God's work as well as they can, they shall be accepted, though they cannot do it as well as those that are aged and experienced. God makes the best of green ears of corn, and so must we.'[2]

By far the most culpable contortion of passages of Scripture out of their natural meaning and connection is found in the history of those theological schools whose pulpits, having rejected the doctrines of sin and grace, were forced to find substitutes for these in semi-religious or wholly secular themes. During the prevalence of

[1] Swift, *Works*, vol. xiv., Sermon x.
[2] Henry, *Com.* on Leviticus ii. 14.

Rationalism in Germany, 'sermons were preached every-where upon such subjects as the care of health, the necessity of industry, the advantages of scientific tillage, the necessity of gaining a competence, the duties of servants, the ill effects of lawsuits, and the folly of, superstitious opinions. It is said that Christmas was taken advantage of to connect the sad story of the child born in a manger with the most approved methods of feeding cattle; and the appearance of Jesus walking in the garden at the break of day on the Easter morning, with the benefit of rising early and taking a walk before breakfast. Not a word was heard regarding atonement and faith, sin and the judgment, salvation, grace, and Christ's kingdom. A selfish love of pleasure, and a selfish theory of life, put a selfish system of morals in the place of a lofty religion. The old-fashioned system of religious service had to be modified and adjusted to this new style of preaching, which was as clear as water, and as thin as water too.'[1] This description, by a very candid writer, of a state of things in Germany in the last century, will apply to some phenomena of the present day both in England and America. The pressure of the evangelical spirit, which is dominant in these countries, restrains the extreme workings of this tendency in the pulpit; and yet it is plainly seen in what is called the 'sensational' discourse, which is commonly founded upon a text torn entirely out of its exegetical nexus, and filled with matter drawn from the four winds, rather than from the Christian revelation.

[1] Hagenbach, *German Rationalism*, p. 105.

A disputed text should not be selected as the basis of a discourse. This rule applies more particularly to doctrinal preaching, yet it has its value for sermonizing generally. The preacher should choose the very plainest, most significant, and pointed passages of Scripture, as the support of his doctrinal discourses. He is then relieved from the necessity of first proving that the doctrine in question is taught in the passage, and can devote his whole time and strength to its exposition and establishment. The less there is of polemics in sacred oratory the better. The more there is of direct inculcation, without any regard to opposing theories and statements, the more efficient, energetic, and oratorical will be the sermon. The controversial tone is unfavourable to the bold, positive, unembarrassed tone of Sacred Eloquence. Disputed texts should, therefore, be left to the philologist and the theologian. When these have settled their true meaning, so far as it can be settled, such texts may be employed to corroborate, and to illustrate, but not to build upon from the foundation.

By this it is not meant that the preacher has no concern with such passages of inspiration. The preacher is, or should be, a philologist and a theologian, and in his study should examine such passages and form a judgment in respect to them. But let him not do this work in the pulpit. The pulpit is the place for the delivery of eloquence, and not of philology, or philosophy, or technical theology. The rhetorical presentation of thought is the mode which the preacher is to employ; and nothing more interferes with this than the minute examinations of criticism, and the slow and cautious processes of pure science.

This maxim is also valuable, not only in reference to strictly doctrinal preaching, but to all preaching. The text is, or should be, the key-note to the whole sermon. The more bold, the more undoubted and undisputed its tone, the better. A text of this character is like a premonitory blast of a trumpet. It challenges attention, and gets it. It startles and impresses by its direct and authoritative announcement of a great and solemn proposition. Nothing remains, then, but for the preacher to go out upon it with his whole weight, to unfold and apply its evident undoubted meaning, with all the moral confidence and all the serious earnestness of which he is capable.

The inference to be drawn from these reasons for the selection of a passage of Scripture as the foundation of a sermon, and these rules for making the selection, is, that *the greatest possible labour and care should be expended upon the choice of a text.* As, in secular oratory, the selection of a subject is either vital or fatal to the whole performance; so, in sacred oratory, the success of the preacher depends entirely upon the fitness of his choice of a text. The text is his subject. It is the germ of his whole discourse. Provided, therefore, he has found an apt and excellent one, he has found his sermon substantially.

All labour, therefore, that is expended upon a text, is wisely and economically expended. Every jot and tittle of painstaking, in fixing upon paper a congenial passage of Scripture, and in setting up all of the skeleton that presents itself at the time; every jot and tittle of pains-taking in examining the passage in the original Hebrew or Greek, and in studying, *in these same languages*, the context and the parallel passages;[1] every particle of care in first obtaining an excellent text, and then getting at, and get-ting out, its real meaning and scope, goes to render the actual construction and composition of the sermon more easy and successful. Labour at this point saves labour at all after points.

The preacher ought to make careful and extensive pre-paration in respect to pulpit themes. His commonplace book of texts should be a large volume in the outset; and if he is faithful to himself and his calling, he will find the volumes increasing. Instead of buying the volumes of skeletons that are so frequently offered at the present day, the preacher must make them for himself. It was formerly the custom, in an age that was more theological than the present, for every preacher to draw up a 'body of divinity' for himself,—the summing up and result of his studies and reflections. Every preacher knew what his theological system was, and could state it and defend it. And although at first sight we might suppose that this custom would lead to great diversities of opinion among the clergy, it is yet a fact that there never was more sub-stantial and sincere unity of belief than among the Pro-testant clergy of England and the continent during those highly theological centuries, the sixteenth and seventeenth.

[1] The rigid observance of this one practice will prevent the Hebrew language (and sometimes, it is to be feared, even the Greek) from becom-ing a 'lost art' to the preacher.

There was no invention of new theories; but the old and established theory, the one orthodox faith of the Christian Church, was made to pass through each individual mind, and so come forth with all the freshness and freedom of a new creation. 'He who has been born,' says Richter, 'has been a first man, and has had the old and common world lying about him, as new and as fresh as it lay before the eyes of Adam himself.' So, too, he who, in the providence and by the grace of God, has become a theologian and a preacher, has no other world of thought and of feeling to move in than that old world of Divine Revelation, in which the glorious company of the apostles, and the goodly fellowship of the prophets and preachers, thought and felt; but if he will open his eyes, and realize where he stands and by what he is surrounded, he will see it as his predecessors saw it, in all the freshness of its real nature, and in all the magnificence of actual infinitude. Whether or not the preacher imitates this example of an earlier day in regard to theologizing, he ought to in regard to sermonizing. Let him not rely at all upon the texts and skeletons of other preachers, but let him cultivate this field by himself and for himself as if it had never been tilled before. Let him pursue this business of selecting, examining, decomposing, and recombining textual materials, with all the isolation and independence of the first preachers, and of all the great original orators of the Christian Church.

CHAPTER VIII.

THE PLAN OF A SERMON.

IN distinguishing the parts of a sermon, the same maxim applies as in distinguishing the different species of sermons. The distinctions should be simple, generic, and as few as possible. We shall adopt the enumeration of Aristotle in his Rhetoric,[1] and regard the sacred oration as made up of the following parts,—namely, the *introduction*, the *proposition*, the *proof*, and the *conclusion*.

1. The Introduction is that part of the sermon which precedes the proposition and the proof. In common with the conclusion, it is a secondary part of an oration, the primary parts being the proposition and the proof. These latter Aristotle denominates 'necessary' parts, 'for,' he says, 'it is absolutely necessary that a discourse should *state* something, and *prove* it.' And it is plain, that if a sermon could have but two parts, the proposition and the proof of it would possess some positive value, taken by themselves; while an introduction and a conclusion, taken by themselves, would be worthless. Hence the exceedingly logical and rigorous Aristotle seems to hesitate at first whether he shall not regard the oration as consisting of but two parts, although he finally admits four.[2]

---

[1] Aristotle's *De Arte Rhetorica*, iii. 13.

[2] Ἀναγκαῖα ἄρα μόρια πρόθεσις καὶ πίστις· ἴδια μὲν οὖν ταῦτα, τὰ δὲ πλεῖστα προοίμιον, πρόθεσις, πίστις, ἐπίλογος.—Aristotle's *De Arte Rhetorica*, iii. 13.

The introduction, in its nature, is preparatory. It does not lay down any truth, it does not establish any doctrine, it simply prepares the way for the fundamental parts and necessary matter of the discourse. In secular eloquence, one very important object of the exordium is to conciliate the hearer towards the speaker; to remove prejudices, and to awaken sympathy with him. There is not, ordinarily, any need of an exordium for this purpose in sacred eloquence. The preacher, unless he has been exceedingly unfaithful to himself and his calling, may presume upon the good-will and the respect of his auditory, and need not waste time or words in endeavouring to secure a favourable attention to himself as a man. It is, however, sometimes necessary that the preacher, in his introduction, should conciliate his audience in respect to his subject. If his theme is a very solemn and awful one, if the proof and discussion of it lead to those very close and pungent trains of thought which are apt to offend fallen human nature, it is well for the sermonizer to prepare the mind of his auditor for this plain dealing with his heart and conscience. The introduction in this case affords an opportunity to remind the hearer that preaching is for the soul's good and the soul's salvation ; that, when the subject requires it, the plainest discourse is really the kindest and most affectionate ; that the truth which is to be established and applied is a part of God's revelation; and that, however severe it may seem, it is the severity of divine wisdom and love.

The ordinary office of the introduction, however, is to exhibit the text in its connections, and to explain its less

obvious meaning. Some writers upon Homiletics assign
this work to a particular part of the discourse, which they
denominate the explanation. It is better to regard it as
belonging to the introduction. In Sacred Eloquence, as we
have already observed, there is generally no need of that
conciliatory matter, either in respect to the speaker or his
subject, which, according to these writers, constitutes the
introduction proper. Hence most sermons can have no
introduction except this explanatory one. Or, again, the
sermon might need to be introduced by some conciliatory
matter, and require no explanation of the text. Hence it
is better to define the introduction as consisting of *all* the
matter, be it conciliatory or explanatory, or both, which
prepares for the necessary and fundamental parts of the
sermon—the proposition and its proof.

The introduction should be short. Of course, it must
be proportioned to the length and general structure of the
discourse. Still, brevity should be a distinguishing characteristic of the exordium ; and where one sermon is faulty
from being too abruptly introduced, one hundred are faulty
from a too long and tiresome preface. It is easier to expand the common thoughts of the introduction than to
fill out full, and thoroughly elaborate the argumentative
parts of the discourse; and hence we too often listen to
sermons which remind us of that Galatian church which
began in the spirit, but ended in the flesh. The sermon
opens with a promising introduction, which attracts attention, conciliates the audience, and paves the way to a
noble and fertile theme. But, instead of bringing the
exordium to a close, and commencing with the develop-

ment of a subject, or the proof of a proposition, the sermonizer repeats, or unduly expands, his introductory matter, as if he dreaded to take hold of his theme. The consequence is, that the theme itself is not handled with any strength or firmness of grasp, and the long and laboured introduction only serves as a foil to set off the brevity and inferiority of the body of the discourse. Rather than take this course, it would be better for the sermonizer to plunge into the middle and depths of his subject at once. This latter method is allowable occasionally. When the subject is a very fruitful and important one, and the preacher can have but a single opportunity of presenting it, it is perfectly proper to dispense with everything like a regular and oratorical exordium, and begin with the treatment of the theme itself.

2. The Proposition is the enunciation of the particular truth which is to be established and applied in the sermon. It is therefore of a positive and affirmative nature. If, consequently, the truth or doctrine to be taught and applied has at first taken on a negative form, it is best to convert it into an affirmation. The demonstration of a position is more favourable to eloquence than of a negation. The proposition should also be stated in the most concise manner possible. It is, or should be, the condensation and epitome of the whole discourse, and should therefore be characterized by the utmost density of meaning. The proposition should also be stated in the boldest manner possible. By this it is not meant that the announcement of the subject of a sermon should be dogmatic, in the bad sense of this word. This should be guarded against. But

every teaching or tenet of revelation ought to be laid down with a strong confidence of its absolute truthfulness. We are told that a certain auditory, upon a certain occasion, were surprised at the doctrine of our Saviour, because He taught them as one having authority, and not as the scribes. Christ spake as never man spake, for He spake with the commanding dignity of a higher consciousness than belongs to a mere man. His doctrines carry a divine weight, decisiveness, and authoritativeness with them, which, when felt, admits no appeal and no gainsaying on the part of the human mind. And this authoritativeness pertains to inspiration as a whole. When, therefore, the proposition of a sermon is a legitimate derivative from a passage of Scripture, it ought to be expressed in such a manner as to preclude all hesitation, doubt, or timorousness in the phraseology. A weighty conciseness and a righteous boldness ought to' characterize the terms and form of the proposition. But in order that this may be the case, the utmost care must be expended upon its phraseology. A propositional sentence is very different from an ordinary sentence. It should be constructed much more elaborately. Its phraseology ought to be as near perfection as possible. The members and clauses of the sentence which is to enunciate the whole doctrine of the discourse should be most exactly worded and most cunningly jointed. The proposition of a sermon ought to be eminent for the nice exactness of its expression, and the hard finish of its diction. As a constituent part of the skeleton, it should be purest bone.

We have thus far spoken of the proposition of a sermon,

as a definite and distinct statement which follows the introduction, and precedes the proof. It is not necessary, however, that a discourse should contain a formal and verbal proposition, in order to its being a true topical sermon, a proper oration. The doctrine may be so inwoven into the proof and discussion, as to render a formal statement unnecessary. The proposition, in this instance, is implied in the body of the discourse. This is generally the case with that large class of sermons which have been denominated subject-sermons. These contain no proposition that is formally announced, although they contain one that is really and organically inlaid. If a discourse does not embody a proposition, either expressly or by implication, it is not topical in its nature. Subject-sermons, as the name denotes, take for their title not a proposition established and applied in them, but the general theme with which they are occupied. From them, however, a proposition can be drawn, to the support and enforcement of which the entire body of the discourse is subservient; and this proves the identity with the topical sermon.

We will illustrate this by reference to a sermon of Saurin, one of the very first of sermonizers, whether we consider the soundness of his thought, the vigour and clearness of his method, or the plain elegance of his rhetoric. The discourse is founded upon 1 Cor. i. 21 : 'After that in the wisdom of God, the world by wisdom knew not God, it pleased God by the foolishness of preaching to save them that believe.' The title of the sermon is, 'The advantages of revelation.' The translator was, probably, led to give it this loose running title, because the author does not for-

M

mally announce a proposition in the discourse. It contains one, however, and, put into a distinct verbal statement, would be this: 'Revealed religion is infinitely superior to natural religion.' This proposition really pervades the whole sermon, and is established by showing that revelation imparts a knowledge infinitely superior to that given by natural religion, in respect—(1) to the nature and attributes of God; (2) to the nature and obligations of man; (3) to the means of appeasing the remorse of conscience; and (4) to a future state.

It is better to vary the structure of sermons by adopting both modes, so far as the proposition is concerned. Invariably to state the proposition, though not so objectionable as invariably to leave it unannounced, imparts an air of stiffness and formality to sermonizing from Sabbath to Sabbath. Whenever, however, the proposition is not verbally stated, the treatment of the subject ought to be of such a character as to leave no doubt in the mind of the hearer respecting the real and positive doctrine of the sermon. The body of the discourse should be made up of such clear and evident matter, that when the hearer asks himself the question, 'What is the proposition of the sermon?' the answer is suggested by its trains of thought, and the general bearing of it as a whole. If, therefore, a sermon contains no outward and formally announced proposition, it should contain an inward and organic one all the more; and the whole mass of its argumentative and illustrative matter should have even a plainer reference, and a stronger drift in one general direction, than when the proposition has been verbally enunciated in the beginning.

3. The Proof is the substance of the sermon. It is the most important part of the discourse, because it is that part, for the sake of which the discourse itself is composed. The introduction, the statement of the proposition, and the conclusion, exist only in order to the demonstration. Separated from that argumentative part of the sermon, which establishes some truth and produces conviction, these other parts are worthless. A logical development of an idea, or a convincing demonstration of a doctrine, always possesses an intrinsic worth. When we can read or hear but one part of a sermon, we always select the body of it, as it is termed.

The proof divides into parts, which are sometimes denominated 'heads,' and sometimes 'divisions.' These divisions should exhibit the following qualities. First, they must possess a true logical force. By this is meant that they must, one and all, go to establish the proposition. It is not enough that they bear some affinity to the theme of the discourse, that they are not heterogeneous. They must be of the nature of demonstration, and carry conviction, as far as they extend, to the hearer's mind. At the conclusion of each head or division of proof, the auditor should feel that the proposition has received an additional and real support. Secondly, each head of the proof ought to exhibit a distinctive character by itself. By this is meant that it should not contain elements of proof that are found in other divisions. It must not be a mere modification of some other head, but a distinct and additional item in the mass of argument. Hence none but the leading arguments should appear in the sermon for the support of a proposition. There is no time in the oration for the numerous exhaustive demonstrations of philosophy, and in reality no need of them. The preacher should seize upon the few prime arguments, and exhibit to the popular audience only the capital proofs.

A close attention to these two fundamental properties in the heads of proof is indispensable to good sermonizing. If a particular argument in support of a proposition is not *genuinely* demonstrative, and *distinctively* demonstrative, it should not constitute a part of the proof. All arguments that do not, so far as they reach and relate, really evince and afford new elements of conviction, ought to be energetically rejected.

The observance of these maxims will secure a proper number of heads. If everything of the nature of proof is employed, without regard to the intrinsic worth and strength of it, the divisions will be too numerous for the nature of oratory. 'Some ministers,' says an old homiletist, 'do with their texts as the Levite with his concubine—cut and carve it into so many pieces.' Some sermons exhibit a body of proof which, owing to the multitude of the divisions and subdivisions, is wholly unsuited to the purposes of persuasive discourse. They are good illustrations of the infinite divisibility of matter, but produce no conviction in the popular mind, because they employ the philosophical instead of the rhetorical mode of demonstration. This fault will be avoided if the sermonizer asks, in respect to each and every head or division, 'Does this proposed head really tend to prove the proposition? and does it afford a positively new item of proof,

that is not contained in any other head ?' These two
questions, rigorously applied, will exclude from the sermon
all second-rate arguments, and the pulpit will bring to bear
upon the popular audience only the strongest, plainest,
and most cogent proofs. By this it is not meant that a
division of the proof may not exhibit another phase of one
and the same general argument. There may be but one
general argument in support of a proposition, and then the
new element of proof, in the new division, must be simply
a new aspect of this. But in this case also the spirit of
the above-given maxim must be obeyed. The new head
or division should exhibit a new aspect, so *distinct* and
diverse from that of all preceding or following heads, as to
impart a marked and distinguishing logical character to it.

In respect to the number of heads or divisions in the
proof, no stiff rule can be laid down. Some rhetoricians
say that they should never exceed five. Probably the
majority of modern sermons contain less than this number,
and the majority of ancient sermons contain more. It is
better to amplify one first-rate argument, than to present
two mediocre ones in the same space. It is more difficult
to do this, because it requires closer and more continuous
reflection, but the sermon is the more excellent for it.
When a rich and fertile argument has been discovered, the
preacher should not leave it until he has made the common
mind feel the whole sum of its force. The instant he has
done this, he should drop it. It is not enough to barely
state a proof. It should be fully unfolded. It should be
revolved in the preacher's mind, and before the hearer's
mind, until all that is latent in it has been elicited. The

maxim, then, in respect to the number of heads or divisions is, 'Amplify rather than multiply.' The effect of this maxim will coincide with what has been said respecting the choice of arguments. The preacher, we have seen, is to choose genuinely demonstrative and distinctively demonstrative proofs; and these are the only ones that can be amplified, and cannot be multiplied. Fertile arguments are few in number, but may be made to cover a wide extent of surface, and furnish a great amount of matter for the body of a sermon.

These same maxims will apply to the subdivisions of proof. These also must possess a real and distinct demonstrative power. They should not repeat each other in any degree. The choice and number of the subdivisions must, therefore, be determined by the same rules that apply to the principal divisions. As a general thing, subdivisions need not be formally announced; they should be so forcible and marked in their character as to announce themselves. Generally speaking, a subdivision that would not attract the attention of a hearer by its own weight and worth should be omitted.

In announcing the divisions and subdivisions of the proof, the greatest pains should be taken with the phraseology. Each one ought to be expressed in the most exact and concise language. The same care which we recommended in wording the proposition should be expended upon the wording of its proofs. These are themselves a species of proposition, and by the old sermonizers are so denominated. The elder Edwards frequently announces a general proposition, under the name of 'doctrine,' and follows with 'proposition first,' 'proposition second,' etc., as the arguments that support it.[1]

It sometimes happens that the matter in the proof is excellent, being both truly and distinctively demonstrative, but the style of expression is exceedingly defective. As an example of a loose and slovenly manner of wording the divisions and subdivisions of the proof, take the following from John Howe, a preacher who, in respect to thought and matter, has no superior in the Ancient or the Modern Church, but is excelled, in respect to form and style, by many of inferior discipline, learning, and spirituality.

In the forty-second of his sermons, he describes the nature of the new birth.[2] The divisions of the discussion are worded thus: '1. As it is a birth, it signifies a real new product in the soul; that there is somewhat really produced anew in it. 2. As this is a real production to be thus born, new born, so it is a spiritual production, in contradistinction to such productions as lie within the sphere of nature. 3. As this is a birth, so we must consider it to be a total production, such an one as carries an entireness with it; for so it is with all such productions that are properly called births. 4. This birth, as it is a birth, signifies a permanent production; an effect that is permanent, lasting, and continued.'

Instead of this loose, incompact phraseology, these divisions would be more forcibly stated and easily remembered in the following form: To be born of God (the text is, 'Whosoever believeth that Jesus is the Christ, is born of

---

[1] Compare Sermon upon 1 Thess. ii. 16. *Works,* iv. 281 sq.
[2] John Howe, *Works,* ii. 894 sq. New York ed.

God) denotes—1. A real true birth. 2. A supernatural or spiritual birth. 3. A permanent birth.[1] The awkwardness of the statement, in this instance, arises from not cleanly separating the head or division from the matter under it, and from attempting some *explanation* or *development* of the head in the head itself. This should never be done. The preacher must reserve the unfolding for its proper place. He should do one thing at a time. When he announces either a proposition or a division, let it be a pure and simple annunciation, in the concisest, clearest, and briefest phraseology. And when he unfolds, or develops, let him do this fully and exhaustively. Milton speaks of the close palm of logic, and the open palm of rhetoric. Now, the statement of a proposition, or of a head, is logical in its nature; it should be the hard, knotty fist. The explanation or development of a proposition, or of a head, is rhetorical in its nature; it should be the open, ample hand. To attempt to unite the two in one sentence, is like attempting to open and shut the hand by a single volition, and by one set of muscles. The hand cannot be shut by the muscles that were made to open it. The statement of a proposition, or of a division of proof, cannot be the development and amplification of it.

Thus far we have spoken of the body of the sermon under the denomination of the proof. When discussing the nature of the proposition, we alluded to a class of sermons, called by some homiletists subject-sermons, which

---

[1] The third head, in Howe's distribution of the matter, is virtually included in the first, and therefore should be omitted in a truly rhetorical plan.

contain no formally announced proposition, although they contain an internal and implied one, and are, therefore, truly topical in their nature. It is obvious, that when the proposition is thus inlaid and implied through the discourse as a whole, the proof takes on a different appearance from that which it wears in a more formally constructed sermon. Sometimes there are no distinctly announced heads. The preacher, from the rapidity of his movement, cannot stop to enumerate, but supplies the lack of formality of statement by emphasizing leading words or clauses. In this case there are subdivisions really, though not formally. Every sermon must contain subordinate thoughts, which flow out of each other, and yet are distinct from each other. Otherwise there are no development, no constant progress, and none of the elements of oratory.

When the body of the sermon is of this informal character, it is termed by some writers the *treatment*, by others the *discussion*. These terms are employed not to denote that there is nothing of the nature of logic or proof in the body of the discourse, but that the logic or proof is less formal, and less formally announced, than in the other instance. The qualities which should characterize the discussion or treatment of a theme, are substantially like those of the proof proper. There must be the same accumulation of genuinely demonstrative material. As this less formal development of the theme goes on, it should acquire additional logical force, and produce a growing conviction in the understanding of the hearer.

In concluding this account of the proof, the question arises, whether all the heads or divisions should be pre-announced by the preacher at the opening of his discourse ? The decision of this question does not affect the structure of the discourse itself, because this pre-announcement is not the addition of any new matter, but simply the repetition of the existing. Without laying down a stiff, undeviating rule, we are inclined to say that *recapitulation* is better than pre-announcement. And this for the following reasons: First, the recapitulation of the proofs at the close of the argumentation is more *intelligible* than the pre-announcement of them at the beginning. After the mind of the hearer has followed the preacher through his proofs, and has listened to their development one by one, it sees their meaning and interconnection much more readily and easily. The full import and connection of an argument cannot be perceived until it has been unfolded in its relations and dependences. Secondly, the recapitulation of the proofs is more *impressive* than the pre-announcement of them. The accurate and rapid repetition of the arguments of a sermon, after they have been clearly and connectedly exhibited, makes a very strong impression upon the hearer. It is a summing up of the demonstration, a grouping and epitomizing of the entire logic of the discourse, which falls with massive, solid weight upon his understanding. This epitome of the proof, read off to the audience before they have become interested in its contents by a course of argumentation, leaves the mind indifferent. It is like perusing the table of contents of a book before reading the book itself. Lastly, the recapitulation of the proof is more easily *remembered* than the pre-announcement of it, for the reason that it is more intelligible and more impressive. That which is most clearly understood, and most forcible and striking, is most easily retained in the memory.[1]

4. The Conclusion is that part of the sermon which vigorously applies the truth which has been established in the proof, or developed in the treatment or discussion. As the introduction is conciliatory and explanatory, the conclusion is applicatory and hortatory. It should, there-- fore, be characterized by the utmost intensity and energy. The highest vitality of the oration shows itself in the per- oration. The onset on the hearer is at this point. If the man's will is ever carried, if this true effect of eloquence is ever produced, it is the work of this part of the sermon. By this it is not meant that the other parts of the discourse may not be excellent, and produce some of their proper effects, even though the conclusion be imperfect. But the crown and completion of the whole oratorical process, the actual persuasion of the auditor, will not ensue if the con- clusion is lame, and not equal to the preceding parts. It must be a true conclusion—a vehement and powerful winding up and finishing. Hence among the ancients the peroration received the utmost attention. The con-

---

[1] 'Our main work is to be the people's remembrancers, to be constant monitors to them of their duty, to bring the contents of it close up to their minds, and to fasten them upon them. To which end it may be sometimes requisite, in the close of our discourses, to *recapitulate* the most important heads and particulars we have been treating of, that our auditors may carry away with them those brief memorials of their duty, which are the sum and abstract of what we have delivered. We should endeavour to refresh their memories, considering that the preaching of the word was not insti- tuted only to inform men of what they were ignorant of before, but to remind them of what they knew well enough, but had forgot.'--JOHN EDWARDS, *The Preacher*, Pt. i. p. 281.

clusions of the orations of Demosthenes and Cicero are constructed in the most elaborate manner, in order that there may be no falling off from the impression made by the preceding portions. At this point in the process of the orator they seem to have exerted their utmost possibility of effort, like a leaper who throws his whole brute force into that one leap which is to save his life from destruction. Indeed, the peroration seems to put the power to spring and smite, the very tendon of Achilles, into oratory.

In sacred eloquence there are two species of conclusions, while in secular eloquence there is, strictly speaking, but one. The sermon may conclude either by *inferences* or by *direct address.* The secular oration employs the latter only. This difference arises from the fact mentioned in the chapter upon the distinctive nature of Homiletics,— namely, that sacred eloquence is more didactic than secular, and hence may vary more from the strict canons of oratory, if it can thereby produce a greater practical impression.

The sermon should have an inferential conclusion, when the principal practical force of the proposition, or the subject, is in the inferences from it. The real strength of some conceptions lies in that which follows from them. They make no very great moral impression of themselves, but they involve, or they imply, or they point to, certain truths that are highly important and serious. Death, for example, is a theme which is much more solemn and effective in its inferences and its implications than in itself. It is, indeed, fearful in itself; but it is the king of terrors only through its concomitants and consequents. The doctrine of the soul's immortality, again, is one that makes its strongest impression by virtue of its inferences and deductions. The mere fact that the soul is to live for ever exerts but little influence upon a man until he has been made to see that he is utterly unfit and unprepared for such an endless existence,—until the doctrines of sin and guilt, of justice and judgment, have sharpened and enforced the doctrine of immortality.

The sermon should also have an inferential conclusion, when the proposition and its proof, or the subject and its discussion, are highly abstract in their nature. There are some doctrines presented in the Scriptures so recondite and metaphysical that they can be made to bear upon the popular mind only in their concrete and practical aspects. Inasmuch as they are revealed truth, they must not be passed over by the preacher. All Scripture is profitable. Yet they are metaphysical in their nature, and in their ultimate reach transcend the powers of the finite intellect. The preacher, therefore, must detect a popular element in them that will make them proper themes for eloquence. He must discover in them a practical quality which will bring them home to the business and bosoms of Christians.

In order to this, the sacred orator must follow the method of Scripture itself. He is to content himself with a brief and succinct statement, which omits nothing essential to the doctrine, but which does not pretend to fully develope and explain it, and from this draw inferences and conclusions respecting the duties of his hearers. In this way the high fundamental dogma is brought down into the sphere of human conduct, and made a practical test of character. It is not fully explained, it is true, because it cannot be by a finite mind ; but it is correctly, that is, scripturally stated. This accurate enunciation of the truth, or doctrine, prepares the way for the inferences,—for that handling of it which brings it into living contact with the affections and will of the hearer. In this way the most abstract and intrinsically metaphysical doctrine of Scripture becomes eloquent, that is, persuasive and influential upon the human mind and heart. The revealed dogma of the Trinity is an example. This is, undoubtedly, the most profound truth that has been presented to the human intelligence. Neither in ancient nor in modern philosophy is there any doctrine that carries the mind down to such central depths. A perfect comprehension of this single truth, such as is possessed by the Divine intelligence, would involve a comprehension of all truth, and would solve at once and for ever those standing problems of the human mind, which have both stimulated and baffled its inquiries ever since the dawn of philosophic speculation. And yet this transcendental truth is a biblical truth, and must be preached to Christian plain men and women. A discourse upon the doctrine of the Trinity, therefore, should be strong in its inferences, rather than its explanations or developments. The relation, for example, which the three distinct Persons in the Godhead sustain to the believer should be insisted upon. The peculiar feelings which he ought to cherish toward the Father, the Son, and the Holy Ghost, should be inferred from the distinctive character and office of each. The duty of an equal adoration and worship in respect to each Person, the part which each performs in the work of redemption—such practical and edifying discussion as this must enter largely into a sermon upon the Trinity, instead of a strictly metaphysical discussion of the doctrine. But such matter as this is inferential, and should constitute the foundation of an address to the affections and will of the hearer. And it falls most properly into the conclusion, because it presupposes the statement and proof of the doctrine itself.

In respect to the character of the inferences themselves, they should possess the following properties : First, they must be *legitimate*. They must originate from the very heart and substance of the proposition or doctrine. Inferences should not be drawn from the accidental or incidental parts of a subject, but from its essentials alone. Then they are lawful inferences, and have the support of the whole fundamental truth from which they spring. There is nothing to be subtracted from them. No allowance is to be made. They are entitled to their full weight. The hearer feels their legitimacy, and he cannot escape their force except by denying the proposition or doctrine of which they are the inevitable consequences. Secondly, inferences must be *homogeneous*. They must all be of the same kind. A conflict in the inferences from a truth destroys their influence upon the mind of the hearer, and a direct contrariety absolutely annihilates them. Hence, the utmost agreement and harmony should appear in the practical inferential matter of a sermon. And this will be the case, provided they each and all possess the pro-

perty of legitimacy. For truth is always self-consistent.
It always agrees with itself. Hence, all matter that is
really derived from the very substance and pith of a fundamental truth is homogeneous and harmonious. Nothing
is then drawn out that was not first inlaid. Thirdly, inferences must be *intensely practical.* The very purpose in
employing them, as we have seen, is to popularize the
abstract, to bring an intrinsically abstruse doctrine or proposition into warm and vital contact with the common
mind and heart. Hence inferences should be entirely
free from a theoretic aspect, and from abstract elements.
Neither is it enough that they be practical in the moderate
sense of the word. They should be *intensely* practical. By
this is meant that their address and appeal should be solely
and entirely to the most moral, earnest, and living part of
man's nature—that is, to his affections and will. The intellectual nature, by supposition, has been addressed by
the proposition and the proof; and now it only remains to
press the doctrine home upon the conscience and feelings,
in the most vivid and vital manner possible. This is done
by legitimate and homogeneous inferences, coming directly
and inevitably from the core of the subject, and containing its concentrated practical substance. Lastly, inferences
must be *cumulative.* They should heap upon each other.
Each succeeding one should not only be an addition to the
preceding, but an advance upon it. The strongest inference should be the last inference. Unless this rule is
observed, it is impossible to construct an excellent inferential conclusion. As we have previously seen, the peroration ought to be the most vivid and impressive part of the

sermon. But it cannot be if the matter of which it is composed is all of equal value, and there is no progress. The peroration should be distinguished by vehemence, by the utmost intensity, energy, vividness, and motion. When therefore, it consists of inferences, these should be of such a nature, and so arranged, as to press with more and more weight, to kindle with hotter and hotter heat, to enlighten with stronger and stronger light, to enliven with intenser and intenser life, and to move with a more and more irresistible force.

Constructed in this manner, the conclusion of a sermon may be in the highest degree eloquent, even although an inferential conclusion, as we have remarked, is not so strictly oratorical as the direct address. For this practical property in inferences, this intense vitality of the material, this constant progress in the arrangement, is the essential element in eloquence. Where these are, there is eloquence; and we see not why the preacher may not make an onset upon the heart and will, through inferences, that will be as vehement and successful as that which is made by a more regularly constructed peroration. At any rate in the instance of such subjects as those which we have specified, and having a proposition whose main practical force lies in its implications, or one which is highly abstract in its own nature, he has no choice left him. He must either pass by such subjects altogether, or else handle them in the manner we have described. But he has no right to omit any truth of Scripture in his sermonizing. He is obligated to employ even the most profound and metaphysical doctrines of Revelation for

N

homiletic purposes, and must, therefore, treat them in the most concrete, popular, and eloquent manner possible, by dealing with their implications and inferences.

The sermon may also conclude with what we have termed the *direct address*. This is more strictly oratorical in its nature than the inferential conclusion. It does not, like this latter, contribute to a further development of the subject of the discourse, while it is applying it to the hearer, but is simply and solely applicatory. The inference, as we have seen, is somewhat didactic. It imparts some further information in respect to the theme of the discourse, while it addresses the affections and will. It is not so with the direct address, or the strictly oratorical peroration. This supposes that the proposition and its proof, or the theme and its treatment, have exhausted the subject in both its theoretic and practical aspects; and in this case nothing remains but to apply it. As a consequence, this species of conclusion is much briefer than that by inferences. It ought not to be at all didactic. It should be purely oratorical and highly hortatory. But such a species of discourse cannot continue long; and perhaps the art of the orator is nowhere more visible than in the skill with which, in the conclusion, he presses his theme upon the affections and will of the hearer. If this vehemence is too prolonged, it defeats itself. If this exhortation goes beyond the proper limits, it not only fatigues but disgusts the mind of the auditor. No preachers are more wearisome than those who are styled hortatory preachers. Their direct address is unsupported by doctrine. Their whole oration is peroration. They omit the proposition and the proof in their plan. It is safer to overdo the address to the understanding than the address to the feelings. The understanding is a cool and sensible faculty, and good sense never tires or disgusts it. But the feelings are both shy and excitable. Addressed too boisterously, they make their retreat; addressed too continually, they lose their tone and sensibility altogether.

The direct address to the hearer should be characterized by the following qualities: First, it must be *appropriate.* By this is meant that the conclusion should enforce the one proposition or the one lesson of the sermon. Every part and particle of the peroration should be pertinent to the discourse as a whole. And this implies, secondly, that the conclusion by direct address be *single.* It cannot be appropriate unless it is characterized by unity. Whatever the doctrine of the sermon may be, the conclusion must apply this and this only. Says that eccentric preacher, Rowland Hill : 'The Gospel is an excellent milch cow, which always gives plenty of milk, and of the best quality. I first pull at justification, then give a plug at adoption, and afterwards a tit at sanctification ; and so on until I have filled my pail with gospel milk.' Now if the body of the sermon has been constructed upon this plan, then an appropriate conclusion would not be one and single in its character. A peroration pertinent to *such* a discourse would be double and twisted. But we have seen that every sermon ought to be characterized by the utmost unity ; that it should approximate to the topical form, even when it does not employ it, and should always approach as nearly as possible to the oration, by containing but one proposition, or developing but one general truth. Hence the conclusion of the sermon is appropriate only as it is single and incomplex in its structure and spirit. It matters not what the proposition or subject may have been, let the direct concluding address be in entire harmony with it. Some homiletists lay down the rule: ' Always conclude with the gospel ; always end with the hopes and promises.' This, we think, is a false rule, both rhetorically and morally. If the law has been preached, then let the conclusion be legal, damnatory, terrible. If the gospel has been preached, let the conclusion be winning, encouraging, and hopeful. Then the sermon is a homogeneous composition, developing one theme, and making a single impression. A preacher should know beforehand the wants of his audience, and deliberately make up his mind in respect to the species of impression which it is desirable to produce. When this point is settled, then let him not be diverted from his purpose, but do what he has undertaken. If he judges that mercy and love are the appropriate themes for the hour, let him present them to the hearer's mind, and apply them to the hearer's heart without any let or hinderance. And if he judges that divine justice needs to be exhibited, and set home to the conscience, let him not temper or soften it by a mixed peroration, in which, *owing to the brevity of the treatment* to which he is now shut up, the two opposite ideas of love and wrath will inevitably neutralize each other in the mind of the auditor.

The rule above mentioned is also indefensible on moral grounds. It is not upright in a preacher, either from fear of man, or from a false kindness, to shrink in the peroration from a plain and solemn application of the subject of his discourse.   He is in duty bound to make the truth which he has established bear with all its weight, and penetrate with all its sharpness. The *spirit* with which he should do this should be Christian.   Let him not dart the lightnings, or roll the thunders, except with the utmost solemnity, the utmost fear of God, the utmost love of the human soul, and the utmost solicitude lest he be actuated by human pride or human impatience.   'Were you able to preach the doctrine *tenderly?*' said M'Cheyne to a friend, who had spoken to him of a sermon which he had delivered upon endless punishment.   Perhaps the imperfection of his own Christian character is never seen more clearly by the preacher than in the manner in which he constructs and delivers the perorations of his solemn discourses. He finds himself running to extremes.   Either he is afraid to be plain and pungent in applying the truth, and thereby puts a sheath upon the sword of the Spirit, and muffles those tones which ought to sound startling as a fire-bell at midnight, or else he is impatient with his drowsy auditors, or is puffed up with self-conceit, and thunders and lightens in his own strength, and, what is worse, for his own purposes. 'Put the lust of *self,*' says Coleridge, 'in the forked lightning, and it becomes a spirit of Moloch.' Self, in all its phases, must be banished from a solemn application of an awful doctrine.   The feeling of the preacher should be that of the timid, shrinking, but *obedient* Jeremiah, when bending under the burden of the Lord.   'Then said I, Ah, Lord God! behold, I cannot speak; for I am a child.   But the Lord said unto me, Say not, I am a child: for thou shalt go to all that I shall send thee, and whatsoever I command thee, thou shalt speak.'

Appropriateness and singleness, then, should characterize the concluding address of the sermon. Bringing all the teachings of the discourse into a single burning focus, it should converge all the rays of truth upon a single spot. That spot is the point in the hearer's soul where the feelings and the conscience come together.· Any auditor whose affections are roused, and whose conscience is stirred, may be left to himself and the Spirit of God; and any peroration which accomplishes this work is eloquent.

The question arises at this point, whether the conclusion by direct address should refer to both classes of hearers, the regenerate and unregenerate. The answer depends upon the contents and character of the sermon. It is possible that a discourse may establish a proposition that admits of a legitimate application to both the regenerate and the unregenerate; though in this case it will generally be found that the application is more easy, natural, and forcible to one class than to the other. The doctrine that man is an accountable being, for example, may be legitimately applied to the Christian, in order to stimulate him to greater fidelity; and yet its strongest and most impressive application is to the impenitent man, who has made no preparation to meet the coming doom. In such an instance as this, good judgment would decide that the address to that party to whom the subject had a less direct application should be very brief—a hint rather than an application; the intensity and energy of the peroration being aimed at that party most immediately and evidently concerned with the subject.

Hence, in laying down a general rule, we would say, in answer to the question that the conclusion should be directed to but one class in the audience, if the proposition or subject applies most plainly to the church, then address the church in the close ; if it applies most significantly to the congregation, then address the congregation. Without, however, laying down this rule as a stiff one, to which there are no exceptions, it is safest, in general practice, to allow that unity of aim and singleness of pursuit, which is unquestionably the constituent principle of eloquent discourse, a free operation. Let unity run clear through the sermon, and clear out. If there be other lessons to be taught from the text, teach them in other sermons. If there be other applications of truth, make them in other discourses. It is not as if the preacher had no other opportunity, as if he must say everything in one sermon, and apply everything in a single discourse. He has the year, and the years before him, in which to make full proof of his ministry, in which to exhibit the truth upon all sides, and to apply it to all classes of men. Let him therefore make each sermon a round and simple unit, and trust to the whole series of his sermons to impart a full and comprehensive knowledge of the Christian system, and to make a complete application of it to all grades and varieties of character.

Having thus considered the two species of conclusion, it may be asked, if it is proper to employ both in one and the same discourse. We answer, that although it may occasionally be allowable to draw inferences from a proposition, and afterwards end with a direct address to the hearer, yet this should be done very rarely. If the inferences do not possess sufficient self-applying power, and need the urgency of direct address to enforce them, this proves that they are defective. In this case it is wiser to bestow more care upon the inferences, and to endeavour to construct a true and adequate inferential conclusion. If the inferences are intrinsically feeble, no amount of earnest peroration can remedy this defect. Generally speaking, therefore, it is an indication of inferiority in a sermon if it has a mixed conclusion, and yet there may be an exception to this general rule. If, owing to the abstruse nature of the proposition or the subject, the inferential matter in the sermon, though more practical and plain than the argumentative matter, is yet considerably recondite and abstract, the preacher may do the most he can towards impressing his subject upon the audience by a direct address to them. In some such case as this, which should be a rare one, and must be, from the fact that but few themes of this highly abstruse nature come within the province of sermonizing, the preacher may employ both species of conclusion, not because it contributes to the greater perfection of the plan of a sermon, but because it is a choice of evils, and the best that can be done under the difficulties of the particular and rare case.

In closing this discussion of the plan and its several parts, the question naturally arises, whether a plan should invariably be formed before the process of composition begins. It is plain, from what has been said, that there will be a variety in the sermons of the same preacher, in respect to the distinctness with which the plan and its parts show themselves in the discourse. Sometimes the skeleton will appear through the flesh, so as to exhibit some angularity; and sometimes it will be so clothed upon, as to render its presence more difficult of detection. Sometimes the plan will be prominent, and sometimes it will be known to exist only by the general unity and compactness of the sermon. But although there will be this variety in the sermon itself, there should be no variation in the method of constructing it. The sermonizer should *uniformly* form a plan before beginning to compose. The plan may sometimes be fuller and more perfect than at others; but a plan of some sort, of more or less perfection, should invariably be formed in the outset.

By this it is not meant that in every particular the sermonizer must severely confine himself to his skeleton, never modifying the plan after he has begun to compose. It will sometimes occur, and this perhaps quite often, that the endeavour to fill out the plan will reveal faults that were not seen while constructing it. These faults must be removed; and this leads to a modification of the plan itself in and during the process of composition. Indeed, in some instances the first attempt at composition serves merely to introduce the mind into the heart of the subject, and to originate a truly organic method of developing it, —a second process of composition, a re-writing, being necessary to the completion and perfection of the discourse. Probably the masterpieces of eloquence were composed in this manner. The first, second, or even third draught, served principally to elaborate a thorough and perfect plan, to set the mind upon the true .trail, and enable it, in the phrase of Bacon, to 'hound' the nature of the subject, and reach the inmost lurking-place of the truth. When this work was accomplished, the mind of the orator was then ready for that last draught and elaboration, which resulted in the masterpiece and model for all time.

But although the sermonizer may modify his plan after he has begun to compose, he may not begin to compose without any plan. He is to construct the best scheme possible beforehand, and to work under it, as the miner works under his moveable hurdle, never disturbing the outside or the main props, but frequently altering the interior and secondary framework as the progress of his labour may require.[1]

The evils of sermonizing without skeletonizing are many and great. In the first place, the preacher's mind loses its logical and constructive ability. In a previous chapter, attention was directed to the excellent influence exerted

[1] Skeletonizing is to sermonizing what drawing is to painting. The foundation of superior excellence in this art, is talent in sketching the human figure, and a knowledge of its anatomy. In this consisted principally the pre-eminence of Da Vinci and Michael Angelo, both of whom possessed a wonderful anatomical knowledge, and exhibited it in their figures. The lack of this knowledge and skill cannot be compensated for by other excellences. Sir Joshua Reynolds, owing to the defect of his early artistic education in this reference, confined himself to portrait painting, knowing that he could do nothing in historical painting, and the higher ranges of his art. An outline sketch of Angelo is more full of meaning than a hundred paintings in which there is no anatomy. Retzsch's 'Outlines' are wonderfully full of life and meaning, without any filling up from painting, because of the knowledge of the human frame, and the consequent significance of attitudes which they display.

by the analysis of sermons, and the effort to detect the plan contained in them. All that was there said in this reference applies, with even greater force, to the actual construction of plans for the preacher's own purposes. No mind can be methodical that does not actually methodize. No mind can be constructive that does not actually construct. If, therefore, the sermonizer neglects this practice of skeletonizing, and begins to compose without a settled scheme, writing down such thoughts and observations as spontaneously present themselves, his intellect will surely, and at no slow rate, lose all its logical ability, and all its methodizing talent. The fundamental power of the rhetorician and orator, the *organizing* power, will disappear. And if, as is apt to be the case, parallel with this disuse of the understanding and the reason, there is an exorbitant development of the fancy and imagination, the very worst consequences ensue. The preacher becomes a florid and false rhetorician, composing and reciting mere extravaganzas. He degenerates into a rhapsodist, making a sensation for the moment in the sensibilities of a staring audience, but producing no eloquent impression upon their higher faculties. There is no calculating beforehand in respect to the issues of such a mind. Reversing the lines which the poet applied to his own composition, we may say of the discourse of a preacher of this character—

> ' Perhaps 'twill be a sermon,
> Perhaps 'twill be a song.'

Secondly, even supposing that, owing to the fact that the preacher's mind is not imaginative, his preaching does not become rhapsodical and feeble; yet, if he neglects the practice of skeletonizing, he becomes rambling and diffuse. Having no leading idea branching off into natural ramifications by which to guide his mental processes, they run and ramble in every direction. The law of association is the sole law of his intellect. He follows wherever this leads him; and the law of association in an illogical, unreflecting mind, is the most whimsical and capricious of laws. It associates the oddest and most heterogeneous things, and suggests the strangest and most disconnected ideas. The course which trains of thought take in such a mind resembles the trails and tracks of the myriads of worms that are brought up out of ground by a warm June rain. Sometimes such a mind really attempts to be methodical, and then the discourse reminds one of Burke's description of Lord Chatham's cabinet: 'He made an administration so checkered and speckled; he put together a piece of joinery so crossly indented and whimsically dovetailed, a cabinet so variously inlaid, such a piece of diversified mosaic, such a tesselated pavement without cement, here a bit of black stone, and there a bit of white, that it was indeed a very curious show, but utterly unsafe to touch, and unsure to stand on.' [1]

Lastly, the neglect to form a plan previous to composing, results in a declamatory and hortatory style of sermonizing. If an immethodical preacher does not fall into one or both of the faults last mentioned, he falls into this one. If he has no imagination and no ideas, not even rambling and disconnected ones, then there is nothing left for him

[1] Burke, Speech on American Taxation.

but to declaim and exhort; and this manner of preaching is perhaps the most ineffectual and worst of all.

Certainly such evils as the three we have mentioned, constitute the strongest of reasons for not neglecting the plan of an oration, for devoting the utmost attention, and uniform attention, to the logical organization of the sermon. It is a sin for the preacher to be a mere rhapsodist; it is a sin if he is a mere rambling babbler; it is a sin if he is a mere declamatory exhorter. He is solemnly bound to be an orator—a man who speaks on a method, and by a plan.

CHAPTER IX.

THE discussion of the subject of Homiletics would be incomplete if it did not include the topic of Extemporaneous Preaching.

This species of Sacred Eloquence has always existed in the Church, and some of the best periods in the history of Christianity have been characterized by its wide prevalence and high excellence. The Apostolic age, the missionary periods in Patristic and Mediæval history, the age of the Reformation, the revival of evangelical religion in the English Church in the eighteenth century in connection with the preaching of Wesley and Whitefield, and the ' Great Awakening,' in this country, were marked by the free utterance of the extemporaneous preacher. Being now too much neglected by the clergy of those denominations which both furnish and require the highest professional education,—a clergy, therefore, who have the best right to employ this species of sermonizing,—there is reason for directing attention to it. In discussing this subject, we shall first speak of the *nature* of extemporaneous preaching, and then of some of the requisites in order to its successful *practice*.

1. The term ' extemporaneous,' as commonly employed denotes something hurried, off-hand, and superficial, and

general usage associates imperfection and inefficiency with this adjective. There is nothing, however, in the etymology of the word which necessarily requires that such a signification be put upon it. Extemporaneous preaching is preaching *ex tempore*—from the time. This may mean either of two things, according to the sense in which the word *tempus* is taken. It may denote that the sermon is the hasty and careless product of that one particular *instant* of time in which the person speaks; the rambling and prolix effort of that *punctum* temporis, which is an infinitely small point, and which can produce only an infinitely small result. This is the meaning too commonly assigned to the word in question, and hence inferiority in all intellectual respects is too commonly associated with it, both in theory and in practice. For it is indisputable that the human mind will work very inefficiently if it works by the minute merely, and originates its products under the spur and impulse of the single instant alone.

But the phrase 'extemporaneous preaching,' may and should mean preaching from *all* the time, past as well as present. Behind every extemporaneous sermon, as really as behind every written sermon, the whole duration of the preacher's life, with all the culture and learning it has brought with it, should lie. The genuine extemporaneous discourse, as really as the most carefully written discourse, should be the result of a sum-total,—the exponent of the whole past life, the whole past discipline, the whole past study and reflection of the man. Sir Joshua Reynolds was once asked, by a person for whom he had painted a small cabinet picture, how he could demand so much for a work which had employed him only five days. He replied : ' Five days ! why, sir, I have expended the work of thirty-five years upon it.' This was the truth. Behind that little picture there lay the studies, the practice, and the toil of a great genius for more than three decades of years in the painter's studio. It is not the mere immediate effort that must be considered, in estimating the nature and value of an intellectual product, but that far more important preparatory effort that went before it, and cost a lifetime of toil. The painter's reply holds good in respect to every properly constructed extemporaneous oration. It is not the product of the mere instant of time in which it is uttered, but involves, *equally with the written oration*, the whole life and entire culture of the orator.

Taking this view of the nature of extemporaneous preaching, it is plain that there is not such a heaven-wide difference between it and written preaching as is often supposed. There is no *material* difference between the two. The extemporaneous sermon must be constructed upon the same general principles of rhetoric and homiletics with the written sermon, and must be the embodiment and result of the same literary, scientific, and professional culture. The difference between the two species of discourses is merely *formal*. And even this statement is too strong. There is not even a strictly formal difference, for the very same style and diction, the very same *technically* formal properties, are required in the one as in the other. The difference does not respect the form as distinguished from the matter of eloquence, but merely the form of the form. In extemporaneous preaching the form is oral, while in other species it is written. There is, therefore, not only no material difference between the two, but there is not even a rigorously and strictly formal difference. Both are the results of the same study, the same reflection, the same experience. The same *man* is the author of both, and both alike will exhibit his learning or his ignorance, his mental power or his mental feebleness, his spirituality, his unspirituality. An ignorant, undisciplined, and unspiritual man cannot write a good sermon; neither *need* a learned, thoroughly disciplined and holy man, preach a bad extemporaneous sermon. For nothing but the want of *practice* would prevent a learned mind, a methodical mind, a holy mind, from doing itself justice and credit in extemporaneous oratory.

A moment's consideration of the nature and operations of the human mind, of its powers by nature, and its attainments by study, is sufficient to show that the difference between written and unwritten discourse is merely formal, and less than strictly formal; is secondary, and highly secondary. The human intellect is full of living powers of various sorts, capable of an awakened and vigorous action, which expresses and embodies itself in literary products, such as the essay, the oration, the poem. But is there anything in the nature of these powers which renders it necessary that they should manifest themselves in one, and only one way? Is there anything in the constitution of the human mind that compels it to exhibit the issues of its subtle and mysterious agency uniformly, and in every instance, by means of the pen? Is there anything in the

o

intrinsic nature of mental discipline, which forbids its utterance, its clear, full, and powerful utterance, by means of *spoken* words? Must the contents of the heart and intellect be of necessity discharged only by means of the written symbol of thought? Certainly not. If there only be a mind well disciplined, and well stored with the materials of discourse, the chief thing is secured. The manner, whether written or oral, in which it shall deliver itself, is a secondary matter, and can readily be secured by practice. If the habit of delivering thought without pen in hand were taken up *as early in life*, by the educated clergy, and were as *uniform* and *fixed*, as is the habit of delivering it with pen in hand, it would be just as easy a habit. If it be supposed that unwritten discourse is incompatible with accuracy and finish, the history of literature disproves it. Some of the most elaborate literary productions were orally delivered. The blind Homer extemporized the *Iliad* and *Odyssey*. Milton, in his blindness, dictated to his daughter the *Paradise Lost*. Walter Scott often employed an amanuensis, when weary of composing with the pen in hand. Cæsar, it is said, was able to keep several amanuenses busy, each upon a distinct subject; thus carrying on several processes of composition, without any aid from chirography. The private secretary of Webster remarks of him: 'The amount of business which he sometimes transacted during a single morning may be guessed at, when it is mentioned that he not unfrequently kept two persons employed writing at his dictation at the same time; for, as he usually walked the floor on such occasions, he would give his chief clerk in one room a sentence to be incorporated in a diplomatic paper, and marching to the room occupied by his private secretary, give him the skeleton, or perhaps the very language of a private letter.'[1]   A writer in the *Quarterly Review* remarks, that 'it was in the open air that Wordsworth found the materials for his poems, and it was in the open air, according to the poet himself, that nine-tenths of them were shaped. A stranger asked permission of the servant, at Rydal, to see the study.   "This," said she, as she showed the room, " is my master's library, where he keeps his books, but his study is out of doors."   The poor neighbours, on catching the sound of his humming, in the act of verse-making, after some prolonged absence from home, were wont to exclaim, "There he is ; we are glad to hear him *booing* about again."   From the time of his settlement at Grasmere, he had a physical infirmity which prevented his composing pen in hand.   Before he had been five minutes at his desk, his chest became oppressed, and a perspiration started out over his whole body, to which was added, in subsequent years, incessant liability to inflammation in his eyes.   Thus, when he had inwardly digested as many lines as his memory could carry, he usually had recourse to some of the inmates of his house to commit them to paper.'[2]

There is, therefore, nothing in the *nature* of extemporaneous preaching incompatible with thoroughness of insight, clearness of presentation, or power of expression.   Whether an unwritten sermon shall be profound, lucid, and impres-

[1] Lanman, *Private Life of Webster*, p. 84.
[2] *London Quarterly Review*, vol. xcii. p. 212.

sive, or not, depends upon the preacher. If, after the due amount of immediate labour upon it, it fails to possess the qualities of good discourse, it is because the author himself lacks either learning, discipline, or practice, and not because there is anything in the nature of the production in question to preclude depth, clearness, and effectiveness.

The truth of these remarks will be still more apparent, if we bear in mind that the extemporaneous sermon has not had the due amount of work expended upon it. It has too often been resorted to in idle and indolent moods, instead of being the object upon which the diligent and studious preacher has expended the best of his power, and the choicest of his time. Again, the extemporaneous sermon has not been the product of persevering practice, and of the skill that comes from persevering practice. The preacher, in the tremor of his opening ministry, makes two or three attempts to preach extempore, and then desists. Remembering the defects of these first attempts, and comparing them with the more finished discourses which he has been in the *habit* and *practice* of writing, he draws the hasty and unfounded inference that, from the nature of the case, oral discourse must be inferior to written discourse. But who can doubt that, with an equal amount of practice, of patient, persistent practice, this species of sermon might be made equal to the other in those solid qualities in which, it must be confessed, it is too generally inferior? Who can doubt that if the clergy would form the habit, and acquire the self-possession and skill of the lawyer in respect to unwritten discourse, and then would expend the same amount of labour upon the unwritten that they do upon the written sermon, it would be as profound, as logical, as finished, and more effective ? The fact is, that there is nothing in the oral any more than in the written method of delivering thought, that is fitted to hamper the operations of the human mind. If an educated man has truth and eloquence within him, it needs nothing but *constant practice* to bring it out in either form he pleases—in written, or in extemporaneous language. Habit and practice will, in either case, impart both ability and facility. Take away the skill which is acquired by the habitual practice of composing with the pen in hand, and it would be as difficult for one to deliver his thoughts in writing as it is for one who has acquired no skill by the practice of extemporaneous discourse to deliver his thoughts orally. Nay, how often, when the thoughts flow thick and fast, is the slow pen found to impede the process of composition ! In such a case the mind yearns to give itself vent in unwritten language, and would do so, if it had only acquired the confidence before an audience, and the skill, which are the result, not of mere nature, but of habit and practice.

II. The truth of these assertions respecting the intrinsic nature of extemporaneous preaching, will be still more evident by considering the chief requisites in order to the attainment of the gift. It will be found that, provided these exist, the unwritten sermon affords an opportunity for the display of all those substantial qualities which are commonly supposed to belong to written sermons alone, and, in addition, of all those qualities which coexist only with the burning words and free delivery of the orator untrammelled by a manuscript and the effort to read it.

1. The first requisite, in order to extemporaneous preaching, is *a heart glowing and beating with evangelical affections.* The heart is the seat of life, the source of vigour, the spring of power. From this centre, vitality, energy, and impulse go out, and pervade the whole system. To the heart, whether in physiology or psychology, we must look for the central force. If profound feeling, the feeling that is grounded in reason and truth, pervade discourse, it will surely attain the end of eloquence, and produce deep movement in the hearer. That peculiar energy, issuing from the heart, which we designate by the word emotion, must mix and mingle with the energy issuing from the intellect, in order to the highest power of speech. It was because, as Macaulay says, 'his reason was penetrated and made red-hot by his passion,' that Fox was one of the most effective and overwhelming of orators. And the same truth will be evident if, instead of looking at the discourse itself, we contemplate the action of the discourser's mind. In order that the human faculties may work with the greatest energy and harmony, the heart must be in the head, and the head in the heart. Never does the mind operate so powerfully, and with such truth and beauty of result, as when the faculty of cognition co-works with the faculty of feeling. If these two faculties become one and indivisible in action, the result is not merely truth, but *living* truth—truth fused and glowing with all the feeling of the heart, and feeling mingled with, and made substantial by, all the truth of the head. The light is heat, and the heat is light.

These remarks respecting the function and agency of the

heart are true in every province, but especially in that of religion. The inmost essence of religion itself has been placed by Schleiermacher, one of the profoundest of the German theologians, solely in feeling. It is, probably, an error to make either knowledge or feeling, *by itself, and apart from the other*, the ultimate essence of religion. Religion is neither knowledge in isolation nor feeling in isolation, but a most original and intimate synthesis of both. If either element by itself be regarded as the sole and single constituent, theology becomes either rationalistic and speculative, or else mystical and vague. And yet, even those theologians whose scientific spirit has led them to emphasize creeds, and made them shy of sentimental religion, have always acknowledged that the heart is not only the seat of piety, but one important source of theological science itself.

If this is true in reference to the theologian, it is still more so in reference to the preacher. He needs the strong stir and impulse of holy affections in order to succeed in his vocation, and especially when he has not the written discourse upon which to rely. A heart replete and swelling with the grand emotions of Christianity, is a well of water springing up into everlasting life and power, for it is fed from infinite fountains. With what force, vividness, and natural method, also, does the Christian, destitute it may be of mental discipline and culture, sometimes speak upon the subject of religion out of a full heart! What wonderful insight does he oftentimes display into the very depths of religion and theology!—thus proving the truth of the saying, 'The heart sees further than the head.' Or, to take another instance, with what power and fresh originality does the convicted sinner utter himself upon the doctrine of human guilt when he is full of the awful feeling itself! Given, a heart filled with intelligent rational emotion respecting any subject, and the primal power by which effective discourse upon it is to be originated is given also.

Now so far as this first requisite in order to the practice of extemporaneous preaching is concerned, it can most certainly be secured by every preacher. Nay, he is presumed to possess it, as that which, in a great degree, justifies him in entering the ministry. Let him by prayer and meditation first purify the feeling of his heart, and then render it more deep and intense by the same means, and he will be prepared to speak freely and forcibly to the human heart. Let him take heed that his feeling be *spiritual*—an affection in distinction from a passion,[1] the product of God's Word and Spirit, and not the mere excitement of the sensibilities,—and he will preach with the demonstration of the Spirit and with power, as did Paul, ' without notes,' though it may be in weakness, and in fear, and in much trembling, and not with enticing words.

2. In the second place, *a methodizing intellect* is requisite in order to successful extemporaneous preaching. By a methodizing intellect is meant one which *spontaneously* works in a logical manner, and to which consecutive reasoning has become *natural*. All truth is logical. It is logically connected and related ; and that mind is metho-

---

[1] See the account of this important distinction by Theremin, *Rhetoric*, p. 131 sq.

dical which detects this relation and connection as it were by instinct. This natural logic, this spontaneous method, is one great source of mental power. How readily do we listen to one who unfolds truth with a facile and effortless precision, and how easily does his discourse win its way into us !

We have said that truth is logical in its essential nature. But it is equally true that the human mind is logical in its essential nature. For the truth and the mind are correlatives. One is set over against the other. The truth is the object to be known, and the mind is the subject or agent to know it; and subject and object are antitheses, like hunger and food, like thirst and water. Consequently in its idea, or, in other words, by its creation, the human intellect is as logical in its structure as the truth is in its nature. By its constitution, the mind is designed to be methodical and consecutive in its working, and to apprehend logical truth logically.

Now, by reason of discipline and practice, the human intellect works towards this true end of its creation, and acquires an instinctive ability to think methodically, and to unfold consecutively any subject presented to it. The exhibition of truth by a methodizing intellect is *exhaustive* (to use a term of Mackintosh) ; and the whole truth is thus unfolded in its substance, its connections, and relations. This methodizing talent *developes* a subject, unrolling it to the centre, and showing the whole of it. Kant has a chapter upon the architectonic nature of the pure reason, by which he means that innate system of laws which reason follows, in building up architecturally

its conclusions; and shows, that when these laws are followed, a logical whole is as certainly and *naturally* produced,
as is the honeycomb with its hexagonal cells, when the
bee follows the architectonic laws of its instinct.[1] Now a
methodizing mind is one which, by discipline and practice,
has reached that degree of philosophic culture, in which
these systematizing laws work *spontaneously*, by *their own
exceeding lawfulness*, and instinctively develope, in a systematic and consecutive manner, the whole truth of a subject. The results of the operation of such a mind may
well be called architecture; for they are built up according to eternal law in order and beauty. There is no
grander fabric, no fairer architectural structure, than a
rational, logical system of truth. It is fairer and more
majestic than St. Peter's. A great system of thought rises
like that cathedral with a

> ' Vastness which grows, but grows to harmonize,
>   All musical in its immensities.'

In speaking of the heart as the seat of feeling, we had
occasion to allude to its influence in modifying the operations of the mind considered as a whole. It was seen that
it imparts vitality to the total mental action, and infuses
vigour through all the products of this action. A methodizing intellect exerts a very important influence in the
same reference. Feeling, though vivific and energizing, is
not precise and clear in its own nature. The man of all
feeling has a vague and mystic tendency. Hence the need
of logic, in order that the energy issuing from the heart

[1] Kant, *Kritik der reinen Vernunft*, p. 641 sq. (Die Architektonik der
reinen Vernunft.)

may be prevented from diffusing itself over too wide a surface, and may be guided into channels and flow along in them. When a beating heart is allied with a methodizing mind, there are at once vigour and life, with clearness and precision. The warm emotions are kept from exhaling and becoming vapoury and obscure by the systematizing tendency of the logical faculty, and the hard dry forms of logic are softened and enlivened by the vernal breath of the emotions.

It is evident that if the sacred orator possesses such a discipline of head and heart as has been described, it will be easy for him to apply it to any theme he chooses, and speak upon it in any manner he may elect. The human mind, when highly trained, can labour with success in almost every direction. Education is, in truth, not a dead mass of accumulations, but the power to work with the brain. If this power be acquired, it is a matter of secondary consequence what be the special topic upon which the work is expended, or the particular manner, oral or written, in which the result is embodied. In the ancient gymnasium the first purpose was to produce a muscular man—an athlete. When this was accomplished, it mattered little whether he entered the lists of the wrestler, or of the boxer, or of the racer. Nay, if he were thorough-bred, he might attempt the *pancratium* itself, and carry off the laurels. Assuming the existence of such a salient heart, and such a methodical head, nothing but habitual practice is needed to permit their employment before any audience whatsoever, and without the aid of a manuscript. If the preacher has attained this facility of methodizing, and is under the impulse of ebullient, swelling affections, awakened by the clear vision of divine truths and realities, he will be able to speak powerfully in any presence, and *extempore.* The furnace is full, and the moulds are ready. Nothing is needed but to draw off; and when this is done, a solid and symmetrical product is the result.

3. A third requisite, in order to the practice of extemporaneous preaching, is *the power of amplification.*[1] By this is meant the ability to dwell upon an important point or principle until the hearer shall feel the whole force of it. It is the tendency of a thoughtful, and especially of a methodizing mind, to be satisfied with the great leading principles of a theme, and not to tarry long upon any one idea, however capital it may be. Such a mind is able to pass over a subject with great rapidity, by touching only the prominent parts of it, as the fabled Titans stepped from mountain to mountain without going up and down the intervening valleys. But the common hearer, the popular audience, cannot follow; and hence the methodical and full mind must learn to enlarge and illustrate until the principle is perceived in all its length and breadth, and the idea is contemplated in all its height and depth. Just in proportion as the methodizing mind acquires this amplifying talent does it become oratorical; without it, though there may be philosophy, there cannot be eloquence.

But this talent will be rapidly acquired by careful pains and practice in regard to it. The speaker needs merely to

[1] Compare the Author's *Discourses and Essays,* p. 96.

stop his mind in its onward logical movement, and let its energy head back upon the idea or the principle which his feeling and his logic have brought out to view. Indeed, the tendency, after a little practice, will be to dwell too long, to amplify too much, when once the intellect has directed its whole power to a single topic. As matter of fact, the preacher will find, altogether contrary to his expectations, that his oral discourse is more expanded and diffuse than his written, that his extemporaneous sermon is longer than his manuscript. An undue amplification is the principal fault in the eloquence of Burke, who was one of the most methodical and full minds in literary history. In the language of Goldsmith, he

. . . 'went on refining,
And thought of convincing, while they thought of dining.'

Hence, although never unwelcome to his readers, his magnificent amplification was sometimes tedious to his hearers. Though the British House of Commons, at the close of the last century, was not a 'fit audience' for Burke, because it had but small sympathy with that broad and high political philosophy out of which his masculine and thoughtful eloquence sprang, like the British oak from the strong black mould of ages; though Burke would not be the 'dinner bell' for the present British Parliment; still his excessive amplification undoubtedly somewhat impedes that rapid rush and Demosthenean vehemence of movement which distinguishes eloquence from all other species of discourse.

4. A fourth requisite in order to successful extemporaneous preaching, is *a precise mode of expression.* A

methodical mind thinks clearly, and therefore the language should be select and exact, that it may suit the mental action. If the orator's thoughts are distinct and lucid, he needs carefully to reject any and every word that does not convey the precise meaning he would express. Indeed, *rejection* is the chief work in clothing the thoughts of a highly disciplined mind. It is an error to suppose that the main difficulty in extemporaneous preaching lies in the want of words, just as it is an error to suppose that great natural fluency is an indispensable aid to it. Dr. Chalmers never acquired the ability to speak extempore in a manner at all satisfactory to himself, or to his auditors when they remembered his written discourses. And the cause of this, according to his own statement, was the unmastered and overmastering fluency of his mind. Thoughts and words come in on him like a flood. In extemporaneous utterance, they impeded each other, to use his own expression, like water attempted to be poured all at once out of a narrow-mouthed jug. A more entire mastery of his resources, a power to repress this fluency, to control the coming deluge, which might have been acquired by patient practice, would have rendered Chalmers a most wonderful extemporaneous preacher, at the same time that it would have improved his written sermons, by rendering them less plethoric and tumid in style, and more exact and precise in phraseology.

Uncontrolled fluency is equally a hindrance to excellent poetical composition. Byron speaks of the 'fatal facility' of the octo-syllabic verse. It runs too easily to be favourable to the composition of thoughtful poetry.

Some of Byron's own poetry, and a great deal of Scott's, betray this fatal facility in a too abundant use of what Goldsmith humorously calls 'the property of jinglimus.' The melody is not subordinated to the harmony, the rhythm is monotonous, and the reader sighs after a more stirring and varied music.

Natural fluency is a fatal facility in the orator also, unless he guards against it by the cultivation of strict logic and precise phraseology. Men generally, even those who are reputed to be men of few words, are fluent when *roused*. When the feelings are awakened and the intellect is working intensely, there are more thoughts and words than the *unpractised* speaker can take care of. What is needed is coolness and entire self-mastery in the midst of this animation and inspiration, so that it may not interfere with itself and impede its own movement. What is needed is the ability in this glow of the heart, this tempest and whirlwind of feeling, to *reject* all thoughts that do not strictly belong to the subject, and all words that do not precisely convey the cool, clear thought of the cool, clear head. The orator must be able to check his thunder in mid volley. This is really the great art in extemporaneous discourse; and it cannot be attained except by continual practice and careful attention with reference to it. The old and finished speaker always uses fewer and choicer words than the young orator. The language of Webster during the last half of his public life was more select and precise than it was previously. He employed fewer words to convey the same amount of meaning, by growing more nice and careful in the rejection of those vague words which come thick and thronging when the mind is roused. Hence the language he did use is full of meaning; as one said, 'every word weighs a pound.'

We have thus discussed the principal requisites in order to successful extemporaneous preaching. It will be evident that the subject has not been placed upon a weak foundation, or that but little has been demanded of the extemporaneous preacher. A heart full of devout and spiritual affections, a spontaneously methodizing intellect, the power of amplification, and a precise phraseology are not small attainments. A great preparation has been required on the part of him who preaches unwritten sermons, but only because it is precisely the same that is required in order to the production of excellent written discourse. If this preparation has actually been made; if his heart is full, and his intellect spontaneously methodical in its working; if he can dwell sufficiently long upon particular points, and can express himself with precision,—then, with no more *immediate* preparation than is required to compose the written sermon, and NO LESS, the preacher may speak as logically as he does when he writes, and even more freshly and impressively. But, as was remarked in the beginning of the chapter, the extemporaneous sermon will be the product, not of the particular instant, but of all the time of the speaker's life,—of all the knowledge and culture he has acquired by the sedulous discipline of his intellect, and the diligent keeping of his heart. Whether, then, all may preach unwritten sermons, depends upon whether all may acquire the requisites that have been described; and to assert that the clergy, generally, cannot acquire them, would be a libel upon them. There have been instances of men so thorough in their learning, and so spontaneously methodical in their mental habits, that, even with little or no immediate preparation, they could speak most logically and effectively. It is related of John Howe, that, 'such were his stores of thought, and so thoroughly were they digested, he could preach as methodically without preparation, as others after the closest study.' Robert Hall composed his singularly finished and elegant discourses lying at full length upon chairs placed side by side, a device to relieve acute pain. It is true that these were extraordinary men; but not a little of their power arose from the simple fact, that they felt strongly, thought patiently, and practised constantly.

And this brings us to the last, but by no means least important point in the discussion of this subject; and this is, the patient and persevering *practice* of extemporaneous preaching. These requisites to unwritten discourse that have been mentioned may all be attained, and, as matter of fact, are attained in a greater or less degree, by every preacher who composes written sermons, and yet there be no extemporaneous discourse. Many a preacher is conscious of possessing these capabilities, and can and does exert them through the pen, who would be overwhelmed and struck dumb if he should be deprived of his manuscript, and compelled to address an audience extemporaneously. These requisites must, therefore, *actually be put into requisition.* The preacher must actually speak extemporaneously, and be in the habit of so doing. And there

P

is one single rule, and but one, the observance of which
will secure that uniform practice, without which the finest
capacities will lie dormant and unused.   At the very
opening of his ministry the preacher must begin to deliver
one extemporaneous sermon on the Sabbath, and do so
uniformly to the close of it.   A resolute, patient, and
faithful observance of this rule will secure all that is
needed.   The preacher must pay no regard to difficulties
in the outset, must not be discouraged or chagrined by the
bad logic or bad grammar of his earlier attempts, must not
heed the remarks and still less the advice of fastidious
hearers ; but must prepare as carefully as possible for the
task as it comes round to him, and perform it as earnestly,
seriously, and scrupulously, as he does his daily devotions.[1]

[1] The following was the method of Dr. Blackburn, a distinguished
Southern preacher, in making the *immediate* preparation for unwritten
discourse, and we do not know of any better one.   'In his studies
and preparation for the pulpit, his plan was to fold a sheet of paper and
lay it on his writing-desk, and then commence walking backward and
forward across the room, occasionally stopping to note down a head or
leading subdivision of his thoughts, leaving considerable space under each
note.   Having thus arranged the plan of his discourse, which he called
"blazing his path," borrowing a figure from backwoods life, he then pro-
ceeded to take up each head and subdivision separately and amplify it
in his mind, until he had thought his whole discourse through and
through, stopping occasionally, as before, to jot down a word or thought,
sometimes a sentence or an illustration, under each division, until he had
finished.   Then taking up the paper, he would usually con it over again
and again, now blotting out, now adding something.   Thus he continued,
until every part of the discourse was satisfactorily arranged in his mind.
The notes thus prepared he usually took with him into the pulpit, but he
rarely had occasion even to glance at them.   He used to remark, "I try
to get the thoughts fully into my mind, and leave the language generally
to the occasion."'—*Presbyterian Quarterly Review*, March 1853.

The importance of an *early beginning*, as well as of a constant practice,
in order to extemporaneous speaking, is illustrated by the following

In course of time he will find that it is becoming a pleasant process, and is exerting a most favourable influence upon his written sermons, and, indeed, upon his whole professional character. In each week he should regularly preach one written sermon and one unwritten sermon to 'the great congregation.' If the preacher must be confined to but one kind of discourse, then he should write. No man could meet the wants of an intelligent audience, year after year, who should always deliver unwritten discourses. But the clergy would be a more able and influential body of public teachers, if the two species of sermonizing were faithfully employed by them. The vigour and force of the unwritten sermon would pass over into the written, and render it more impressive and powerful than it now is, while the strict method and finished style of the written discourse would pass over into the unwritten. If the young clergyman lays down this rule in the outset, and proceeds upon it, it is safe to prophesy a successful career of extemporaneous preaching in his case. But if he does not lay it down *in the very outset,* if he delays until a more convenient season occurs for going up into the pulpit, and speaking without a manuscript, then it is almost absolutely certain that, like the majority of his

remark of Mr. Clay to the students of a law school : 'I owe my success in life to one single fact, namely, that at the age of twenty-seven I commenced, and continued for years, the practice of daily reading and speaking upon the contents of some historical or scientific book. These off-hand efforts were made sometimes in a corn-field, at others in the forest, and not unfrequently in some distant barn, with the horse and the ox for my auditors. It is to this early practice of the great art of all arts that I am indebted for the primary and leading impulses that stimulated me forward, and have shaped my entire subsequent history.'

associates in the ministry, he will go through life **never** delivering a really excellent extemporaneous sermon.

We are confident that extemporaneous preaching should engage, far more than it does, the labour and study of the clergy. The more we think of it, the more clearly shall we see that, as a species, it comes nearest to ideal perfection. It is a living utterance out of a living heart and intellect to living excited men, through no medium but the free air. It was the preaching of Christ and his apostles, of many of the early Fathers, of Luther and the Reformers. And whenever any great movement has been produced, either in Church or State, it has commonly taken its rise, so far as human agency is concerned, from the unwritten words of some man of sound knowledge and thorough discipline, impelled to speak by strong feeling in his heart.

If the clergy would study the Bible with a closer and more penetrating exegesis,[1] and that theological system which has in it most of the solid substance of the Bible with a more patient and scientific spirit; if they would habituate their intellects to long and connected trains of thought and to a precise use of language, then, under the impulse of even no higher degree of piety than they now possess, greater results would follow from their preaching.

[1] The relation of exegetical study to extemporaneous speaking deserves a separate discussion. Nothing is more certain to make a fluent and ready speaker than the analytic examination of the revealed Word. He who is accustomed to read a Gospel or an Epistle *over and over and over again*, in the original Greek, becomes so saturated with its revelations, that he is as full of matter as Elihu, the friend of Job, and must speak that he may be refreshed. A *single* philological perusal will not have this effect; but ten or twenty will.

When the clergy shall pursue theological studies, as Melancthon says he did, for personal spiritual benefit; when theological science shall be wrought into the very soul, inducing a theological mood; when thorough learning and diligent self-discipline shall go hand in hand with deep love for God and souls; and when the clergy shall dare to *speak* to the people with extemporaneous boldness out of a full heart, full head, and clear mind, we may expect, under the divine blessing, to see some of those great movements which characterized the ages of extempore preaching,—the age of the apostles, the age of the Reformers, the age of John Knox in Scotland, the age of Wesley and Whitefield in England and America.

CHAPTER X.

THE exposition of the methods and maxims by which homiletical discipline may best be acquired, demands, at its conclusion, some consideration of their practical application in the actual work of the clerical profession. With what spirit ought the preacher to deliver his message? what should be its main drift and lesson? how should the manner of his utterance compare with that of other professions? These are some of the questions, upon the right answer to which depends very greatly the success of the clergyman. For though his theory of Sacred Eloquence may be high and true, yet a false spirit carried into his work will vitiate all his science, and bring him short of his ideals. His great work is to speak to the popular mind upon the subject of religion with a view to influence it; and therefore his oratorical efforts ought to be marked by that practical, and, so to speak, business-like manner which is seen in the children of this world, who, in their generation, are oftentimes wiser than the children of light. The preacher has much to learn from the legal profession. A lawyer goes into the court-room in order to establish certain facts, and impress certain legal truths upon twelve men in the jury box. He

is generally an earnest and direct man. He may be somewhat diffuse and circuitous in his representations, but it
will be found that, in the end, he comes round to his case,
and makes everything bear upon the verdict which he
desires. In like manner the Christian minister is to go
into the pulpit in order to establish certain facts in regard
to God and man, and to impress certain religious truths
upon all who come to hear him. He, too, ought to be
marked by great energy and simplicity of aim. He should
start upon his professional career with a true and positive
conception of the work before him. The theme, then, is
a wide one, and in order to convey the particular thoughts
which we would present in the briefest and most concise
manner possible, we propose to speak of the *matter*, the
manner, and the *spirit* of preaching.

1. In respect to the matter, the ideas and truths which
the preacher shall bring before the popular mind, during
ten, twenty, or forty years in which he may address it,
we affirm that he ought to confine himself to evangelical
doctrine. If he is to err in regard to the range of subjects,
let him err upon the safe side. It is undesirable and
unwise for the pulpit to comprehend anything more, in its
instructions, than that range of inspired truth which has
for its object the salvation of the human soul. It is true
that Christianity has a connection with all truth; and so
has astronomy. But it no more follows that the Christian
minister should go beyond the fundamental principles of
the gospel, and discuss all of their relations to science, art,
and government, in his Sabbath discourses, than that the
astronomer should leave his appropriate field of observa-

tion, and attempt to be equally perfect in all that can be logically connected with astronomy. Life is short, and art is long. In the secular sphere, it is conceded that the powerful minds are those who rigorously confine themselves to one department of thought. Newton cultivated science, and neglected literature. Kant wrought in the quicksilver mines of metaphysics for fifty years, and was happy and mighty in his one work. These men made epochs, because they did not career over the whole encyclopedia. And the same is true in the sphere of religion. The giants in theology have dared to let many books go unread, that they might be profoundly versed in revelation. And the mighty men in practical religion, the reformers, the missionaries, the preachers, have found in the distinctively evangelical elements of Christianity, and their application to the individual soul, enough, and more than enough, to employ all their powers and enthusiasm.

The Christian minister is not obligated to run out Christianity into all its connections and relations. Neither he nor the Church is bound to watch over all the special interests of social, literary, political, and economical life. Something should be left to other men and other professions, and something should be left to the providence of God. The Christian preacher can do more towards promoting the earthly and temporal interests of mankind by indirection, than by direct efforts. That minister who limits himself, in his Sabbath discourses, to the exhibition and enforcement of the doctrines of sin and grace, and whose preaching results in the actual conversion of human

beings, contributes far more, in the long run, to the progress of society, literature, art, science, and civilisation,
than he does who, neglecting these themes of sin and
grace, makes a direct effort from the pulpit to 'elevate
society.' In respect to the secular and temporal benefits
of the Christian religion, it is eminently true that he that
finds his life shall lose it. When the ministry sink all
other themes in the one theme of the Cross, they are rewarded in a twofold manner: they see the soul of man
born into the kingdom of God; and then, as an inevitable
consequence, with which they had little to do directly, but
which is taken care of by the providence of God, and the
laws by which He administers his government in the
earth, they also see arts, sciences, trade, commerce, and
political prosperity flowing in of themselves. They are
willing to seek first the kingdom of God, and his righteousness, and find all these minor things—infinitely minor
things, when compared with the eternal destiny of man—
added to them by the operation, not of the pulpit, or of
the ministry, but of divine laws and divine providence.
But, whenever the ministry sink the Cross, wholly or in
part, in semi-religious themes, they are rewarded with
nothing. They see, as the fruit of their labours, neither
the conversion of the individual nor the prosperity of
society. That unearthly sermonizing of Baxter and Howe,
so abstracted from all the temporal and secular interests of
man, so rigorously confined to human guilt and human
redemption,—that preaching which, upon the face of it,
does not seem even to recognise that man has any relations
to this little ball of earth, which takes him off the planet

entirely, and contemplates him simply as a sinner in the presence of God,—that preaching, so destitute of all literary, scientific, economical, and political elements and allusions,—was, nevertheless, by indirection, one of the most fertile causes of the progress of England and America. Subtract it as one of the forces of English history, and the career of the Anglo-Saxon race would be like that of Italy and Spain.

The preacher must dare to work upon this theory, and make and keep his sermons thoroughly evangelical in their substantial matter.   The temptations are many, in the present age, to multiply topics, and to introduce themes into the pulpit, upon which Christ and his apostles never preached.   It is enough that the disciple be as his master. And if the Son of God, possessing an infinite intelligence, and capable of comprehending, in his intuition, the whole abyss of truth, physical and moral, natural religion and revealed, all art, all science, all beauty, and all grandeur,— if the Son of God, the Omniscient One, was nevertheless reticent regarding the vast universe of truth that lay outside of the Christian scheme, and confined himself to that range of ideas which relate to sin and redemption,—then, who are we that we should venture beyond his limits, and counteract his example !

2. Secondly, in respect to the manner in which the preacher is to address the popular mind, upon these fundamental truths of Christianity, he ought to use great directness of style and speech.   The connection between the matter and the manner of a writer is one of action and reaction.   Clear, evangelical ideas favour lucid, earnest

style. He who selects semi-religious topics immediately begins to hyperbolize and elocutionize. No Demosthenean fire, no hearty idiomatic English, no union of energy and elegance, naturally issues when poetry is substituted for theology, and the truths of nature are put in the place of the doctrines of grace. A languid and diffuse manner, like that of moral essays, is the utmost that can be attained upon this method.

And, on the other hand, a tendency to a direct, terse, vigorous mode of handling subjects, reacts upon the theological opinions of the preacher, and favours intensity and positiveness in his doctrinal views. Wordsworth, in conversing upon the style of a certain writer, which was peculiar and striking, remarked: 'To be sure, it is the manner that gives him his power; but then, you know, the *matter* always comes out of the manner.'[1] This is reversing the common statement of the rhetorician, who is in the habit of saying, that the manner comes out of the matter. But it contains its side of truth. No man can cultivate and employ a vigorous, direct, and forcible rhetoric, without finding that he is driven to solid and earnest themes, in order to originate and sustain it. Those slender and unsuggestive truths which lie outside of revelation, and which relate more to man's earthly than to his immortal nature, more to his wordly than his eternal destiny, prove too weak for a powerful and commanding eloquence, and thus the rhetorician of an earnest and natural type is driven, by his very idea of style, to those themes of sin, guilt, judgment, atonement, grace, and eternal glory, which constitute

[1] Emerson, *English Traits*, p. 294.

the substance of Christianity, and are full of immortal vigour and power.

As the preacher goes forth to speak, it may be for twenty or forty years continuously, to his fellow-immortals, upon the awful themes of eternity, let him weigh well every word he utters, and make it the direct exponent of a vivid and earnest thought. He lives in an age more inclined to sentiment than to ideas. The vicious and meretricious manner of the fugitive magazine and review is, just now, influencing the public taste, more than the dense and powerful style of the classical standards. Let him pay special attention, therefore, to his own manner. He should be a plain, direct, terse, and bold orator. He must employ the rhetoric which Jael used upon Sisera, putting his nail to the *head* of his auditor, and driving it sheer and clear through his brain.

3. And, finally, in respect to the spirit with which the preacher should deliver his ideas, we sum up all that can be said upon this point when we urge him to speak the truth in love. An affectionate spirit is the type and the model for the Christian herald. The greatest of the graces is charity. This we are toiling after all our days, and this comes latest and slowest into the soul. If those who have preached the word for years were called upon to specify the one particular in respect to which they would have their ministry reconstructed, it would be their deficiency in this mellow, winning, heavenly trait of St. John. Perhaps they can say that they have been measurably positive, earnest, plain, and truthful preachers; but alas! they cannot be so certain in their affirmation that they have been

affectionate heralds of the Lord Jesus. Their love for God's honour and glory, and the welfare of the human soul, has been too faint and feeble. This is the weak and not the strong side of their service in the pulpit.

It is well for the clergyman to know this in the outset of his ministry, so that his efforts may be directed accordingly. That trait in which the human soul is most deficient, because it is most directly contrary to human selfishness,—that Christian trait which is the most difficult both to originate and to maintain,—is certainly the one that should be before the eye of the Christian minister from the beginning of his course. Other traits, unless toned down by this one, are liable to run into extremes that become positive faults. The preacher's lucid energy, for example, unless tempered by a tender affectionateness, may issue in an exasperating vehemence that defeats all the ends of preaching, and renders it impossible to 'persuade' men to become reconciled to God, or even to 'beseech' them to become so.

The preacher, then, must cultivate in himself a genuine and sincere affection for man as man, for man as sinful and lost, and for God as the blessed and adorable Saviour of man. And among the several means of educating himself in this direction, none is more effectual than that strict confinement of his mind and heart to *evangelical* themes, which we have already recommended. If he would feel love for man's soul, he must distinctly see how precious the soul is by its origin, and how deeply wretched and lost it is by its sin. If he would feel love towards God as the Redeemer of man, he must distinctly see how great a self-sacrifice He has made, in order to the remission and removal of man's sin. If such topics as these are the infrequent themes of his study and sermonizing,—if they are crowded out by other topics, which have no direct tendency to fill him with tender emotions in reference to God and man, but, on the contrary, puff up with pride, or perhaps lead to an undervaluation of evangelical doctrine,—then, he cannot be an affectionate preacher. He will never be able to say, as St. Paul did of himself, in reference to the Thessalonians: 'We were gentle among you, even as a nurse cherisheth her children: so, being affectionately desirous of you, we were willing to have imparted unto you, not the gospel of God only, but also our own souls, because ye were dear unto us.'[1]

Of all the New Testament truths, none is equal to the doctrine of forgiveness through the blood of the dying Lord, in eliciting this divine and holy love. And therefore the preacher's meditation must be much upon this, and his speech very frequent upon it. The Roman Catholic theologians, in their classification of the gifts and graces of the believer, mention the *donum lachrymarum,* the heavenly gift of tears. By it they mean that tender contrition of soul which weeps bitterly, like Peter, under the poignant recollection of transgression, and the sweet sense of its forgiveness. It is that free and outgushing sorrow which flows from the strange unearthly consciousness of being vile when tried by a perfect standard, and yet of being the justified and adopted child of God. It is that relief which a Christian man craves for himself, when, after much

[1] 1 Thess. ii. 7, 8.

meditation upon his sin, he still finds the heart is hard, and the soul is parched with inward heat that 'turns the moisture into the drought of summer.' This gift of tears is most intimately connected with the gift of love. From that soul which is forgiven much, and whose consciousness of the divine mercy flows in the tears of the Magdalene, there issues a most profound affection. We love the soul of man, and are willing to toil and suffer for its welfare, when we are melted down in gratitude and affection because we have ourselves been forgiven.

If, therefore, the Christian preacher would suffuse his thoughts with that yearning charity which St. Paul describes, let him live in the light of the Cross, let him feel the virtue of expiating blood in his conscience. The immediate intuition of the great Atonement arms the preacher with a wonderful tenderness and power of entreaty. Other doctrines are powerful, but this carries him beyond himself, and fills him with a deathless affection for God and the soul of man that seems madness itself to the natural mind. Whitefield's, Summerfield's, and M'Cheyne's glowing and seraphic fervour was inspired almost wholly by this single truth. And what a pathetic earnestness, what a tender and gentle sympathy, ever mingled with the strong flood-tide of Chalmers' emotion, after that memorable sickness, when he sat for weeks upon the brink of eternity, and there, in the face of endless doom and death, obtained the first clear calming view of his dying Redeemer!

The age and condition of the world demand ministers of this type. The preacher of this age is appointed to proclaim the gospel at a period when the Christian religion and Church are assailed by materialism in the masses, and scepticism in the cultivated. These are the two foes of Christ, whose presence he will feel wherever he goes. He will meet them in Christendom, and he will meet them in Paganism. It looks now as if Antichrist were making his final onset. Let him therefore adopt a positive method. He should not waste his strength in standing upon the defensive. Christianity is not so much in need of apologetic as of aggressive efforts. *State* its doctrines with plainness, and they will hold their ground. Fuse them in the fire of personal convictions, and utter them with the confidence of an immediate perception, and they will not need the support of collateral argument. They are their own evidence, when once enunciated, and lodged in the conscience of man—as much so as the axioms of science.

The Christian herald should go forth with faith and hope, remembering that the gospel of the Son of God is the only system that is not subject to fashions and changes. It is the same now that it was when St. Paul carried it to Athens, and St. John taught it in Ephesus. It will be the same system down to the end of the world. He is to be a co-worker with a mighty host in the rear, and another mighty host in the front. Why should he not be courageous, standing as he does in the centre of a solid column, whose ranks are closed up, and which presents an impregnable front from whatever side the foe may approach? And why should he not be the boldest and most commanding of orators, when he remembers, still more, that the gospel of the Son of God is the only system of truth, for whose triumph the Eternal One is pledged? He hath sworn by himself, and the word has gone out of his mouth in righteousness, and shall not return: 'Unto Him every knee shall bow.'

CHAPTER XI.

RECIPROCAL RELATIONS OF PREACHER AND HEARER.

THE orator is not an isolated person, but one who stands in living sensitive *rapport* with an auditory, and therefore the discussion of the subject of Eloquence cannot be regarded as complete, without some account of the mutual relations of the parties. And there is more need of this exposition in reference to sacred than to secular oratory, because one whole side of the message which the Christian herald carries to man is unwelcome. He must preach the condemning law, and present the severe aspects of truth. This renders it more difficult for him to establish a harmonious relation between himself and his audience than it is for the secular orator. The difficulty in the case will be most easily overcome, if both speaker and hearer have a clear understanding of the attitude which each is morally bound to take towards the other. 'Preach the preaching that I bid thee,' is God's explicit command to the herald. 'Take heed how ye hear,' is his solemn message to the congregation. Both parties must hear the message, and endeavour to come into right relations to each other, if they would receive the divine blessing. 'For,' says Richard Baxter, 'we bring not sermons to church as we do a corpse for a burial. If there be life in them, and life in the hearers, the connaturality will cause such an amicable closure, that, through the reception, retention, and operation of the soul, they will be the immortal seed of a life everlasting.'[1] This passage, from one of the most fervid and effective of preachers, gives the clue to Christian eloquence. Life in the preacher, and life in the hearer,—vitality upon both sides,—this, under God, is the open secret of successful speech.

For the relation which properly exists between the Christian preacher and the Christian hearer is a *reciprocal* one, or that of action and reaction. Yet it is too commonly supposed that eloquence depends solely upon the speaker; that the hearer is only a passive subject, and as such is merely to absorb into himself a mighty and powerful influence that flows out from the soul of the orator, who alone is the active and passionate agent in the process. It will be found, however, upon closer examination, that eloquence, in its highest forms and effects, is a joint product of two factors—of an eloquent speaker and an eloquent hearer. Burning words presuppose some fuel in the souls to whom they are addressed. The thrill of the orator, however exquisite, cannot traverse a torpid or paralysed nerve in the auditor. It is necessary, therefore, as all the rhetoricians have said, in order to the highest effect of human speech, that the auditor be in a state of preparation and recipiency ; that there be an answering chord in the mass of minds before whom the single solitary individual comes forth with words of warning or of consolation, of terror or of joy.

[1] Baxter, Sermon on Christ's absolute dominion. (Preface.)

It follows, consequently, that if there be a true tone in preaching, there is also a true temper in hearing. If it is incumbent upon the sacred ministry to train itself to a certain style of thinking and utterance, it is equally incumbent upon the sacred auditory to school itself into the corresponding mood, so that its mental attitude, its prejudgments, its intellectual convictions, its well-weighed fears and forebodings, shall all be, as it were, a fluid sea, along which the surging mind of the public teacher shall roll its billows. What, then, is the true tone in preaching, and what is the true temper in hearing religious truth?

The divine interrogatory, 'Is not my word like as a fire?'[1] suggests the true tone which should at all times characterize public religious address to the natural man; and the decided utterance of the Psalmist, 'Let the righteous smite me, it shall be a kindness,'[2] on the other hand, indicates the temper which the public mind should maintain in reference to such a species of address. From the voice of God speaking through the most shrinking, yet the most impassioned of his prophets, from the voice of God emitted from the deepest, clearest, widest religious experience under the old economy, we would get our answer. The purpose, then, of this chapter will be to specify, in the first place, some distinctly biblical views of truth that are exceedingly intense in their quality and penetrating in their influence, and should therefore enter as constituent elements into preaching; and, in the second place, to indicate the proper attitude of the popular mind towards such preaching.

[1] Jer. xxiii. 29. [2] Ps. cxli. 5.

I. The prophet Jeremiah, in the well-known interrogatory to which we have alluded, directs attention to those elements in Revelation which are adapted to produce a keen and pungent sensation, like fire, whenever they are brought into contact with the individual or the general mind. Just in proportion, consequently, as public address upon religious themes emits this subtle and penetrating radiance, because the preacher has inhaled the vehement and fiery temper of the Scriptures respecting a certain class of subjects, will it speak to men with an emphasis that will startle them and hinder them from sleep.

1. Commencing the analysis, then, we find these elements of force and of fire, in the biblical representation of God as an *emotional person,* or, in Scripture phrase, as the ' *living* God.'

And here we shall pass by all those more general aspects of the divine personality, which have been abundantly brought to view in the recent and still existing contest between theism and pantheism, and confine ourselves to a notice of those more specific qualities which have been somewhat overlooked in this controversy, and which constitute the core and life of the personal character of God. For the biblical representation of the Deity not merely excludes all those conceptions of Him which convert Him into a Gnostic abyss, and place Him in such unrevealed depths that He ceases to be an object of either love or fear, but it clothes Him with what may be called individuality of emotion or feeling. Revelation is not content with that inadequate and frigid form of theism, that deism which merely asserts the divine existence and

unity with the fewest predicates possible, but it enunciates the whole plenitude of the divine nature upon the
side of the *affections* as well as of the understanding.   When
the Bible denominates the Supreme Being the '*living*
God,' it has in view that blending of thought with emotion,
that fusion of intellect with feeling, which renders the
Divine Essence a throbbing centre of self-consciousness.
For subtract emotion from the Godhead, and there
remains merely an abstract system of laws and truths.
Subtract the intellect, and there remains the mystic and
dreamy deity of sentimentalism.   In the Scriptures we
find the union of both elements.   According to the Bible,
God possesses emotions.   He loves, and He abhors.   The
Old and New Testaments are vivid as lightning with the
feelings of the Deity.   And these feelings flash out in the
direct, unambiguous statement of the Psalmist, 'God loveth
the righteous; God is angry with the wicked every day;'
in the winning words of St. John, 'God is love;' and in the
terrible accents of St. Paul, ' Our God is a consuming fire.'
Complacency and displeasure, then, are the two specific
characteristics, in which reside all the vitality of the
doctrine that God is personal.   These are the most purely
individual qualities that can be conceived of.   They are
continually attributed to the Supreme Being in the Scriptures, and every rational spirit is represented as destined
for ever to feel the impression of the one or the other of
them, according as its own inward appetences and adapta-
tions shall be.   While, therefore, the other truths that enter
into Christian theism are to be stated and defended in the
great debate, the philosopher and theologian must look

with a lynx's eye at these emotional elements in the Divine nature. For these, so to speak, are the living points of contact between the Infinite and Finite; and that theory of the Godhead which rejects them, or omits them, or blunts them, will, in the end, itself succumb to naturalism and pantheism.

There are no two positions in Revelation more un-qualified and categorical, than that 'God is love,' and that 'God is a consuming fire.' Either one of these affirmations is as true as the other; and therefore the complete un-mutilated idea of the Deity must comprehend both the love and the displeasure in their harmony and reciprocal relations. Both of these feelings are equally necessary to personality. A being who cannot love, is impersonal; and so is a being who cannot abhor. Torpor in one direction implies torpor in the other. 'He who loves the good,' argued Lactantius fifteen centuries ago, 'by this very fact hates the evil; and he who does not hate the evil, does not love the good; because the love of goodness flows directly out of the hatred of evil, and the hatred of evil springs directly out of the love of goodness. There is no one who can love life without abhorring death; no one who has an appetency for light without an antipathy to darkness.'[1] He who is able to love that which is lovely, cannot but hate that which is hateful. One class of emotions towards moral good implies an opposite class towards moral evil. Every ethical feeling necessitates its counterpart; and therefore God's personal love towards

[1] Lactantius, *De ira Dei*, c. 5. Compare also Tertullianus, *De testimonio animæ*, c. 2.

the seraph necessitates God's personal wrath towards the fiend.

There is therefore no true middle position between the full scriptural conception of God and the deistical conception of Him. We must either, with some of the English deists, deny both love and indignation to the Deity, or else we must, with the prophets and apostles, attribute both love and indignation to him. Self-consistency drives us to one side or the other. We may hold that God is mere intellect, without heart and without feeling of any kind; that He is as impassive and unemotional as the law of gravitation or a geometrical axiom; that He neither loves the holy nor hates the wicked; that feeling, in short, stands in no kind of relation to an Infinite Essence;—or we may believe that the Divine Nature is no more destitute of emotional than it is of intellectual qualities, and that all forms of righteous and legitimate feeling enter into the divine self-consciousness,—we may take one side or the other, and we shall be self-consistent. But it is in the highest degree illogical and inconsistent, to attribute one class of emotions to God, and deny the other; to postulate the love of goodness, and repudiate the indignation at sin. What reason is there in attributing the feeling of complacency to the nature of the Infinite and Eternal, and denying the existence of the feeling of indignation, as so many do, in this and every age? Is it said that emotion is always, and of necessity, beneath the Divine Nature? Then why insist, and emphasize, that 'God is *love?*' Is it said that wrath is an unworthy feeling? But this, like love itself, depends upon the nature of the object upon which it is expended. What species of feeling ought to possess the Holy One, when He looks down upon the orgies of Tiberius ? when He sees John the Baptist's head in the charger ? Is it a mere illicit and unworthy passion, when the wrath of God is revealed from heaven against those sins mentioned in the first chapter of Romans, and continually practised by mankind ? And may not love be an unworthy feeling ? Is not this emotion as capable of degenerating into a blind appetite, into a mere passion, as any other one ? Which is most august and venerable—the pure and spiritual abhorrence of the seraphim, wakened by the sight of the sin and uncleanness of fallen Babylon, or the selfish fondness and guilty weakness of the un-principled affection of earth ? Which is most permeated with eternal truth and reason, and so most worthy of entering into the consciousness of a Divine and Supreme Mind—the wrath of law, or the love of lust ?

So the Scriptures represent the matter; and upon the preacher's thorough belief in the strict metaphysical truth of this biblical idea of God, and his solemn reception of it into his mind, in all its scope and elements, with all its implications and applications, depend his power and energy as a religious thinker and speaker. He must see for himself, and make his hearers see, that God is just that intensely immaculate SPIRIT, both in his complacency and his displeasure, in all his personal qualities and on both sides of his character, which Revelation represents Him to be. No other energy can make up for the lack of this. With this, though his tongue may stammer and his heart often fail him, the preacher will go out before his accountable, guilty, dying fellow-men, with a spiritual power that cannot be resisted.

For man's mind is startled, when the divine individuality thus flashes into it, with these distinct and definite emotions: ' I thought of God, and was troubled.' The human spirit trembles to its inmost fibre, when God's personal character darts its dazzling rays into its darkness. When one realizes in some solemn moment, that no blind force or fate, no law of nature, no course and constitution of things, but a being as distinctly self-conscious as himself, and with a personality as vivid in feeling and emotion towards right and wrong as his own identity, has made him, and made him responsible, and will call him to account; when a man, in some startling but salutary passage in his experience, becomes aware that the intelligent and the emotional I AM is penetrating his inmost soul—he is, if ever upon this earth, a roused man, an earnest, energized creature. All men know how wonderfully the faculties of the soul are quickened, when it comes to the consciousness of guilt; what a profound and central activity is started in all the mental powers, by what is technically termed ' conviction.' But this conviction is the simple consciousness that God is one person, and man is another. Here are two beings met together,—a holy One, with infinite and judicial attributes, and a guilty one, with finite and responsible attributes: the two are in direct communication, as in the garden of Eden; and hence the shame, the fear, and the attempt to hide.

If, however, it is supposed that there must be some abatement and qualification in order to bring the biblical representation of the Deity into harmony with some theory in the head or some wish in the heart, it loses its incisive and truthful power over the human mind. If the full-orbed idea be so mutilated, that nothing but the feeling of love is allowed to enter into the nature of God, the mind softens and melts away into moral imbecility. If nothing but the emotion of displeasure makes up the character of the Deity, as was the case with the sombre and terrible Pagan religions, the mind of the worshipper is first over-whelmed with terror and consternation, and finally para-lysed and made callous by fear. But if both feelings are seen necessarily to co-exist in one and the same Eternal Nature, and each exercised towards its appropriate and deserving object, then the rational spirit adores and burns like the seraph, and bows and veils the face like the arch-angel.

2. In close connection with the doctrine of the living God, the Bible teaches the doctrine of the *guilt of man ;* and this is the second element of force and fire alluded to by the prophet in his interrogatory.

We have already noticed the close affinity that exists between a vivid impression of the divine character and the conviction of sin. When that comparatively pure and holy man, the Prophet Isaiah, saw the Lord, high and lifted up, he cried, ' I am a man of unclean lips.' And just in proportion as the distinct features of that divine countenance fade from human view, does the guilt of man disappear. But here, again, as in the preceding instance of the divine emotions, the difficulty does not relate so much to the bare recognition of the fact, as to the degree and thoroughness of the recognition. We have observed that there is a natural proneness to look more at the complacent than at the judicial side of the divine nature; to literalize and emphasize the love, but convert the wrath into metaphor and hyperbole. In like manner, there is a tendency to extenuate and diminish the degree of human guilt, even when the general doctrine is acknowledged. To apprehend and confess our sin to be our pure self-will and *crime*, is very difficult. We much more readily acknowledge it to be our disease and misfortune. Between the full denial on the one hand, that there is any guilt in man, and the full hearty confession on the other, that man is nothing but guilt before the Searcher of the heart and Eternal Justice, there are many degrees of truth and error; and it is with regard to these intermediates that the preacher especially needs the representations of the Bible. It is by the dalliance with the shallows of the subject that public religious address is shorn of its strength.

The Scriptures, upon the subject of human guilt, never halt between two opinions. They are blood-red. The God of the Bible is intensely immaculate, and man in the Bible is intensely guilty. The inspired mind is a rational and logical one. It either acquits absolutely and eternally, or condemns absolutely and eternally. It either pronounces an entire innocency and holiness, such as will enable the possessor of it to stand with angelic tranquillity amidst the lightnings and splendours of that countenance from which the heavens and the earth flee away, or else it pronounces an entire guiltiness in that Presence of such scarlet and crimson dye, that nothing but the blood of incarnate God can wash it away. The Old Testament, especially, to which the preacher must go for knowledge upon these themes, because the Old Dispensation was the educational dispensation of law, is full, firm, and distinct in its representations. Its history is the history of an economy designed by its rites, symbols, and doctrines, to awaken a poignant and constant consciousness of guilt. Its prophecy looks with eager-straining eye, and points with tremulous and thrilling finger to an Atoner and his atonement for guilt. Its poetry is either the irrepressible mourning and wail of a heart gnawed by guilt, or the exuberant and glad overflow of a heart experiencing the joy of expiated and pardoned guilt.

And to this is owing the intense vitality of the Old Testament. To this element and influence are traceable the vividness and energy of the Hebrew mind,—so different, in these respects, from the Oriental mind generally. The Hebrews were a part of that same great Shemitic race which peopled Asia and the East, and possessed the same general constitutional characteristics. But why did the Hebrew mind become so vivid, so intense, so dynamic, while the Persian and the Hindoo became so dreamy, so sluggish and lethargic? Why is the religion of Moses so vivific in its spirit, and particularly in its influence upon the conscience, while the religions of Zoroaster and Boodh exert precisely the same influence upon the conscience of the Persian and the Hindoo that poppy and mandragora do upon his body? It is because God subjected the Hebrew mind to this theistic, this guilt-eliciting education. From the very beginning, this knowledge of God's unity

and personality, and of God's emotions towards holiness
and sin, was kept alive in the chosen race. The people of
Israel were separated purposely, and with a carefulness
that was exclusive, from the great masses of the Oriental
world. Either by a direct intercourse, as in their exodus
from Egypt, with that personal Jehovah who had chosen
them in distinction from all other nations, or else by the
inspiration of their legislators and prophets, the truth that
God is a sovereign and a judge, 'keeping mercy for thousands, forgiving iniquity and transgression, and that will
by no means clear the guilty,' was made more and more
distinct and vivid in the Hebrew intuition, while it grew
dimmer and dimmer, and finally died out of the rest of the
Oriental populations. This education, this biblical education of the Hebrews, was the source of that energy and
vitality which so strikes us in their way of thinking and
modes of expression, and the absence of which is so noticeable in the literatures of Persia and India.

And here it is obvious to remark upon the importance
of a close investigation of those parts of the Old and New
Testaments which treat of the subject of atonement as
antithetic to that of sin and guilt. For this doctrine of
expiation in the Christian system is like a ganglion in
the human frame; it is a knot of nerves; it is the oscillat-
ing centre where several primal and vital truths meet in
unity. This single doctrine of sacrificial oblation is a vast
implication. It implies the personality of God, with all
its elements of power. It involves the absolute self-will
and responsibility of the creature in the origin of sin. It
implies the necessary, inexorable nature of justice. And

if we analyse these again, we shall find them full of the
'seeds of things,'—full of the substance and staple of both
ethics and evangelism. Those portions of the Bible, therefore, which treat of this central truth of Christianity,
either directly or indirectly, should receive the most
serious and careful investigation. The Mosaic system of
sacrifices should be studied, until its real meaning and
intent is understood. The *idea* of guilt—we employ the
word in the Platonic sense—and the *idea* of expiation, as
they stand out pure and simple, yet vivid and bright, in
the Prophets and Psalms, and in their inspired commentary the Epistle to the Hebrews, should be pondered,
until their intrinsic and necessary quality is apprehended.
For there is danger that the very ideas themselves may
fade away and disappear in an age of the world and
under a dispensation in which there is no daily sacrifice,
and frequent bleeding victim, to remind men of their debt
to eternal justice. The Christian religion, by furnishing
the one great sacrifice to which all other sacrifices look
and point, has of course done away with all those typical
sacrifices which cannot themselves take away guilt, but
can remind of it.[1] And now that the daily remembrancers
of the ritual and ceremonial are gone, the human mind
needs, more than ever, to ponder the teachings, and breathe
in the spirit of the legal dispensation, in order to keep the
conscience quick and active, and the moral sense healthy
and sound, in respect to the two great fundamental ideas
of guilt and retribution.

[1] 'In those sacrifices there is a *remembrance* again made of sins every
year.'—HEB. x. 3.

It has been an error, more common since the days of Grotius than it was in the time of the Protestant Reformation, that the doctrine of the atonement has been explained and illustrated too much by a reference to the attribute of benevolence and the interests of the creature, and too little by a reference to the attribute of justice and the remorseful workings of conscience. There is hazard, upon this method, that the simple, uncomplex ideas of guilt and atonement, as they operate in the very moral being of the individual sinner, and as they have their ground in the very nature of God, may be lost sight of, and the whole transaction of reconciliation be transferred into a region which, during the first exercises of an awakened soul, is too distant for a vivid apprehension and impression. Man must in the end, indeed, come to understand the bearings of the sacrifice of the Son of God upon what Chalmers calls 'the distant places of God's creation;' but he will be more likely to attain this understanding, if he first comes to apprehend its bearings upon his personal guilt and remorse, and how the blood of the Lamb expiates crime within his own burning self-consciousness. For, guilt and expiation are philosophical correlates, genuine correspondencies, set over against each other, like hunger and food, like thirst and water. 'My flesh,' saith the Atoner. 'is meat indeed; my blood is drink with emphasis.' He who knows with a vivid and vital self-consciousness what guilt means, knows what atonement means as soon as presented; and he who does not experimentally apprehend the one, cannot apprehend the other. If, therefore, any man would see the significance and necessity of sacrificial expiation, let him first see the significance and reality of crime, in his own personal character and direct relationships to God. The doctrine grasped and held *here* presents little difficulty. For the remorse, now felt, necessitates and craves the expiation; and the expiation, now welcomed, explains and extinguishes the remorse.

Now, it is the peculiarity of the biblical representation of this whole subject, that it handles it in the very closest connection with the personal sense of sin; that is to say, in its relation to the conscience of man on the one side, and the moral indignation of God on the other. In the Scriptures the atonement is a *propitiation;* and by betaking himself to this representation, and making it his own spontaneous mode of thinking and speaking upon this fundamental doctrine, the preacher will arm his mind with a preternatural power and energy. Look at the preaching of those who, like Luther and Chalmers, have been distinguished by an uncommon freedom and saliency in their manner of exhibiting the priestly office and work of Christ, and see how remarkably the Old Testament atonement vitalizes the conception and the phraseology. There is no circumlocution or mechanical explanation. The *remorse* of man is addressed. The simple and terrible fact of guilt is presupposed, the consciousness of it elicited, and then the ample pacifying satisfaction of Christ is offered. The rationality of the atonement is thus seen in its inward necessity; and its inward necessity is seen in the very nature of crime; and the nature of crime is seen in the nature of God's justice, and felt in the workings of man's conscience. In this way, preaching becomes in-

R

tensely personal, in the proper sense of the word. It is made up of personal elements, recognises personal relationships, breathes the living spirit of personality, and reaches the heart and conscience of personal and accountable creatures.

Is not, then, the Word of God as a fire, in respect to this class of truths, and its mode of presenting them? As we pass in review the representations of God's personal emotions, and of man's culpability, which are made in those living oracles, from which the clergyman is to draw the subject-matter of his discourses, and the layman is to derive all his certain and infallible knowledge respecting his future prospects and destiny, is it not plain, that if there be lethargy and torpor on the part of either the preacher or the hearer, if there be a lack of eloquence, it will not be the fault of the written Revelation? As we look abroad over Christendom, do we not perceive the great need of a more incisive impression, from those particular truths which relate to these personal qualities, these moral feelings of the Deity, which cut sharply into the conscience, probe and cleanse the corrupt heart, and induce that salutary fear of God which the highest authority assures us is the beginning of wisdom? Is there in the visible Church such a clear and poignant insight into the nature of sin and guilt, such reverential views of the divine holiness and majesty, and such a cordial welcoming of the atonement of God, as have characterized the more earnest eras in Church history? And if we contemplate the mental state and condition of the multitude who make no profession of godliness, and in whom the naturalism of the age has very greatly undermined the old ancestral belief in a sin-hating and a sin-pardoning Deity, do we not find still greater need of the fire and the hammer of the Word of the Lord ?

II. Having thus described the preacher's duty in regard to a certain form and aspect of revealed truth, we pass now, in the second place, to consider the hearer's duty, and thereby evince the reciprocity of the relation that exists between them. We shall direct attention in the remainder of the chapter to that sort of understanding, with regard to this mode of preaching, which ought to exist between the hearer and the preacher,—that intellectual temper which the popular mind should adopt and maintain towards this style of homiletics. For if, as we remarked in the outset, the effectiveness of the orator is dependent upon the receptivity of the auditor, then there is no point of more importance to the Christian ministry than the general attitude of the public mind towards the severer truths and doctrines of revelation. What, then, is the proper temper in hearing which is to stand over against this proper tone in preaching ?

In order to answer this question, we must, in the outset, notice the relation that exists between divine truth and an *apostate* mind like that of man, and the call which it makes for moral earnestness and resoluteness. For we are not treating of public religious address for the seraphim, but for the sinful children of men ; and we shall commit a grave error if we assume that the eternal and righteous truth of God, as a matter of course, must fall like blessed genial sunlight into the corrupt human heart, and make none but pleasant impressions at first. It is therefore necessary, first of all, to know precisely what are the affinities, and also what are the *antagonisms*, between the guilty soul of man and the holy Word of God.

It is plain that such an antagonism is implied in the prophet's interrogatory. For if the Word of God is 'as a fire,' the human mind, in relation to it, must be as fuel. For why does fire exist, except to burn? When, therefore, the message from God breathes that startling and illuminating spirit which thrilled through the Hebrew prophets, and at times fell from the lips of Incarnate Mercy itself, still and swift as lightning from the soft summer cloud, it must cause

> 'Anguish, and doubt, and fear, and sorrow, and pain,
> In mortal minds.'

The posture, consequently, which the 'mortal mind' shall take and keep in reference to such a painful message and proclamation from the heavens, is a point of the utmost importance. Many a human soul is lost, because, at a certain critical juncture in its history, it yielded to its fear of mental suffering. The Word of God had begun to be 'a fire' unto it, and foreseeing (oh, with how quick an instinct!) a painful process of self-scrutiny and self-knowledge coming on, it wilfully broke away from all such messages and influences, flung itself into occupations and enjoyments, and quenched a pure and good flame that would have only burnt out its dross and its sin,—a merely temporary flame, that would have superseded the necessity of the eternal one that is now to come. For there is an instinctive and overmastering shrinking in every man from suffering, which it requires much resolution to overcome. The prospect of impending danger rouses his utmost energy to escape from it, and his soul does not recover its wonted tranquillity until the threatening calamity is overpast. In this lies all the power of the drama in its higher forms. The exciting impression made by a tragedy springs from the steadily increasing danger of suffering, which thickens about the career of principal characters in the plot. The liability to undergo pain, which increases as the catastrophe approaches, united with the struggles of the endangered person to escape from it, wakens a sympathy and an excitement in the reader or the spectator stronger than that produced by any other species of literature. And whenever the winding-up of any passage in human history lifts off the burden of apprehension from a human being, and exhibits him in the enjoyment of the ordinary happy lot of humanity, instead of crushed to earth by a tragic issue of life, we draw a breath so long and free, as to evince that we share a common nature, one of whose deepest and most spontaneous feelings is the dread of suffering and pain.

And yet, when we have said this, we have not said the whole. Deep as is this instinctive shrinking from distress, there are powers and motives which, when in action, will carry the human soul and body through scenes and experiences at which human nature, in its quiet moods and its indolent states, stands aghast. There are times when the mind, the rational judgment, is set in opposition to the body, and compels its earth-born companion to undergo a travail and a woe from which its own constitutional love of ease and dread of suffering shrink back with a shuddering recoil.

This antagonism between the sense and the mind is seen in its more impressive forms within the sphere of ethics and religion. Even upon the low position of the Stoic, we sometimes see a severe dealing with luxurious tendencies, and a lofty heroism in trampling down the flesh, which, were it not utterly vitiated by pride and vainglorying, would be worthy of the martyr and the confessor. But when we rise up into the region of entire self-abnegation for the glory of God, we see the opposition between the flesh and the spirit in its sublimer form, and know something of the terrible conflict between mind and matter in a fallen creature, and, still more, of the glorious triumph in a redeemed being, of truth and righteousness over pain and fear. 'If thy right eye offend thee, pluck it out and cast it from thee,' is a command that has actually been obeyed by thousands of believers,—by the little child, and by the tender and delicate woman, who would not adventure to set the sole of her foot upon the ground, for delicateness and tenderness,—not in stoical pride and self-reliance, not with self-consciousness and self-gratulation, but in meekness and fear and much trembling, and also in the spirit of power, of love, and of a sound mind.

There is a call, therefore, on the part of the hearer of religious truth, for that sort of temper which is expressed in the words of the Psalmist: 'Let the righteous smite me, it shall be a kindness.' In this resolute utterance, suffering is not deprecated, as it would be, if these instincts and impulses of human nature had their way and their will, but is actually courted and asked for. That in the Psalmist which needs the smiting of the righteous and of righteousness, and which, for this reason, shrinks from it, is rigorously kept under, in order that the infliction may be administered for the honour of the truth and the health of the soul.

And such, it is contended, should be the general attitude of the public mind towards that particular form and aspect of divine revelation which has been delineated in the first part of this chapter. Every human being, the natural as well as the spiritual man, ought to say, ' Let the righteous smite me, it shall be a kindness ; let the truth and law of God seize, with their strongest grasp and bite, upon my reason and conscience, it shall be an eternal blessing to me.' We do not suppose that the natural man, as such, can make these words his own in the high and full sense in which they were uttered by the regenerate and inspired mind of David. But we do suppose that every auditor can control his impatience, and repress his impulses to flee away from the hammer and the fire, and conquer his prejudices, and compel his ear to hear doctrinal statements that pain his soul, and force his understanding to take in truths and arguments that weigh like night upon his feelings, and that say to him, as did the voice that cried in the tortured soul of Macbeth, ' Sleep no more ; rest and peace for thee, in thy present state, are gone for ever.' Has not the Christian ministry a right to expect a tacit purpose and a resolute self-promise upon the part of every attendant upon public worship, to hold the mind close up to all logical and self-consistent exhibitions of revealed truth, and take the mental, the inward consequences, be they what they may ? One of the early Fathers speaks of the 'ire of truth.' Ought not every thinking, every reasoning man, to be willing to resist his instinctive and effeminate dread of suffering, and expose his sinful soul to this 'ire,' because it is the ire of law and righteousness ?

1. In presenting the argument for this sort of resolute temper in the public mind towards the cogent representations of the pulpit, it is evident, in the first place, that upon the general principles of propriety and fitness, the sacred audience, the assembly that has collected upon the Sabbath-day and in the sanctuary of God, ought to expect and prepare for such distinctively biblical representations of God and themselves, as have been spoken of. The secular week has been filled up with the avocations of business or the pursuits of science and literature ; and now when the exclusively religious day and duties begin, is it not the part of consistency to desire that the eternal world should throw in upon the soul its most solemn influences, and that religious truth should assail the judgment and the conscience with its strongest energy ? Plainly, if the religious interests of man are worth attending to at all, they are worth the most serious and thorough attention. This sabbatical segment of human life, these religious hours, should be let alone by that which is merely secular or literary, in order that, while they do last, the purest and most strictly religious influences may be experienced. A man's salvation does not depend so much upon the length of his religious experience and exercises, as upon their

thoroughness. A single thoroughly penitent sigh wafts the soul to the skies and the angels and the bosom of God. But such exhaustive thoroughness in the experience is the fruit only of thoroughness in the previous indoctrination. He, therefore, who is willing to place himself under the religious influences of the Sabbath and the sanctuary, should be willing to experience the very choicest of these influences. He who takes pains to present himself in the house of God, should expect and prepare for the most truthful and solemn of all messages. Professing to devote himself to the subject of religion, and no other, and to listen to the ministration of God's Word, and no other, his utterance should be that of the Psalmist: 'Let the righteous smite me, it shall be a kindness.' Seating himself in the house of God, it should be with an expectation of plain dealing with his understanding, and with the feeling of the stern yet docile auditor, whose uniform utterance before the preacher was, 'Now let the Word of God come.' We lay it down then, as a maxim of fitness and self-consistency, that the public mind ought ever to expect and require from the public religious teacher, the most distinctively religious and strictly biblical exhibitions of truth upon the Sabbath-day, and in the house of God. Other days and other convocations may expect and demand other themes and other trains of thought; but the great religious day of Christendom, and the great religious congregation, insist upon an impression bold and distinct from the world to come. 'He has done his duty, now let us do ours,' was the reply of Louis XIV. to the complaint of a fawning and dissolute courtier, that the sermon of

Bourdaloue had been too pungent and severe.   There were
manliness and reason in the reply.   The pulpit had discharged its legitimate function, and irreligious as was the
grand monarch of the French nation, his head was clear,
and his judgment correct.

If, now, the auditor himself, of his own free will, adopts
this maxim, and resolutely holds his mind to the themes
and trains of thought that issue from the Word of God, a
blessing, and not a curse, will come upon him.   Like the
patient smitten with leprosy or struck with gangrene, who
resolutely holds out the diseased limb for the knife and the
cautery, this man shall find that good comes from taking
sides with the divine law, and subjecting the intellect (for
we are now pleading merely for the human understanding)
to the searching sword of the truth.   There is such a
thing as common grace; and that hearer who is enabled
by it, Sabbath after Sabbath, to overcome his instinctive
fear of suffering, and to exercise a salutary rigour with his
mind respecting the style and type of its religious indoctrination, may hope that common and prevenient grace
shall become renewing and sanctifying grace.

Probably no symptom of the feeling and tendency of the
popular mind would be witnessed and watched with more
interest by the Christian philosopher or the Christian
orator, than a growing disposition on the part of the masses
to listen to the strict truths, the systematic doctrines of
Christianity, and to ponder upon them.   And why should
there not be this disposition at all times?   That which
is strictly true is entirely true; is thoroughly true—true
without abatement or qualification.   Why, then, shall a

thinking creature shrink back from the exactitudes of theology, the severities of righteousness? Why should not the human mind follow out everything within the province of religion, to its last results, without reference to the immediate painful effect upon the feelings? If a thing be true, why confer with flesh and blood about it? If certain distinctly revealed doctrines of revelation, accurately stated and logically followed out, do cut down all the cherished hopes of a sinful man with respect to his future destiny, why not let them cut them down? Why not, with the unsparing self-consistence of the mathematician, either take them as legitimate and inevitable conclusions, from admitted sources and premises, in all their strictness and fearful meaning, or else throw sources, premises, and conclusions all away? How is it possible for a thinking man to maintain a middle and a neutral ground in doctrinal religion, any more than in science.

2. But, leaving this mainly intellectual argument for the Psalmist's temper towards the stern side of Revelation, we pass, in the second place, to the yet stronger moral argument, drawn from the nature of that great spiritual change, which the Founder of Christianity asserts must pass upon every human being, in order to entrance into the kingdom of heaven.

Man, though self-ruined, is helplessly, hopelessly ruined. Loaded with guilt which he cannot expiate, and in bondage to a sin from which he can never deliver himself, he cannot now be saved except by the most powerful methods, and the most thorough processes. What has been done outside, in the counsels of eternity, and in the depths of the triune God, to bring about human redemption, evinces the magnitude and the difficulty of the work undertaken. But of this we do not propose to speak. We speak only of what is to be done *inside*, in the mind and heart of the individual man, as evincing, conclusively, that this salvation of the human soul cannot be brought about by imperfect and slender exhibitions of truth, or by an irresolute and timorous posture of the auditor's mind. No man is compelled to *suffer* salvation. Pardon of all sin from the eternal God, and purity for eternal ages, are offered to him, not as a cheap thing to be forced upon an unwilling recipient, but as a priceless boon. Our Lord himself, therefore, bids every man count the cost, and make up the comparative estimate, before he commences the search for eternal life. ' Either make the tree good, and his fruit good ; or else make the tree corrupt, and his fruit corrupt.' Be *thorough* in one direction or the other. Either be a saint or a sinner. The Redeemer virtually advises a man not to begin the search at all unless he begin in earnest. The entire Scripture representation is, that as man's salvation cost much on high and in the heavens, so it must cost much below, and in the soul of man. If, then, religion be not rejected altogether, and the hearer still expects and hopes to derive an everlasting benefit from it, he should take it precisely as he finds it, and allow its truths to wound first, that they may heal afterwards ; to slay in the beginning, that they may make alive in the end.

For such is the method of Christianity. Conviction is the necessary antecedent to conversion. But how is this great process to be carried through, if the public mind shrinks away from all convicting truth, as the sensitive plant does from the touch ?   How is man to be conducted down into the depths of a humbling and abasing self-knowledge, if he does not allow the flashing and fiery illumination of the law and the prophets to drive out the black darkness of self-deception ?   It is impossible, as we have already observed, that divine truth should pour its first rays into the soul of alienated man without producing pain.   The unfallen seraph can hear the law proclaimed amidst thunders and lightnings, with a serene spirit and an adoring frame, because he has perfectly obeyed it from the beginning.   But Moses, and the children of Israel, and all the posterity of Adam, must hear law, when first proclaimed, with exceeding fear and quaking, because they have broken it.   It is a fact too often overlooked, that divine truth, when accurately stated and closely applied, cannot leave the mind of a sinful being as quiet and happy as it leaves that of a holy being.   In the case of man, therefore, the truth must, in the outset, cause foreboding and alarm.   In the history of the human religious experience, soothing, consolation, and joy, from the truth, are the subsequents, and not the antecedents. The plain and full proclamation of that Word of God which is ' as a fire,' must at first awaken misgivings and fears, and until man has passed through this stage of experience, must leave his sinful and lost soul with a sense of danger and insecurity.   There is consequently no true option for man, but either not to hear at all, or else to hear first in the poignant and anxious style.   The choice that is left him is either that of the Pharisee or the Magdalene; that of the self-righteous or the self-condemned; either to hate the light, and not come to the light, lest painful disclosures of character and conduct be made, or else to come resolutely out into the light, that the deeds may be reproved.

For this work of reproval is the first and indispensable function of religious truth in the instance of the natural man. If there be self-satisfaction and a sense of security in the unrenewed human soul, it is certain that, as yet, there is no contact between it and the Divine Word. For it is as true of every man as it was of the Apostle Paul, that when the law shall come with plainness and power to his mind, he will ' die.' His hope of heaven will die ; his hope of a quiet deathbed will die; his hope of acquittal and safety in the day of judgment, and at the bar of God, will die. That apostolic experience was legitimate and normal, and no natural man must expect that the truth and law of God, when applied with distinctness and power to his reason and conscience, will leave him with any different experience, in the outset, from that which has initiated and heralded the passage from darkness to light, and from sin to holiness, in every instance of a soul's redemption. There is no royal road across the chasm that separates the renewed from the unrenewed man. In order to salvation, every human creature must tread that strait and narrow path of self-examination, self-condemnation, and self-renunciation, which was trodden by the goodly fellowship of the prophets, the glorious company of the apostles, and the noble army of the martyrs.

In subjecting the mind and conscience to the poignant influence of keen and pure truth, and doing everything in his power to have the stern and preparatory doctrines of the legal dispensation become a schoolmaster, to lead him to the mercy and the pity that are in the blood of Christ, the hearer in the sanctuary is simply acting over the conduct of every soul that, in the past, has crossed from the kingdom of darkness to the kingdom of light. He is merely travelling the King's highway to the celestial city; and whoever would climb up some other way, the same is a thief and a robber. Even the thoughtful pagan acknowledged the necessity of painful processes in the human mind, in order to any moral improvement. Over the Delphic portal were inscribed these words: ' Without the descent into the hell of self-knowledge, there is no ascent into heaven.' We do not suppose that this remarkable saying exhibits its full meaning within the province of the pagan religion, or of natural religion. The heathen sage often uttered a truth whose pregnant significance is understood only in the light of a higher and supernatural dispensation. But if the anguish of self-knowledge is postulated by paganism, in order to the origin of virtue within the human soul, much more, then, is it by Christianity. If the heathen moralist, with his low view of virtue, and his very indistinct apprehension of the spirituality of the moral law, and his utterly inadequate conception of a holy and happy state beyond the grave, could yet tell us that there is a hell of self-knowledge to be travelled through, a painful process of self-scrutiny and self-condemnation to be endured, before moral improvement can begin here, or the elysiums of the hereafter be attained,—if this be the judgment of the heathen moralist from his low point of view, and in the mere twilights of natural religion, what must be the judgment of the human mind, when, under the Christian dispensation, the moral law flashes out its nimble and forked lightnings upon sin and pollution, with a fierceness of heat like that which consumed the stones and dust, and licked up the water in the trench, about the prophet's altar,—when divine truth is made quick and powerful by the superadded agency of the Holy Ghost, so as to discern the very thoughts and intents of the heart,—when the pattern-image of an absolute excellence is seen in Him who is the brightness of the Father's eternal glory,—and when the heaven to be sought for, and, what is yet more, to be prepared for, is a state of spotless and sinless perfection in the light of the divine countenance! Plainly, self-knowledge within the Christian sphere implies and involves a searching and sifting examination into character, motive, thought, feeling, and conduct, such as no man can undergo without shame, and humiliation, and self-condemnation, and remorse, and, without the blood of Christ, everlasting despair.

The same course of reasoning, respecting each and all of the remaining processes that enter into the change from sin to holiness, and the formation of a heavenly character, would in each instance help to strengthen the argument we are urging in favour of the plainest preaching and the most resolute hearing of religious truth. The more a man knows of sin and of holiness, of the immense gulf between them, and of the difficulty of the passage from one to the other, the more heartily will he believe that the methods and the processes by which the transition is effected are each and all of them of the most energetic and thorough character. And the deeper this conviction, the more hearty and energetic will be his adoption of the Psalmist's utterance : ' Let the righteous smite me, it shall be a kindness.'

We have thus considered the mutual relations of the Sacred Orator and the Christian Auditor. In doing this, we have passed rapidly over a very wide field, and have touched upon some of the most momentous themes that can engage the human mind. What, and how, we are to conceive of God, and, particularly, how we are to represent Him as affected in his own essential being, towards the holiness or the sin of his creatures, is of all subjects the most serious and important. In closing the discussion, we are more than ever impressed with the importance of a bold and biblical theism in the Christian pulpit. Whenever the preacher asserts that God loves the righteous, let him assert it with energy and warmth and momentum. Let him make his hearers see and know that the great God is personal in this emotion ; that He pours out upon those who are in filial sympathy with Him and his law, the infinite wealth of his pure and stainless affection, and that it permeates the whole being of the object so beloved with warm currents of light and life eternal. And whenever he asserts that God hates sin, and is angry with the sinner, let him assert it without any abatement or qualification. Let him cause the impenitent and sin-loving man to see and know, that upon him, as taken and held

s

in this sinful character and condition, the eternal and holy Deity is pouring out the infinite intensity of his moral displeasure, and that, out of Christ, and irrespective of the awful passion of Gethsemane and Calvary, this immaculate and stainless emotion of the divine essence is now revealed from heaven against his unrighteousness, and is only awaiting his passage into the eternal world, to become the monotonous and everlasting consciousness of the soul.

Amidst the high and increasing civilisation and over-refinement that are coming in upon Christendom, and especially amidst the naturalism that threatens the Scriptures and the Church, the Christian ministry must themselves realize, as did the Hebrew prophets, that God is the *living* God, and by God's own help and grace evoke this same consciousness in the souls of their hearers. Let, then, these two specific personal qualities—the divine wrath and the divine love—be smitten and melted into the consciousness of the nations. Then will there be the piercing wail of contrition preceding and heralding the bounding joy of conscious pardon.

CHAPTER XII.

HAVING discussed the principal topics in the department of Homiletics, we are brought now to a
subject which lies outside of it, but which is intimately
connected with it, in the services of the Christian sanctuary. It is *Liturgics.* In passing to this theme, we leave
the subject of Eloquence, and consider that of Worship.
In treating of Sacred Rhetoric, we were occupied with the
address of an individual to an audience ; but in considering
the nature and province of Liturgics, we are concerned
with the address of the audience itself to Almighty
God.

The liturgical services of the sanctuary are those parts
which relate to divine worship. As the etymology denotes, the liturgy is the work of the people λεῖτον, *publi-
cum, populare ;* ἔργον, *opus.* The appropriate work of the
auditor is worship, as the appropriate work of the orator
is eloquence. Not that the two may not sometimes inter-
penetrate,—especially in the instance of the preacher, who
is himself to worship, while he instructs, and moves his
audience to acts of worship. Yet, as it is the peculiar
function of the preacher, as such, to address an audience,
so is it the peculiar function of the audience, as such, to

address God, as the result of the preacher's address to them. Preaching should always end in worship. While the rhetorical processes of instruction, conviction, and persuasion belong to the speaker, the liturgical acts of supplication, adoration, and praise belong to the hearer. But the preacher is to lead them in these acts of worship ; and hence the need of principles and rules by which he may be guided in the discharge of this part of his duty. Hence arises the department of Liturgics, in the general course of clerical discipline.

It is necessary, in the outset, to remark that this department, though an important one, cannot be made so prominent in those Churches which adopt no complicated formulary of public devotions. It naturally becomes more complex and comprehensive of rules and regulations, in Churches which, like the Romish, the English, and the Lutheran, use a liturgy. Hence, in the German treatises upon Practical Theology, that part denominated Liturgics is very thoroughly elaborated ; and if we do not find the same thing true of Romish and Episcopal treatises, it is because there is in these communions little disposition to examine into the speculative grounds of ecclesiastical usages, and not because the department itself is undervalued by them in actual practice. As matter of fact, in both the Romish and English Churches, the liturgy overshadows the sermon ; the forms and formularies of worship receive more attention than the principles and canons of eloquence. This branch of the subject consequently demands a briefer and less elaborate treatment, so far as the wants of those Protestant Churches which are distinguished by a simple ritual are concerned; and we shall be able to exhibit its leading topics in a single chapter.

The liturgical services of the Sanctuary, in those Protestant communions which have no liturgy, are left very much to the choice of the preacher. In the Episcopal and Lutheran Churches, the passages of Scripture to be read, the prayers that are to be offered, and, to some extent, the praises that are to be sung, are prescribed by regulation, and are embodied in a collection called the Liturgy. In the other Protestant Churches, this choice is left to the individual clergyman; and hence there is, in reality, more need of a careful liturgical discipline in the instance of the Presbyterian or Congregational clergyman, than in that of the Episcopalian, or Lutheran, or Romish. For even if the established and appointed liturgy should not in all its parts be appropriate, the officiating clergyman has no option; and when its arrangements are appropriate, he has only passively to adopt them as his own. But the minister of a simpler worship, inasmuch as he is deprived of these external aids, needs, all the more, the internal aids of a good taste and a cultivated mind, that he may make all that part of the services of the sanctuary which relates to worship, as distinguished from discourse, harmonize with itself, and with the service as a whole. There are three topics which fall within this department of Liturgics —namely, *selections from Scripture, selections of hymns,* and *public prayer.* We shall discuss them in the order in which they have been mentioned.

1. The reading of a portion or portions of Scripture, though not so strictly a liturgical act, is nevertheless not

a rhetorical one.   It is true that praise is not always offered to God, in and by this service.   On the contrary, preceptive instruction is very often imparted to the people in the Scripture lessons; and, in this respect, the service seems to belong more to the work of the orator than to the work of the audience.   Still, it does not properly fall within the province of rhetoric; the principles and canons of Homiletics have nothing to do with this part of divine service.   It must be regulated by the principles of taste. The matter is already formed and fixed in the Scriptures, and there is no call for original composition.   It only remains, therefore, to make a suitable choice; and hence the topic itself falls most properly into the general department of Liturgics.   The principal directions to guide the clergyman in the selection of Scripture lessons are the following:—

In the first place, when there is nothing that specially calls for a different selection, he should choose a portion of Scripture that gives expression to some feeling—such as the feeling of praise, of thanksgiving, of adoration, of contrition.   The Psalms are largely composed of such matter, and ought to be selected for the reading before sermon, more often than they are, by the clergy of most Protestant denominations.   The great excellence of the English liturgy consists in the size of the Psalter embodied in it.   <u>The</u> Psalms are better adapted than any other compositions to elicit the Christian feeling of an assembly.   They range over the whole field of the affections, and every mood of the Christian heart finds a full and gushing utterance in them.   'The harp of David was full-stringed, and every angel of joy and of sorrow swept over the chords as he passed.' They ought, therefore, to be made the means of worship, of stirring the emotions of a Christian assembly, and preparing it for the lyrical hymn or psalm. There are other portions of the Scriptures also, like the glowing predictions of the prophets concerning the future of the Church, which partake of this characteristic of the Psalms. These should be selected by the preacher, so that the Bible, in all its variety of emotional utterance, may become the organ through which the Christian assembly gives expression to its own emotions in the sanctuary. In this way the Bible itself becomes the liturgy.

Secondly, there may be occasionally a special reason for selecting a doctrinal or historical portion of Scripture ; and hence the clergyman ought not to be rigidly confined to such portions of the Bible as we have mentioned. It may be that his sermon is of such a special character as to require the reading of a long passage, which stands in close connection with it. In this particular instance, if he think proper, he may make this service of reading somewhat less liturgical, and more didactic, than would ordinarily be desirable.

Lastly, whether a liturgical or a didactic portion of Scripture be chosen, it should be congruous with the general tone of the services. If, for example, the attention of the audience is to be directed in the sermon to an encouraging, cheering, joyful subject, the psalm selected should be one of thanksgiving. To preface a sermon of such a character with a mournful and penitential psalm, would be inapposite, and would defeat the end in view. The passage to be read should be carefully chosen, and carefully perused beforehand by the preacher. He should never look up his Scripture lessons in the pulpit.

II. The choice of Hymns is the second topic under the head of Liturgics. The principal directions which we mention for securing an excellent selection, are the following: First, the clergyman must acquire a correct knowledge of the nature of lyric poetry. Many educated men are deficient in a thorough understanding of this species. Epic and dramatic poetry absorb the interest of students, to the neglect of lyric. They are more familiar with Homer, Shakspeare, and Milton, than with Pindar and Burns. This is owing partly to the fact that, as a species, lyric poetry is of a lower grade than epic or dramatic, and has engaged less eminent poetic powers. But, after allowing that the epic and the drama are loftier performances than the ballad and the song, and that the genius of Pindar and Burns is not equal to that of Homer and Shakspeare, it is still true that lyric poetry does not commonly receive that degree of attention from educated men which its intrinsic excellence and importance deserve. For in some respects the lyric comes nearer to the ideal perfection of poetry than any other species. As works of art, as exquisitely complete wholes, the hymns of Pindar stand at the head of human compositions. The range of thought is very limited, it is true, in the lyrical ode, but this permits the poet to impart an ideal completeness and finish to it, that are not to be found in works that are more extended in their range. We never shall see a perfect epic or a perfect drama, because of the variety and amount of the contents. But the hymns of Pindar and the odes of Horace, if they are not absolutely perfect, do yet, it is universally conceded, approach so near to the ideal, that he should possess the very highest æsthetic culture who presumes to assert their imperfection, and ventures to attempt to make good his assertion by pointing out defects.

The clergyman must devote a proper attention to this species of poetry, in order to know, both by natural feeling and cultivated instinct, what is lyrical, and what is not. This kind of verse is made to be sung. Other species have no special connection with music; but this is nothing, unless it can be set to tune. That poetry which is not fitted to be accompanied with the human voice, and the musical instrument, is not lyrical. Tried by this test, much poetry which bears this name is not worthy of it. It is too didactic, or it is not the expression of feeling; or it may be emotive, yet not a tuneful utterance of emotion. The preacher must therefore understand the general subject of lyric poetry. He ought to familiarize his mind with the best specimens in ancient and in modern literature, and with the most philosophic and genial criticism upon them. He should study the odes of Pindar and Horace, for the sake of the perfusive grace, the high artistic finish, and, in the instance of Pindar, the impassioned fire and energy. He should study the old English Ballads, not so much for their artistic merits, as for the simplicity, artlessness, and heartiness. He should study the little gushes of song, that are scattered like gems here and there, in the pages of Shakspeare,—wonderful compositions which, in the midst of the complexity and combinations of the mighty drama, strike the mind, very much as the sweet liquid notes of the human voice fall upon the ear, in the lull of the tumult of the orchestra,—musical as golden bells heard in the silence of the band. He should study the songs of Burns, until he feels their immeasurable superiority to the artificial sentiment and melody of Thomas Moore.

In the second place, while seeking this knowledge of the nature of lyric poetry from profane literature, the clergyman should examine very carefully the lyric poetry of the Christian Church. Doctor Johnson has asserted that devotional poetry not only does not please, but, from the nature of the case, cannot please. Probably this is the greatest blunder ever made by a critic. For what judgment could be more erroneous, than that religious feeling, the purest and highest form of emotion, is incompatible with a melodious utterance of itself? The fact that universally the higher we ascend in the scale of existence, the more rhythmical, melodious, and harmonious we find everything becoming, would lead to the exactly contrary judgment, and to the affirmation that the sacred ode is, in its own nature, as much superior to the secular as the ideas of eternity are grander than those of time, and the emotions of heaven higher than those of earth.

The preacher must begin the study of sacred lyrics by imbuing his mind with the spirit of the Hebrew poetry. If a man like Milton drew inspiration from this source for the purposes of his merely human art, most certainly should the preacher go to it for liturgical culture. The

lyric writers of the Christian Church have been distinguished for excellence in proportion as they have re-
produced the Hebrew Psalter, in the forms of modern
metrical composition. The finest hymns of Watts are
Hebrew in their matter and spirit. Modern poetry, it
is true, exhibits a variety in its forms that renders it a
more complex and elaborate portion of literature than
Hebrew poetry ; but it is far inferior to the Hebrew, in
respect to the lyrical tone,—especially that *solemn* lyrical
tone which alone is suited to the sanctuary. The modern
poet must go to the song of Deborah and the psalms of
David for triumphant and jubilant praise, for the ' seven-
fold chorus of hallelujahs and harping symphonies.'

Next in order, the preacher ought to study the hymns of
the Patristic and the Mediæval Church. His examination
of these should be discriminating, as his examination of
the Fathers and the Schoolmen themselves should be. The
modern theologian and preacher, too generally, has committed an error in regard to this portion of Christian history.
He has either neglected these ages altogether, or else he has
devoted an exclusive and extravagant attention to them.
Both of these periods belong to the history of the Christian Church, and, as such, in their proper place, deserve
and challenge the attention of the Modern. They contain,
as everything human does, a mixture of truth and error ;
and probably a more confused and remarkable mixture
than other ages. This characteristic appears in their
hymnology. Some of the Greek hymns of Synesius, for
example, are a mixture of pantheism and theism. The
piercing wail of guilt and cry for mercy is blended with

the dim and dreamy worship of mere naturalism.　Much of the later devotional poetry of the Latin Church is vitiated by Mariolatry and saint worship.　But such grand chants as the *Gloria in excelsis* and the *Te Deum laudamus*, if frequently read and meditated on in the sounding and rhythmical Latin, lift up the mind for praise and adoration, like the pealing tones of an organ, and impart a craving for simple and lofty verse in the sanctuary.　The solemn majesty and mystery of the Trinity, as expressed in the hymns of Hilary and Ambrose, awe the soul in profound reverence and self-abasement; while the earnest and vivid Christology of St. Bernard imbues the heart with a tender and precatory feeling.　The two greatest lyrics of the Mediæval Church are the *Stabat Mater* and the *Dies iræ*.　The former exhibits too much of the peculiar doctrine of Romanism, in combination with gospel truth, to be expressive of a pure religious feeling; but the *Dies iræ* is a most spiritual utterance of human guilt, without any reference to the intercession of the saints, or of the Virgin Mother.　This latter hymn is worthy of the frequent perusal of any Protestant.　It is sometimes employed in Protestant services on the Continent of Europe. Tholuck, in a note to one of his sermons, alludes to the sensation produced by the singing of this hymn in the University Church at Halle, and remarks, that 'the impression which was made by the last words, as sung by the University choir alone, will be forgotten by no one.' An American clergyman who happened to be present on this occasion, says that ' it was impossible to refrain from tears when, at the seventh stanza, all the trumpets ceased, and the choir, accompanied by a softened tone of the organ, sung those touching lines :

> ' Quid sum miser tunc dicturus ?
> Quem patronum rogaturus,
> Cum vix justus sit securus ?'

The hymnology of the German Church is extremely rich. Some of the hymns of Luther and Paul Gerhardt stand second to none in all the Christian centuries. But the English hymnology must of course receive most attention from the preacher, in order to a proper liturgical cultivation. It is the product of that English mind in whose characteristics he shares, and belongs to that English literature which has done more than any other to make and mould him, intellectually and morally. There is much religious poetry, and some of it lyric, composed by the writers of Elizabeth's age, that deserves constant and careful perusal. The works of Spencer, Raleigh, Ben Jonson, Herbert, Vaughan, Herrick, Drummond, and Milton, contain devotional hymns of high merit, both as respects matter and form ; and he who looks through a collection of English poetry, like that of Chambers for example, will be surprised to discover, here and there, a religious lyric breathing a most penitential or adoring spirit in the very midst of the most earthly and perhaps erotic poetry.[1]

The hymn-book of the Church to which he ministers should, however, receive most of the clergyman's study. After deducting all the prosaic matter that is to be found in it, there still remains a large remainder of genuine

[1] Herrick, and Drummond of Hawthornden, afford examples.

lyric poetry. With this the preacher ought to be intimately familiar, occasionally enlivening his own discourse
with a glowing or a swelling or a thrilling stanza, and
always selecting, for purposes of worship, those hymns
which, while they give vivid and vital expressions to Christian emotions and affections, also 'voluntary move harmonious numbers.' That acquaintance with the denomi-
national hymn-book, and that deep interest in it, which are
seen in the Methodist clergy and the Methodist Church,
deserve to be imitated by all. It is a much safer and
more truly rational interest than that which some clergies
and denominations show toward formularies of worship.
The hymns of Charles Wesley, the sweet singer of
Methodism, have done much towards the production of
that peculiar intensity of the religious life in Methodism
which led Chalmers to define it as 'Christianity in earnest.' By thus studying the hymnology of the Church
—of the Jewish and the entire Christian Church—the
preacher is to obtain that taste and feeling for sacred lyric
poetry which will guide him, as by a sure instinct, to the
choice of the best and most appropriate hymns.

Without laying down a rule to be servilely followed,
perhaps the choice of hymns for public worship should be
somewhat as follows: The first hymn should be one of
general praise, serving to inspire feelings of worship and
adoration towards God as the Being to be worshipped.
The second may be either of the same character as the
first, or may refer to the discourse which is to follow.
The third and last hymn should have this reference.
Whether the second hymn should be didactic or not, will

depend upon the character of the sermon. Probably, in the majority of instances, the first and second hymns should be strictly liturgical, offerings of praise and thanksgiving ; the last hymn alone being didactic and applicatory of the sermon.

III. The third topic under the head of Liturgics is Prayer. This subject deserves a fuller treatment than is possible within these limits. Bishop Wilkins, Dr. Watts, and Witsius, have composed very sensible treatises upon it; but a good work, suited to the wants of those Protestant Churches which use extemporaneous prayers, is still a desideratum. The following rules involve perhaps the principal points to be regarded by the clergyman in his public petitions.

First, he ought to study *method* in prayer, and observe it. A prayer should have a plan as much as a sermon. In the recoil from the formalism of written and read prayers, Protestants have not paid sufficient attention to an orderly and symmetrical structure in public supplications. Extemporaneous prayer, like extemporaneous preaching, is too often the product of the single instant, instead of devout reflection and premeditation. It might, at first glance, seem that premeditation and supplication are incongruous conceptions ; that prayer must be a gush of feeling, without distinct reflection. This is an error. No man, no creature, can pray well without knowing what he is praying for, and whom he is praying to. Everything in prayer, and especially in public prayer, ought to be well considered and well weighed.[1]

[1] Chalmers was accustomed occasionally to write out the prayer in full which he was to offer up. See Appendix B. to the second volume of his life.

So far as concerns the method and plan of prayer in the sanctuary, the following from Bishop Wilkins' treatise is judicious : ' the first thing in a form of prayer is the *preface*—consisting first of the titles of invocation, together with some brief amplification of them, mostly in Scripture phraseology, sufficient to impress the divine character upon the mind, both of him who leads and those who accompany in public worship; secondly, of some general acknowledgment of personal unworthiness; and, thirdly, of supplication for the divine assistance and attention. After this preface, follow the principal *parts* of prayer : 1. Confession; 2. Petition; 3. Thanksgiving. The order in which these come is not uniform. There will be transposition according to circumstances. In some prayers, confession will predominate ; in others petition ; in others thanksgiving. The preacher should study his prayer in order that he may vary and change, with the circumstances in which he is called to officiate. Some clergymen pray but one prayer through their whole ministry. It contains just so much preface, and just so much confession, petition, and thanksgiving, and always in the same order. In reality it is a form which is repeated from habit and memoriter. It is destitute of the excellences of written prayers, and yet is as monotonous and uniform as they are.'

Secondly, the clergyman must *avoid verbiage and repetition* in prayer. ' Vain repetitions ' are denounced by our Saviour; and although He probably referred primarily to conscious and intended repetitions, the spirit of his direction would exclude that thoughtless and indolent reiteration of the same thoughts, which is one of the principal faults in extemporaneous prayers. It is better to stop, even before the time allotted to prayer has expired, than to attempt to fill it up with verbiage. In this connection, the habit of didactically discoursing in prayer should be guarded against. The suppliant for the divine mercy sometimes turns into the instructor of the divine omniscience. The clergyman should ever remember that God ' knows what we have need of, before we ask Him,' and not enlarge and explain to Him. No one *can* do this, while under a realizing sense of the character of Him with whom he has to do. It is only when the clergyman forgets God and addresses the congregation, that the prayer degenerates into a sermon.

Thirdly, the preacher must study *directness* in matter and manner. This does not imply familiarity, but simple earnestness, in the creature's address to the throne of grace. Familiarity is the worst of faults in prayer. Circumlocution, paraphrase, and repetition are not so reprehensible, as irreverent approach to the Eternal Jehovah. On the contrary, a direct address to God is commanded, and is proper, in the creature. The suppliant should first know clearly what he needs and what he wants; and the more importunate his entreaty, the more immediate his petition for it, the more appropriate and acceptable is his prayer. One chief reason why supplication for spiritual blessings, such as the conversion of men, is not answered, lies in the fact, that too often there is no clear understanding of the nature of the blessing, and no direct petition for it. That Being who searches the heart, and knows the entire consciousness of the man in the attitude of prayer sees that

T

there is no distinct conception of the thing implored, therefore no strong desire, and therefore no strong cry and supplication. Such a prayer is continually discoursing about the topic or enlarging upon the blessing, but does not *ask* for it. 'Ask,' really *ask*, 'and ye shall receive.'

The clergyman should not only school himself in respect to this point, but he should school his Church likewise. A word upon this topic, though not strictly in place, in this connection, may perhaps be allowable. There is nothing which infuses such life into the prayer-meeting as earnestness and directness. In times of awakened religious feeling, this characteristic appears. The same blessings that have been the subject-matter of prayer, for many years it may be, are still prayed for—there is no great change in the general phraseology of the petitioners; but their minds are awake, and they now know what they need and what they desire, and a direct, earnest, and comparatively brief prayer is the consequence. The clergyman, by his own example, and if need be by precept, should seek to impress this characteristic upon his Church, so that the assemblings together for meditation and prayer may be efficacious means of grace and of blessing. He ought to cultivate, in the minds and hearts of Christians, a disposition to be distinct, direct, sincere, and brief in supplication.

In this way, the number of those who participate in this exercise will become much greater than it now is. The entire Church will pray, instead of a few persons; there will be more variety in the petitions, and more pertinency in them; and through the action and reaction of mind upon mind, greater fervour and sincerity will mark the devotional services of the Christian brotherhood.

We have thus passed rapidly over the department of Liturgics, touching upon those principal topics which are connected with worship, as distinguished from discourse or address to the audience.   The subject deserves special attention from the clergy of a simple ritual.   The impressiveness and effectiveness of non-liturgical worship must depend mainly upon the taste and judgment of the individual clergyman.   He has no fixed and imposing forms by which to be guided, inevitably, in the conduct of public worship.   He therefore specially needs a judicious discipline in this direction,—a liturgical culture obtained in the general manner that has been indicated.   The clergyman, then, carries his rule with him.   He has an unwritten liturgy in his own cultivated and pure taste, which he is at perfect liberty to vary, with times and circumstances. One who has acquired this true liturgical sense and feeling will render the services of the sanctuary impressive by their appropriateness, by their symmetry, and by that unity which we have seen to be the inmost essence of beauty.   Without drawing away the attention of the congregation from more important matters, as a formal and splendid ritual is apt to do, such a minister will throw a sacred and spiritual atmosphere over the entire services of the sanctuary, more impressive than even the dim religious light of the cathedral.

PASTORAL THEOLOGY.

PASTORAL THEOLOGY.

CHAPTER I.

DEFINITION OF PASTORAL THEOLOGY.

IT is a convenient and accurate classification which distinguishes the scientific part of clerical discipline from the practical. All that side of the clergyman's training which relates to strictly theoretic branches—for example, to philology, philosophy, and theology—falls under the denomination of Theological Science, while all that part which relates to the public application of this theoretic culture is Practical Theology. The subject of Homiletics would therefore be comprehended under this latter, because sermonizing is the popular presentation of theological science. Sacred rhetoric supposes that the speculative principles of the Christian religion have been previously mastered by means of studies and methods that are more abstract than its own. Having been made a theologian by the severer training and the more fundamental discipline, the clergyman is then to be made an orator by the more popular and practical culture of Homiletics.

But the clergyman bears still another character, and performs still another kind of labour, which likewise belongs to the practical side of his profession. He is not only a preacher, whose function it is to impart public instruction before an audience, but he is also a *pastor*, whose office it is to give private and personal advice from house to house, and to make his influence felt in the social and domestic life of his congregation. The clergyman is an orator, and therefore needs the homiletical education that corresponds. He is also a pastor, and hence requires the special discipline that qualifies him to watch over the personal religious interests of his flock. It is the object of the department of Pastoral Theology, to prepare him for this part of his work. The formation of clerical character, and the discharge of strictly parish duties, are, then, the principal topics in this branch of the inquiry.

We define Pastoral Theology to be that part of the clerical curriculum which relates to the clergyman's *parochial* life. It contemplates him in his more retired capacity, as one who has the care of individual souls. The pastor is a *curate*, and Pastoral Theology relates to the clergyman's *curacy*. These terms, which are not so familiar to the American as to the English ear, if taken in their etymological signification, denote precisely the more private character and duties of the clergyman. They are derived from the Latin *curare*, to take care of. A curate is one who has the care of souls.[1] The Apostle Paul speaks of 'watching for souls.' The pastor, or curate, is a watcher for souls.

Having regard, then, as it does, to this important side

[1] The German Seelsorger expresses the same idea.

of the clerical vocation and these important aspects of clerical labour, the department of Pastoral Theology deserves very careful study. In its own place, it is as necessary to a complete professional discipline as the more imposing departments of sacred philology and dogmatic theology. Imperfect education, in respect to the pastoral and parochial duties of the clergyman, must lead to the neglect of them; and this will seriously impair his influence, and, in the review of his ministry, awaken many poignant regrets. The limits of this treatise do not allow more than the briefest discussion of a few cardinal points; but we feel that we shall have accomplished much, even if we should do nothing more than direct attention to the well-known work of Richard Baxter. The *Reformed Pastor* of this wonderful and successful minister should be read through once in each year by every clergyman. 'If,' says John Angell James, 'I may, without impropriety, refer to the service which, during fifty-four years, I have been allowed to render to our great Master, I would express my thankfulness in being able, in some small degree, to rejoice that the conversion of sinners has been my aim. I have made, next to the Bible, Baxter's *Reformed Pastor* my rule, as regards the object of my ministry.' [1]

[1] A valuable collection in one volume of tracts and treatises pertaining to Pastoral Theology has been published at Oxford, by Rivington and Co.

CHAPTER II.

THE foundation of influence in parochial life is in the clergyman's character, and the root of clerical character is piety. The first theme, consequently, that demands attention in the discussion of the subject of Pastoral Theology, is the *religious character and habits* of the clergyman.

The calling and profession of the clergyman demand eminent spirituality. An ordinary excellence is not sufficient. The Christian minister, by his very vocation, is the sacred man in society. By his very position, he is forbidden to be a secular member of the community, and hence he must not be secular either in his character or his habits. It is true that the clergy are not a sacred caste, yet they are a sacred profession. Hence society expects from them a ministerial character and bearing, and respects them just in proportion as they possess and exhibit it. The clergyman is sometimes called the 'parson.' Though the word has fallen into disuse, owing to the contemptuous employment of it by the infidelity of the eighteenth century, its etymology is instructive in this connection. Parson is derived from the Latin *persona*. The clergyman is the person, by way of emphasis, in his parish. He is the marked and peculiarly religious man in the community.[1] His very position and vocation, therefore, make it incumbent upon him to be eminently spiritual. His worldly support is provided by the Church to whom he ministers, and his acceptance of it is an acknowledgment upon his part that a secular life is unsuitable for him, and a demand upon their part that he devote himself entirely to religion, and be an example to the flock. Every clergyman ought to be able to say to his congregation, with the sincerity and the humility with which St. Paul said to the Thessalonians, ' Ye are witnesses, and God also, how holily and justly and unblameably we behaved ourselves among you.'

Not only does the ministerial calling and profession require eminent piety, but it tends to produce it. By his very position, the clergyman is greatly assisted in attaining to a superior grade of Christian character ; and if, therefore, he is a worldly and unspiritual man, he is deeply culpable. For, so far as his active life is concerned, his proper professional business is religious. The daily labour of the clergyman is as truly and exclusively religious as that of the farmer is agricultural, or that of the merchant is mercantile. This is highly favourable to spirituality. Ought not one to grow in grace whose daily avocations bring him into communication with the anxious, the thoughtful, the convicted soul, the rejoicing heart, the bereaved, the

---

[1] One reference, also, was to the temporalities of the Church. ' He is called parson (*persona*), because, by his person, the Church, which is an invisible body, is represented, and he is himself a body corporate in order to protect and defend the rights of the Church which he personates.'

sick, and the dying ? Ought not that man to advance in the love and knowledge of God whose regular occupation from day to day it is to become acquainted with the strictly religious wants and condition of the community, and to minister to them ? If the daily avocations of the mechanic have a natural tendency to make him ingenious and inventive, if the daily avocations of the merchant tend to make him enterprising and adventurous, do not the daily avocations of the clergyman tend to make him devout ? The influence of active life upon character is, in its own place and manner, as great as that of contemplative life. A man is unconsciously moulded and formed by his daily routine of duties, as really as by the books he reads, or the sciences he studies. Hence a faithful performance of clerical duties contributes directly to spirituality.

Again, so far as the contemplative life of the clergyman is concerned, his profession is favourable to superior piety. In discussing the subject of Homiletics, we have seen that the clergyman, in order to successful sermonizing, must absorb himself in theology, must induce and maintain a theological mood, must acquire the homiletic spirit and talent, and make all his culture subservient to preaching. But such a life as this from day to day naturally affects the moral character. The studies of the theologian and preacher work directly towards the growth of piety. Those who unduly magnify the practical to the undervaluation of the doctrinal and theoretic in theology, are wont to make the objection, that study is unfavourable to devotion. There cannot be a more erroneous judgment than this. The studious, thoughtful Christian is always more unwordly and sincere than the Christian who reads but little, and thinks still less. The pastor can employ no means more certain to sanctify his flock than reading and reflection upon their part. Just in proportion as he is able to induce the habit of studying the Scriptures, and of perusing religious and doctrinal books, will he spiritualize the Church to which he ministers.

This is equally true of the clergyman. Study—close, persevering study—improves his religious character. An indolent minister is not a spiritually-minded man. He who neglects his library, and passes by biblical and theo- logical science to occupy himself with the frivolities of society, or with the light literature of the day, cannot keep his mind and heart in a very high state of devotion. There is something in a regular routine of careful investi- gation eminently fitted to deepen and strengthen the reli- gious character. The mind converses with solid verities, and is thereby preserved from what the Scriptures call ' vain imaginations.' It does not ramble and wander in the fields of fancy, but is busy with sober, serious truth. How much more favourable to the growth of piety is such a studious life than an indolent and day-dreaming one! For the mind must do something. If it is not occupied with great and good themes, then it will be busy with small and frivolous ones. This is especially true of the clergyman. He has no secular occupations to engross him, like those of the farmer, the mechanic, and the merchant. He does not rise up in the morning and go out among men to his work until the evening. His time is all at his own disposal; and if he does not devote it with fidelity to the active and contemplative duties of his profession, it will hang upon his hands. The consequence will be a restless, vagrant, and inefficient mental action. So far as his intellect is concerned, he will drag out a feeble and unhappy life. And is this favourable to growth in holiness? Is this the sort of mortification that is profitable to godliness? It is no more profitable than the dull, paralytic existence of the monk in his dark, damp cell.

The fact is, that the holiest men in the Christian Church have been the most studious men. Those spiritual and heavenly-minded divines who accomplished most in the ministry of their own day, and who have been the lights and guides of the ministry up to this time, were men of great learning. Augustine, Calvin, Owen, Baxter, and Edwards, were hard students. Henry, in his *Life of Calvin*—a work which deserves to be read and pondered by every clergyman—furnishes striking examples of the studiousness of this great and intensely spiritual man. He was so assiduous in completing his *Institutes*, that he often passed whole nights without sleeping, and days without eating. Beza remarks, that for many years Calvin took only one meal a day, and then only a very sparing one, assigning, as a reason, the weakness of his stomach. Though, from his connection with the Reformation generally, and his relation to the Genevese commonwealth particularly, Calvin was compelled to perform as much public civil labour as a modern secretary of state, he yet found time to write a commentary upon nearly the whole Bible, to carry on learned and powerful controversies with all sorts of errorists and heretics, to compose a system of divinity which has exerted more influence in the world than any other uninspired production, and, besides all this, to preach probably more than three times the number of sermons delivered by the minister of the present day, in the same length of time. Henry remarks of his labours at Geneva, that in addition to his literary employments, such as the composition of treatises, didactic and polemic, and an extensive correspondence with kings and cabinet ministers, in behalf of the Church, he had to attend to the business of the court of morals, or the consistory, to that arising from the assembly of the clergy, and from his connection with the congregation,—a great amount of local, legislative, and judicial business. Three days in the week he lectured on theological subjects, and every alternate week he preached daily. When the day had been wholly occupied in business, the quiet hours of the night remained to him, and, allowing himself a brief repose, he would continue his studies. Writing to Farel from Strasburg, Calvin says : ' When the messenger was ready to take the beginning of my work with this letter, I had about twenty leaves to look through. I had then to lecture and preach, to write four letters, make peace with some persons who had quarrelled with each other, and answer more than ten people who came to me for advice. Forgive me, therefore, if I write only briefly.' [1]

Baxter has left a larger body of theological composition for the use of the Church than any other English divine ; and how much he accomplished in the way of preaching and of pastoral work, is well known. Though his early

[1] Henry, *Life of Calvin,* i. p. 424.

education was neglected, and he did not receive a collegiate training, he was one of the most studious and learned of men.   He is generally known by his more popular and practical writings ; and one who had read these alone might infer that Baxter was distinguished only for a vivid intellect and a zealous heart.   But if any one will study his strictly theological treatises, he will discover evidence, in every line, of the most severe discipline and the most patient and extensive reading.   Besides the close and critical study of the Scriptures in the original tongues, Baxter was well versed in the pagan theologies and philosophies, in the speculations of the Christian Fathers, and in the theology and philosophy of both the Schoolmen and the Reformers.   The familiarity which Baxter shows with the Scholastic philosophy and theology is remarkable. His own mind was eminently analytic ; and one of the English prelates remarks of him, that if he had lived in the Middle Ages, he would have been one of the Schoolmen.   The plain, unadorned, and pungent periods of the *Saint's Rest*, and the *Call to the Unconverted*, came from a mind that was entirely master of the subtle metaphysics of Thomas Aquinas.[1]

Now we hold and affirm, that this severe study fostered the piety of Calvin and Baxter.   If we could suppose that, in the economy of grace, the same degree of divine influence is bestowed without the use of means as is bestowed

[1] 'Next to practical divinity, no books so suited with my disposition as Aquinas, Scotus, Durandus, Ockham, and their disciples, because I thought they narrowly searched after truth, and brought things out of the darkness of confusion.   For I could never, from my first studies, endure confusion.'—BAXTER, *Narrative of his Life and Times.*

with it, and should assume the existence of the same degree, in the instances of Calvin and Baxter, that was actually enjoyed by them, while subtracting the influence of this close studiousness upon their Christian character, it would undoubtedly lose much in depth, thoroughness, and ripeness. God bestows a blessing upon intellectual serious-ness, upon devotion to good books, and upon a meditative spirit. It is true that the learned man is oftentimes proud and unevangelical; but would ignorance render him any less so? In order to convert a proud scholar into a meek and lowly Christian, is it only necessary to take away his library, and strip him of his acquisitions? Is ignorance the mother of devotion?

Having thus seen that the clerical calling and profession itself demands and is favourable to a superior religious character, we proceed to mention some practical rules for its cultivation in the clergyman.

1. The first rule is that which is to be given in every age and clime to all grades of cultivation, and all varieties of occupation and profession. That which is the first maxim for any and every Christian in keeping the heart, is also the first for the clergyman. He must maintain regular habits of communion with God, in prayer. The lettered Christian is more liable to neglect this duty and privilege than the unlettered, because his mind is con-stantly conversant with divine truth, and he is exposed to the temptation of substituting this for the direct expres-sion of desires and wants. But in order to growth in religion, it is not enough for him to meditate upon the divine character and religious doctrines; he must actually

address God in supplication. Undoubtedly a serious mood may be maintained, by being familiar with great and lofty subjects, especially with the deep themes of metaphysical philosophy. The merely natural attributes of the Deity have power to elevate and solemnize the human mind. Pantheism itself, introducing the soul to the immensity of nature, and bringing it under the mysterious impression of vast forces and laws and processes, operating in infinite space and everlasting time, throws a shadow over the spirit, and renders it grave in its temper. Spinoza was a serious-minded person; so much so, that Novalis, one of the most thoughtful of the secular German poets, named him the ' God-intoxicated man;' and Schleiermacher himself, in one of his discourses upon religion, calls him the ' holy persecuted Spinoza.'[1] But the very delineation of his character which follows, shows that this solemnity of Spinoza's intellect originated in the awe and worship of the impersonal Infinite,—a worship that is meditative, indeed, but never supplicatory.

But this is not religion. It has no root in the knowledge and acknowledgment of the I AM. It never holds actual communion with the living and true God. Naturalism never prays. There is no *address* of one person to another person. For this communion with the Infinite, this ' mingling with the universe,' and feeling, in the phrase of Byron, ' what one cannot express, yet cannot all conceal,' this worship of mere immensity, is not religion. There is no personality upon either side. The man who worships loses his individuality, and the God who is worshipped has

---

[1] Schleiermacher, *Reden über Religion*, p. 48.

none, to begin with.[1]   And this holds true as we go up the scale.   It is not sufficient to commune with the truth, for truth is impersonal.   We must commune with the God of truth.   It is not enough to study and ponder the contents of religious books, or even the Bible itself.   We must actually address the Author of the Bible, in entreaties and petitions.[2]

There can consequently be no genuine religion without prayer.   And the degree of religion will depend upon the depth and heartiness of prayer.   It does not depend so much upon the length, as the intensity of the mental activity. A few moments of real and absorbing address to God will accomplish more for the Christian in the way of arming him with spiritual power, than days or years of reflection without it.   Hence the power of ejaculatory prayer.   In the brief instant, the eye of the creature catches the eye of the Creator; glances are exchanged; and the divine

[1] That there can be no penitence for sin and confession in pantheism, is self-evident; and, therefore, so far as this is an element of religion for man, religion is impossible for the pantheist.

[2] Coleridge, during that pantheistic period in his mental history which is so interesting in its psychological aspects, fell into this error respecting prayer, but afterwards criticised and corrected it, with a depth of insight into the nature of prayer, all the more profound, perhaps, for the previous experience.   A writer in *Tait's Magazine* informs us, that on his first introduction to Coleridge, 'he reverted with strong compunction to a sentiment which he had expressed in earlier days upon prayer.   In one of his youthful poems, speaking of God, he had said—

> ". . . . Of whose all-seeing eye,
> Aught to demand, were impotence of mind."

This sentiment he now so utterly condemned, that, on the contrary, he told me, as his own peculiar opinion, that the act of praying was the very highest energy of which the human heart was capable,—praying, that is, with the total concentration of the faculties; and the great mass of worldly men and of *learned* men he pronounced absolutely incapable of prayer.' Henry Nelson Coleridge corroborates this statement in the following interesting

power and blessing flow down into the soul. It is this
direct vision of God, and this direct imploring something
of Him, which render the brief broken ejaculations of
the martyr so supporting and triumphant over flesh and
blood, over malice and torture. The martyr might meditate never so intensely and long upon the omnipotence
and the wisdom of God, and still be unable to endure the
flame and the rack. But the single *prayer*, 'Lord Jesus
receive my spirit,' lifts him high above the region of
agony, and irradiates his countenance with the light of
angelic faces.

The most holy and spiritual teachers and preachers in
the Church have been remarkable for the directness and
frequency of their petitions. They were in the habit of
praying at particular times in the day, and also of ejaculatory prayer. Some of them began the day with hours

anecdote :—'Mr. Coleridge, within two years of his death, very solemnly
declared to me his conviction upon the same subject. I was sitting by his
bedside one afternoon, and he fell (an unusual thing for him) into a long
account of many passages of his past life, lamenting some things, condemning others, but complaining withal, though very gently, of the way in which
many of his most innocent acts had been cruelly misrepresented. "But I
have no difficulty," said he, "in forgiveness ; indeed, I know not how to
say with sincerity the clause in the Lord's prayer which asks forgiveness *as we forgive*. I feel nothing answering to it in my heart. Neither
do I find or reckon the most solemn faith in God, as a real object,—the
most arduous act of the reason and will. Oh no, my dear, it is to PRAY,
to PRAY as God would have us; this is what, at times, makes me turn
cold to my soul. Believe me, to pray with all your heart and strength,
with the reason and the will, to believe vividly that God will listen to
your voice through Christ, and verily do the thing He pleaseth thereupon,
—this is the last, the greatest achievement of the Christian's warfare upon
earth. *Teach* us to pray, O Lord !" And then he burst into a flood of
tears, and begged me to pray for him.'—COLERIDGE, *Table Talk, Works*,
vi. 327.

of continuous supplication, and then interspersed their labours with brief petitions. Luther was distinguished for the urgency and frequency of his supplications. His maxim, *bene orasse est bene studuisse,* is familiar. So easy and natural was it for him to pray, that even in company with friends, and in the midst of social intercourse, he would break out into petitions. This was often the case in times of trouble to the Church and the cause of the Reformation. God was then present, without intermission, to his anxious and strongly exercised soul; and hence he talked with Him as a man talketh with his friend. The peculiar vigour and vitality of Luther's religion should be traced not solely to his reception of a doctrine, even so vital a doctrine as justification by faith, but to direct intercourse with God.

Consider, again, for an illustration, the *Confessions* of Augustine,—the most remarkable book of the kind in all literature; a book in which the religious experience of one of the subtlest and deepest of human minds, allied with one of the mightiest and most passionate of human hearts is portrayed in letters of living light. But it is full of prayer. The autobiography is intermingled, all through, with petitions and supplications. So natural had it become for that spiritual and holy man to betake himself to his God, that the reader feels no surprise at this mixture of address to man and address to God. This work is well entitled *Confessions,* for in it Augustine pours out his whole life, his entire existence, into the divine ear.

Well, therefore, may we lay down, as the first rule for the promotion of piety in the clergyman, the great and standing rule for all Christians. Let him not be satisfied with studying and pondering the best treatises in theology, or with studying and pondering even the Bible itself. Besides all this, and as the crowning and completing act in the religious life, let him actually and really pray. Let him not be content with a theological mood, with a homiletic spirit, with a serious and elevated mental habitude. Besides all this, and as a yet higher and more enlivening mental process, let him truly and personally address his Maker and Redeemer in supplication. Let him not attempt to promote piety in the soul by a merely negative effort,—by neglecting the cultivation of the mind, and undervaluing learning and study. If the clergyman is not spiritually-minded and devotedly religious with learning and studiousness, he certainly will not be so without it. Neglect of his intellectual and theological character will not help his religious character. Let him constantly endeavour to advance the divine life in his soul by a positive and comprehensive method. Let him consecrate and sanctify all his study, and all his meditativeness, and all his profound and serious knowledge, with prayer.

2. The second rule for the cultivation of the religious character of the clergyman is, that he pursue theological studies for personal conviction and improvement. Melancthon, one of the most learned and contemplative of divines, as well as one of the most spiritual and best of men, makes the following affirmation respecting himself: 'I am certain and sure that I never investigated theology as a science for any other purpose, primarily, than to

benefit myself.'[1]   If the clergyman would advance in
spirituality, he must seek, first of all, in the investigation
of divine truth, to satisfy his own mind, and put it at rest,
in respect to the great themes of God's purposes and man's
destiny.   He must make the theology of the Bible contribute to his own mental peace.   That which a man knows
with certainty will affect his character.   If theological
studies result in an undoubted belief, a belief in which
there is no wavering or tremulousness, they will result in
solid religious growth.   To say nothing of the influence of
such a mode of pursuing the truth upon the manner of
communicating it, its effect is most excellent upon the
preacher himself.   We are. in reality influenced by
divine truth only in proportion as we thoroughly know
it and thoroughly believe it.   Suppose that the theologian
wavers in his mind in respect to the doctrine of endless
punishment, will not his own religious character be dam-
aged in proportion to the degree of his mental wavering ?
Suppose that his mind is not made up and at rest, suppose that he hesitates not outwardly, but in the thoughts
of his heart, in respect to the absolute perdition of the
impenitent, will not his own sense of the malignity of sin
be less vivid, and his own dread and abhorrence of it less
intense ?   Of course he not only cannot preach the doctrine
to another with that solemn earnestness, and that impetus
and momentum of statement which causes the hearer to
believe and tremble, but he cannot preach the doctrine
to himself.   He cannot fill his own soul with a profound

---

[1] Compare a similar remark which Baxter makes respecting himself
in his *Narrative of his Life and Times.*

fear of sin.   Thorough knowledge, and thorough personal belief of the truth, are indispensable to the existence of sincere, unhypocritical religion.

3. The third rule for the promotion of the religious character of the clergyman is, that he perform every clerical duty, be it in active or contemplative life, with punctuality, uniformity, and thoroughness.   There is discipline in labour.   The scrupulous and faithful performance of work of any kind improves both the mind and heart. A thorough and punctual mechanic is a man of character. He possesses a mental solidity and strength that render him a noticeable man and a reliable man in his sphere. The habit of doing work uniformly well, and uniformly in time, is one of the best kinds of discipline.   He who has no occupation or profession, must be, and as matter of fact is, an undisciplined man.   And in case one has an occupation or a profession, the excellence of his discipline is proportioned to the fidelity with which he follows it.   If he half does his work, his moral character suffers.   If he does his work thoroughly, when he does it at all, but does not perform it with punctuality and uniformity (a thing which is, however, not likely to happen), it is at the expense of his moral power.

All this is true, in an eminent degree, of professional labour.   Consider, for example, the contemplative side of the clergyman's life, the duties of his profession so far as concerns the preparation of sermons, and see how directly thoroughness and uniformity in this department promote his religious growth and character.   It is his duty as a preacher to deliver two public discourses in each week.

There may be, and there will be, more or less of informal religious instruction to be imparted besides this; but the substance of the clergyman's professional service, in the present state of society, is performed if he preaches two sermons, two oratorical discourses, every Sabbath-day. This is the regular and established routine of clerical life on its literary and contemplative side.

Now we affirm that the careful and uniform preparation of two sermons in every six days is a means of grace. It is in its very nature adapted to promote the piety of the clergyman. Punctual and faithful sermonizing fixes his thoughts intently upon divine truth, and preserves his mind from frivolous and vain wandering. It brings his feelings and emotions into contact with that which is fitted to enliven and sanctify them: it overcomes the natural indolence of human nature, and precludes a great deal of temptation to employ the mental powers wrongly; it leaves no room for the rise of morbid and unhealthy mental exercises; it makes the clergyman happy in his profession and strong in the truth, because he becomes, in the process, a thorough-bred divine; it gives him a solid weight of character and influence that does not puff him up with vanity, as mere popularity always does, but makes him devoutly thankful and humble before God; and, lastly, it promotes his piety by promoting his permanence in the ministry, for the piety of a standard man is superior to that of a floating man. And thus we might go on specifying particulars, in regard to which the conscientious performance of clerical duties in the study tends directly to build up a solid and excellent religious character.

There is a variety in the means which the clergyman must employ in order to spiritual growth, and they differ in the degree of their importance. We have assigned the first place to prayer, but we do not hesitate to assign the second place to conscientious and thorough sermonizing. For what is such sermonizing as we are pleading for but religious meditation of the very best kind—patient thought upon that divine truth which is the food and nutriment of holiness, bringing out into the clear light of distinct consciousness in our own minds, and for the minds of others, the doctrines of salvation? There is no surer way to become interested in a truth than to write a well-considered discourse upon it. The careful composition of a sermon oftentimes brings the heart into a glow of feeling that gives itself vent in prayer. Hence we find some of the greatest preachers among the Fathers and the Reformers writing down the prayer that rose spontaneously from their overflowing souls, making it the conclusion of their sermon. Many of the sweetest and loftiest hymns of Watts were the lyrical utterance of what had passed through his mind in sermonizing, and were originally appended to his discourses. And the same thing appears still more remarkably in the writings of the Schoolmen. In these strictly scientific treatises, which do not pretend to be oratorical, or applicatory to an audience, we meet here and there with a short prayer, full of earnestness, and full of vitality. In Anselm, in Aquinas, and in Bernard, the reader sees the spirit of these analytic metaphysical men, at the close of its intense meditation upon some mystery in the Divine Being or the divine administration, subdued and awed, hushed and breathless, in supplication and adoration. The intensely theoretic turns into the intensely practical, pure reason into pure emotion, dry light into vivid life.

What has been said of the contemplative life of the clergyman, applies with equal force to his active life. A thorough and punctual performance of pastoral duties is a direct means of grace. In the first place, the conscientious delivery of the two sermons that have been composed in the conscientious manner spoken of, ministers to edification. Although this is not strictly a pastoral work, yet it belongs to the active rather than the contemplative side of clerical life. That clergyman who *preaches* his sermons with earnestness, feeling the truth of every word he utters, will be spiritually benefited by this part of his labours. Elocution, the mere delivery of truth, which is too often destitute of both human nature and divine grace, when emphatic and sincere, promotes piety. Speaking in and by a sermon with ardour and feeling to an audience in respect to their spiritual interests, as really sets the Christian affections into a glow, as speaking in the same spirit to an individual in private intercourse.

In the second place, a faithful and constant performance of the duty of pastoral visiting is a means of grace. No one who has had any experience in this respect will deny this for a moment. There is nothing better adapted to develope piety, to elicit the latent principles of the Christian, than going from house to house, and conversing with all varieties of character and all grades of intelligence upon the subject of religion. The colporteur's piety is active and zealous; and the missionary, who is generally obliged to teach Christian truth to individuals, is a fervid and godly man. The clergyman, then, will grow in grace by simple assiduity in the discharge of this part of his professional labours. Whenever he is called to the bedside of an impenitent sinner, let him be thorough in dealing with that endangered sinner's soul, affectionate but solemn in probing his consciousness, perseveringly attentive to the moral symptoms of the unregenerate man on the bed of languishing; let him be a faithful pastor in each and every such instance, and he will be enriched with heavenly wisdom and love. Let him stand with the same uniform fidelity at the bedside of the dying Christian, dispelling momentary gloom by the exhibition of Christ and his atonement, supplicating for more of the comfort of the Holy Ghost in the soul of the dying saint, listening to the utterances of serene faith, or of rapturous triumph; let him submit his own soul to the great variety of influences that come off from the experience of the sick and the dying, and he will greatly deepen and strengthen his own religious character. And, lastly, the same fidelity and constancy in conversing with well and happy men, and therefore thoughtless men, respecting their eternal interests, and in catechizing the children, conduces powerfully to the formation of an unearthly and a holy frame of spirit.

Here, then, in the clerical office itself, is a most efficient means of grace. The clergyman needs not to go up and down the earth, seeking for instrumentalities for personal improvement. By his very position and daily labour, he may be made spiritual and heavenly. The word is nigh him, in his mouth and in his heart. A single word is the key to holiness in the clergyman. That word is *fidelity*—fidelity in the discharge of all the duties of his closet, his study, and his parish. A somewhat noted rationalist speaks of some men as being 'aboriginal saints,'—men in whom virtue is indigenous. There is no such man. But we may accommodate this hypothesis of a natural virtue, and say that the clergyman, so far as his calling and position are concerned, ought to be naturally holy. His whole environment is favourable to piety. He ought to be spontaneously religious.

CHAPTER III.

IN the preceding chapter we were led to speak of intellectuality and studiousness in their relations to the religious character of the clergyman, taking the position that, provided he is faithful in other respects, learning and contemplation are in themselves favourable to spirituality and piety. In this chapter we are to consider, first, the *type* of intellectual character which the clergyman ought to form; and, secondly, the *means of forming it*.

In respect to the style of mental culture at which the clergyman should aim, we sum up the whole in the remark, that it should be choice. It should be the product of a very select course of reading and study, and hence of a finer grade than the common intellectuality. In this country, and in this reading age, almost every man is somewhat literary. He is more or less acquainted with books, and may be said to have an intellectual as well as a moral character. Two centuries ago this was less the case. There was then, in society at large, very little of that enlightenment which is the effect of miscellaneous and general reading. Culture was concentrated in a smaller number; and hence in the seventeenth century there was a higher intellectual character in the learned professions, relatively to that of the mass of society, than there is at the present day. The masses have made more advance than the literary circles have. The professional classes and the public are now nearer a common level than they were two centuries ago; because, while the public has enlarged its acquaintance with literature, there has not been a corresponding progress on the part of the professions. The learning and intellectual power of the theologians of the present day are not as much superior to that of Richard Hooker or John Howe, as the popular knowledge of the nineteenth century is superior to that of the sixteenth and seventeenth. Neither is the mental culture of the upper class in the literary world as choice now as formerly, because it partakes more of the indiscriminateness of the common enlightenment. The great multiplication of branches of knowledge and of books has made the professional man more of a miscellaneous reader than he once was. The consequence is, that the intellectual character of the professions, while it has gained something in variety and versatility, has lost in quality.

In view of this fact, as well as on account of the intrinsic desirableness of the thing itself, the clergyman ought to aim at choiceness in his education. He should strive after ripe scholarship, and such mental traits as profundity, comprehensiveness, clearness, and force. These are too often neglected for a more superficial culture, and a class of qualities like versatility, vivacity, and brilliancy. These latter are much more easily obtained than the former. They do not task the persevering power of the mind, and consequently do not draw out its best capacity. The natural indolence of human nature is inclined to that species of intellectuality which is most readily acquired, and which makes the greatest momentary impression upon others. The clergyman, the lawyer, and the author, are too content with a grade of knowledge that is possessed by society at large. They are too willing to read the same books, and no more; to look from the same point of view, and no higher one; in short, to reflect the general culture of the masses. But a professional man has no right to pursue this course. Society does not set him upon an elevation above itself, and maintain him there by its institutions and arrangements, merely to have him look through their eyes and from their own lower position. Society does not, for example, place a man upon the high position of a public religious teacher, expecting that he will merely retail the current popular knowledge. Society looks up to the clergyman as its religious instructor, and requires that he be in advance of its own information. It does not indeed insist that he know all things, and be ahead in all respects. The lawyer, as he listens to his clergyman, does not look for a more extensive and accurate knowledge of law than he himself possesses. The man of business—the farmer, the manufacturer, and the merchant —does not expect from his minister a shrewder and wider information in the department of active life than he has himself. But each and all expect that, in regard to religion, and all those portions of human knowledge which are most closely connected with theology, the clergyman will be in advance of themselves. They demand that, in its own sphere, clerical culture be superior to that of society at large.

The clergyman should not therefore be content with the average intellectuality. He ought not to loudly profess a choicer culture than that of the community, but he ought actually to possess it. As the clerical position and calling demands a superior and eminent religious character, so it demands a superior and eminent intellectual character. If the clergyman may not supinely content himself with an ordinary piety, neither may he content himself with an ordinary culture.

These remarks upon the kind and type of intellectual character, at which the clergyman must aim, prepare the way for considering the chief means and methods of forming it. And these may all be reduced to one—namely, the *daily, nightly, and everlasting study of standard authors.* 'Few,' remarks John Foster, 'have been sufficiently sensible of the importance of that economy in reading which selects almost exclusively the very first order of books. Why should man, except for some special reason, read a very inferior book at the very time that he might be reading one of the highest order? A man of ability, for the chief of his reading, should select such works as he feels beyond his own power to have produced. What can other books do for him, but waste his time and augment his vanity?'

Choice and high culture is the fruit of communion with the very finest and loftiest intellects of the race. Familiarity with ordinary productions cannot raise the mind above the common level. Like breeds like; and mediocre literature, that neither descends deep nor soars high, will leave the student mediocre and commonplace in his thoughts. The preacher must love the profound thinkers,

w

and meditate upon them. But these are not the multitude. They are the few. They are those who make epochs in the provinces in which they labour. As we cast our eye along the history of a department, be it poetry or philosophy or theology, a few names represent and contain the whole pith and substance of it. Though there are many others who are respectable, and many more who are mere sciolists and pretenders, still an acquaintance or unacquaintance with them all would not materially affect the sum of his knowledge, who should be thoroughly familiar with these leading and standard writers.

The clergyman, therefore, must dare to pass by all second-rate authors, and devote his days and nights to the first-rate. No matter how popular or brilliant a cotemporary may be, no matter how active may be the popular mind in a particular direction, it is his true course to devote his best powers to mastering those authors who have been tried by time, and are confessedly the first intellects of the race. If a great thinker actually arises in our own age, we are not to neglect him because he is a cotemporary. Greatness should be recognised whenever it arises. But it must be remembered that a single age does well if it produces a single historic mind,—a mind that makes an epoch in the history of the department to which it devotes itself. And, moreover, it must be remembered, that we are more liable to be prejudiced in favour of a cotemporary than of a predecessor, and hence, that cotemporary judgments are generally modified, and sometimes reversed, by posterity. The past is secure. A student who bends his energies to the comprehension of an author who is acknowledged to be standard by the consent of ages and generations of scholars, takes the safe course to attain a choice culture.

It is not possible to go over the whole field of literature in a single chapter, and we shall therefore confine ourselves to those three departments which exert the most direct and important influence upon the intellectual character of the clergyman. These are poetry, philosophy, and theology. In each of these we shall mark out a course of reading and study which we think adapted to result in a ripe culture. And, assuming that the Bible, from its difference in kind from all other literature, and its peculiar and paramount claims upon the study of the clergyman, will be the object of supreme attention,—the Book of books, —we shall confine our remarks to uninspired literature.

In poetry the clergyman should study all his days the great creative minds—namely, Homer, Virgil, Dante, Shakspeare, and Milton. A brief sketch of their characteristics, and specification of the elements of culture furnished by each, to go into the combination we are seeking, will be in place here. Homer is to be studied as the head and representative of Greek poetry. The human mind reached the highest grade of culture that is possible to paganism in the Greek race; and the inmost spirit and energy of the Greek intellect are concentrated in the blind bard of Chios. Long-continued familiarity with the *Iliad* and *Odyssey*, imparts force, fire, and splendour to the mental character. It also imparts freshness, freedom, and enthusiasm. Bouchardon said that, while reading Homer, his whole frame appeared to himself to be enlarged, and all surrounding nature to be diminished to atoms. The function of Homer is to dilate and kindle the intellect.

Virgil is to be studied as the embodiment of dignity and grace. Though hardly severe and massive enough to be a full representative of the Roman mind, yet, upon the whole, he contains more of its various characteristics than any other single Roman poet. He adequately represents imperial Rome, if he does not monarchical and republican. The dignity of the Roman character is certainly exhibited in the Virgilian poetry. The influence of familiarity with the *Æneid* is highly refining. Men of elegant traits, like Canning and Robert Hall, relish and quote Virgil. Everything in him is full of grace and propriety. Even in the *Georgics*, though the theme is not favourable to the exhibition of such qualities, they yet appear in their height. As Addison says, the farmer in the *Georgics* tosses his dung about with an air of dignity.

Dante is the great poet of the Middle Ages. Though a Papist by birth and position, he is yet a Protestant in temper and spirit. Dante and Michael Angelo, so far as the fundamental traits of their minds are concerned, were both of them blood-relations of Martin Luther. Intensity is the prominent characteristic of the *Divine Comedy*. Familiarity with Dante imparts a luminous distinctness to the operations and products of the mind. The poetry of Dante is more speculative than that of any other poet.[1]

---

[1] It is also more theological than that of any other, unless we except Milton—if indeed he is to be excepted. Better statements of the doctrines of sin and atonement, for example, have not been made than Dante lays down in the seventh canto of the *Paradise*.

He was well acquainted with Aristotle's philosophy, and exhibits the subtlety and analysis of the Schoolmen themselves. Indeed the general literary characteristics of the Middle Ages are all concentrated in the great Italian poet.

Shakspeare and Milton stand upon a common level. The English Parnassus, to use the figure of Coleridge, has twin peaks that crown its summit. Both alike deserve a life-long study,—Shakspeare for the breadth and subtlety of his thinking, Milton for his loftiness and grandeur.

The English poets in this list the clergyman may read in his own tongue. If he would be perfect, he must study the others in the tongues in which they were born and wrote. With the Latin of Virgil he should be ashamed to be unfamiliar; while it is to be remembered that dignity and grace, being formal qualities, are more difficult to be transfused into another language. Dante has been faithfully translated by Cary; and by frequent perusal the student may, even through this medium, thoroughly imbue his culture with the spirit of the *Divine Comedy.* Homer, so far as possible, ought to be read in the original Greek; but if a translation is to be employed, it should be that of Chapman, one of the early English translators. It is exceedingly rugged, yet very faithful to the original. But, what is of most importance, Chapman has caught the Homeric spirit far more than any other translator, be he English, French, German, or Italian. That fiery energy, that rushing life, and that dilation and inspiration which are so characteristic of the Greek, reappear in the Englishman. Familiarity with this version, even without any other knowledge of Homer, will bring the student into a more living sympathy with him than the perusal of Pope's version can, even if helped out with a mere dictionary-knowledge of the original. The spirit of the performance is intensely Homeric. It is, as Lamb says, not so much a translation as an original production, —such a one as Homer himself would have composed had he been compelled to use the less flexible and harmonious English, instead of the pliant and mellifluous Greek. But while we are speaking of translation, it must be remembered that a continuous study of an author, even in versions, naturally results in more or less study of him in the original. Struck with the force, or perhaps the obscurity of translation, the reader takes down the original to compare or explain, and in this way keeps his mind considerably familiar with the original,—certainly more familiar than he would if the writer were entirely neglected.[1]

The authors thus mentioned and sketched are the first and greatest in the province of poetry, in their respective ages and literatures. The clergyman who is thoroughly familiar with these, though he should be ignorant of all others, will be marked by a choice poetical cultivation; while, if he neglects these, though he should be acquainted

---

[1] The prohibition of translations to the young student while acquiring the rudiments of a language, is wise and necessary. But their subsequent use, after the foundations of classical knowledge have been laid, and the scholar is compelled, by the demands of a laborious profession, to make wide excursions over the whole immense field of ancient literature, is a different matter. That a real and vivid knowledge of an author may be acquired even from a translation, is proved by the fact that the English Bible is the only source whence the majority of the Anglo-American world derive their acquaintance with the Hebrew and Greek Scriptures.

with all other poets, this part of his education would betray radical defects.

The department of philosophy next demands our attention. This exerts a very powerful influence upon the intellectual character, and may be said to determine its whole style and tone. If we know the philosophical authors with whom a student is familiar, we know the fundamental and distinguishing characteristics of his education; for philosophy furnishes him with his methods of reasoning and investigating, forms his habits of thought, and to a great extent determines the direction of his thinking, by presenting the objects of thought. Thus it may be said to contain the principles, means, and end of mental development; and therefore, of merely human and intellectual branches of discipline, it is the first and most important. The same injunction to read standard authors applies with full force here also. A few names make up the list of first-class minds in this department. The clergyman should become familiar with the two masters of Grecian philosophy, Plato and Aristotle. Their systems are sometimes represented as radically different from each other; but the difference is only formal, such as naturally arises, when, of two minds, one is synthetic, and the other is analytic, in its nature and tendency. The diligent student of these Grecians will discover in them a material agreement in respect to first principles, together with a formal difference in the mode of investigation and representation, that is for his benefit. Their systems should be studied in connection, as two halves of one coherent whole. He who has mastered them, has mastered all that is true and valuable in the philosophy of the Ancient world. As these authors are voluminous, and in a difficult language, the clergyman needs all the aids possible. Of Plato, there is a good Latin version by the Italian Ficinus, two German versions—one by Schleiermacher, and one by Schwarz,—and an excellent French translation by Cousin. Of the English translations, that which is now published by Bohn, of London, includes the entire works of Plato, and is of unequal merit in its parts. On the whole, the cheap Tauchnitz edition of the Greek, a good Greek lexicon, and Bohn's translations, make up an apparatus for the study of Plato that is within the reach of every clergyman. When he wishes to read rapidly, let him peruse the English version, correcting the mistakes, and elucidating the obscurity of the translators, by the Greek. When he desires to read for the sake of the language and style of the original, let him carefully study this. In this way, the clergyman, notwithstanding the multiplicity of his labours, may become well acquainted with the philosophy of the Academy.

In reading Aristotle, the same method may be followed. The same publisher is printing, from time to time, translations of this author, and the German publisher Tauchnitz furnishes an equally cheap edition of the Greek. More discrimination is needed in selecting from Aristotle than from Plato. Aristotle wrote extensively upon natural philosophy, and his speculations in this department are not of so much worth to the modern student, surrounded as he is with the achievements of modern science. The Metaphysics and Ethics, the Rhetoric, and, though last not least, the Politics and Economics, are the treatises of Aristotle of most value to the clergyman. The Greek of this author is worthy of special attention, by reason of its affinity with that of the New Testament, and it is much less difficult than the poetic prose of Plato.

The clergyman should peruse the philosophical writings of Cicero. The Roman reproduces, in a genial and elegant manner, the moral philosophy of Plato. He ought to be read in the original altogether, and may easily be. The most valuable of his philosophical treatises are the tract on the *Immortality of the Soul*, the *De Natura Deorum*, and the *De Finibus*, which discusses the nature of good and evil.

There is no writer of the Middle Ages, in philosophy, who stands in a similar relation to his time, with Plato and Aristotle and Cicero to theirs. Philosophy, during this period, passed over into theology ; and hence we shall speak of the Mediæval thinkers under that head. Moreover, as the Aristotelian philosophy was the dominant system of the Middle Ages, the study of Aristotle himself will make the student acquainted with the Mediæval methods of thinking and investigation.

Des Cartes is justly regarded as the father of Modern philosophy, because he gave it its predominant direction towards psychology. His first principle, *Cogito ergo sum*, converts philosophy into an analysis of consciousness. His discourse on the *Method of rightly conducting the Reason*, and his *Meditations*, are of most value to the theological student. Though not chronologically in place, yet, from his intellectual relations, we here mention the

name of Leibnitz. The philosophical speculations of this
writer are highly theological, and therefore are attractive
to the clergyman. Written in the most pellucid style,
such treatises as the *Théodicée* and *Nouveaux Essais* (the
most masterly criticism that has yet been made upon the
philosophy of Locke) well reward the scholar for their
perusal. The clergyman ought to become well acquainted
with the method and system of that sagacious comprehensive, and substantial thinker, Lord Bacon. He also,
like Aristotle, is regarded by some as the antagonist of
Plato; but a perusal of his works, particularly the *Novum
Organum,* in the light thrown upon them by those Essays
of Coleridge in the *Friend,*[1] in which he compares Bacon
and Plato, will convince any one that their philosophical
methods are essentially the same, only applied to different
departments of inquiry,—Plato being the philosopher of
the intellect and spirit, Bacon the philosopher of nature
and matter; the one cultivating intellectual and moral
philosophy, the other investigating natural philosophy and
physical science.

The next system in the historic movement of philosophy is that of Locke. This merits the study of the
clergyman, mainly for negative purposes. Thus far, the
systems which we have mentioned are substantially the
same, and in one straight, though sometimes wide, path of
progress. But this system is out of the line of a true
philosophic advance. It has, however, exerted so great an
influence in the philosophic world, that it deserves to be
thoroughly studied, as the most self-consistent, and at the

[1] Coleridge, *Works,* vol. ii. p. 437 sq.

same time moderate, of all the systems of materialism. A critical mastery of it results in a more immoveable position upon the true philosophic ground. In this reference, the study of Locke is of great negative worth, while, at the same time, it is often of value in repressing that false spiritualism into which the human mind is apt to run, in passing from one extreme to another.

The last name that we mention in this series of philosophers is that of Kant. He who goes to the study of this author after that of Locke, will find himself again in the broad, travelled highway of philosophy, and will come into contact with the most logical mind since Aristotle. The fundamental principles of theism and ethics are laid down with scientific precision in the three critiques of this latest of the great metaphysical thinkers. Kant is most satisfactorily read in the original German; yet such a study of previous philosophers as we have recommended, resulting as it does in what may be called a philosophic instinct and sagacity in detecting the drift of a system, will enable the student to gather his general meaning, even out of the very inadequate translations that have been made of him. Something, moreover, may be learned from the English and French writers who have either adopted or opposed his opinions. Of them all, Coleridge and Hamilton were by far the best acquainted with Kant, and their writings are the best introduction to the German philosopher that is accessible to the merely English reader.

In concluding under this head of philosophy, we make a remark similar to that at the close of the paragraph upon poetry.　Familiarity with these eight authors—Plato, Aristotle, Cicero, Des Cartes, Leibnitz, Bacon, Locke, and Kant —will impart a choiceness to the clergyman's metaphysical discipline, that cannot be obtained without them, and that cannot be obtained by a perusal of the hundreds and thousands of second-rate works in this province.　These are virtually the whole.　The entire department of philosophy is potentially in these eight authors.　They are the fountains whence all others draw.

It now remains to mark out a course of study in the department of theology.　And the first name in the series, both chronologically and intrinsically, with which the clergyman ought to become familiar, is that of Augustine. The position of this writer, in systematic theology, is very central ; so that a clear understanding of him, is a clue to very much that comes after him.　Though not everything in his writings is fully developed or accurately developed, yet the principal seeds and germs of the modern Protestant theology are found in them, and he, more than any other one of the Fathers, and far more than any one of the Schoolmen, constitutes the organic link of connection between scriptural Christianity in the Ancient Church and scriptural Christianity in the Modern.　And besides the scientific interest which the most distinguished of the Christian Fathers awakens, his personal character itself wins upon the admiration of the student all the days of his life.　His entire works are no longer difficult of access, through the cheap reprint in Migne's series of the Fathers and Schoolmen.　Individual writings of his have also been republished, which may be obtained as readily as the

Latin and Greek classics. Of his entire works, may be mentioned the important tenth volume in the Benedictine arrangement, which contains his views upon the great themes of sin and grace, in opposition to Pelagianism and Semi-Pelagianism. To these must be added the *De Civitate Dei*, and the *Confessions*,—the one doctrinal, and the other biographical. The *City of God* is one of Augustine's largest works, and conveys a more adequate impression of him as a systematizer than any other single treatise of his. It is somewhat unequal in structure. This, however, arose in part from the disposition to be exhaustive in the investigation, not only of the principal topics in theology, but of all collateral topics. Augustine, for example, discusses the question, 'How ought the bodies of saints to be buried?' with as much serious earnestness, and as strong a desire to answer it correctly, as he does the question, 'What was the condition of the first man before his fall?' This same inclination to take up every point and exhaust it, is seen in the Schoolmen as well as the Fathers, and accounts for the wood, hay, and stubble mixed with the gold, silver, and precious stones, found in their writings.

The clergyman should next be familiar with the Scholastic theology, so far as is possible for him. Very little is now known of the theologians of the Middle Ages, even by professed scholars and authors. The great minds among them, however, deserve to be read, at least in a few of their best tracts and treatises. On the whole, Anselm deserves most attention, because he unites the speculative and practical tendencies in greatest harmony. Thomas Aquinas has left the most important systematic treatise of the

Middle Ages, and should be associated with Anselm.
Lastly, the spiritual and saintly Bernard, the most contemplative of the Schoolmen, opens many veins of rich
and edifying thought. The following works of these
authors may be the most easily obtained, and deserve to
be pondered in the order in which they are mentioned.
Anselm's *Cur Deus Homo?* is a treatise in which the
philosophic necessity and rationality of the doctrine of
atonement are exhibited for the first time, and which has
been studied by the ablest thinkers upon this subject ever
since. His *Proslogion* and *Monologium* are two closely
reasoned tracts, of which the first contains the most metaphysical *à priori* argument yet made for the divine existence, and the last, an excellent statement of the relation
of reason to revelation. The three tractates, *De libero
arbitrio, De casu diaboli,* and *De virginali conceptu,* hold
the clue to the deep mystery of the finite will and the
origin of moral evil, if that clue has ever been vouchsafed
to the human intellect. The *Summa Theologica* of Thomas
Aquinas is the systematic theology of the Middle Ages.
The *Sententiæ, De Consideratione,* and *De modo bene vivendi*
of Bernard will introduce the student to trains of reflection,
in which there is a rare union of depth with edification.

The next era in the history of theology is that of the
Reformation, including also the succeeding period of
conflict between Calvinists and Arminians. Calvin and
Turrettin are the two leading theological minds of this
period, and the clergyman cannot study the *Institutes* of
the former, and the *Institutio* of the latter, too patiently
or too long. In the former he will find the completion

of the systematic structure whose foundations were laid by Augustine; while in the latter the more minute and thorough elaboration of particular doctrines appears. For controversy compels thorough statements; and that discussion between the Calvinists and Arminians was one of the most analytic and subtle that has ever occurred.

The English divines of the seventeenth century next deserve the study of the clergyman. If he were to be shut up, as he ought not to be, to a single period in the history of theology, and to communion with a single class or school, it would be safe to leave him alone with the theologians of England, both Prelatical and Nonconforming. They were men of the widest reading, the most thorough learning, and the most profound piety. There are many noble names among them; but, in accordance with a parsimonious method, and having special reference to dogmatic theology, we shall mention only Owen, Howe, and Baxter. Though the theoretic and the practical elements wonderfully interpret each other in the writings of all three, yet each has his distinguishing excellence. Owen is the most comprehensively systematic, Howe the most contemplative and profound, and Baxter the most intense and popularly effective.

The last writer in the series is the elder Edwards,—a theologian equal to any that have been mentioned, whether we consider the depth and subtlety of his understanding, the comprehension and cogency of his logic, or the profundity and purity of his religious experience, and who deserves the patient study of the American clergyman in particular, because, more than any other American theologian, he forms a historical connection with the theologies of the past, and stands confessedly at the head of our scientific theology.

We have now passed in review the departments of poetry, philosophy, and theology; and we think that any one would concede that a course of study such as we have marked out would result in a high type of intellectual character. By pursuing it, the mind of the clergyman would be put into communication with all the best culture and science of the human race. Such a choice intellectual discipline would give him influence with the most highly educated men in society, and the respect of the people at large. The people naturally venerate learning. They expect it in their religious teacher, and they are impressed by it. It inspires their confidence. Baxter, in speaking upon this point in his *Reformed Pastor*, goes so far as to recommend the preacher to introduce occasionally into his sermons a scholastic word or a learned term which the people do not understand, in order to show that he is familiar with sciences and branches ·of knowledge with which they themselves are unacquainted. Baxter recommends this in all seriousness and solemnity, as he does everything else. The rule is not worth observing, but the spirit of it is.

Such an intellectual discipline, moreover, leaves room for growth and expansion, and impels to it. The standard minds, as we have remarked, are in one and the same general line of thinking; and hence all the acquisition that is made by the student is homogeneous. He is not compelled to unlearn anything. He is studying one common system of truth, and employs one common method of apprehending and stating it; so that, whatever may be the particular part of the great whole which he is studying for the time being, the results of his study will fall in with all other results, and go to constitute a harmonic and symmetrical education. The plan of clerical study, upon this scheme, is like the plan of a perfect campaign. All the movements are adjusted to each other, and are coherent; so that, at whatever point the individual soldier labours, and however distant from headquarters, he is contributing directly to the one predetermined and foreseen issue. Hence, although we have mentioned the standard authors chronologically, as the most convenient and natural order, it is not necessary that the clergyman should invariably study them in this order. Let him be retrogressive or progressive as he pleases; let him begin anywhere in the series, and with any single writer, and he will be in line, and may form connections with the front and the rear. He may also indefinitely expand his system of study,— widening and deepening the foundations, rearing up and beautifying the superstructure, and yet never essentially varying the form and proportions of the temple of truth and of science.

But how, it may be asked, is the clergyman, with all his public and private occupations, to find time for such an extensive and thorough course of study? We shall devote the short remainder of the chapter to the answer to this question. Before proceeding, however, to give specific rules, let us observe that this is a course of study for life. It is not to be run through in a year, or ten years, and

x

then to give place to another. It is not to be outgrown
and left behind. One of the most eloquent and enthusi-
astic of literary men remarks, that the scholar should ' lay
great bases for eternity ; ' that is, he should adopt a plan
and method of study which possesses compass enough,
and coherence enough, to be ever permanent for purposes
of discipline and scholarship. The clergyman should intellectually, as well as morally, lay great bases for eternity.
He ought not, therefore, to be overwhelmed in the very
outset by the greatness of the proposed edifice, but should
relieve his mind by remembering that he has his whole
life before him.

In order to the successful prosecution of such a course of
study, and the attainment of a high intellectual discipline,
the clergyman must rigorously observe hours of study.
His mornings must be seasons of severe application. By
proper arrangements, the time from eight to one may be
a period of uninterrupted devotion to literary toil. Of
these five hours, two may be devoted to books, and three
to sermonizing; or, in the outset, one hour to books and
four to sermonizing. Supposing that no more than six
hours are devoted to pure study in a week, even this, in
the course of twenty, thirty, forty, or fifty years, would
carry the clergyman over a very wide field of investigation,
and carry him thoroughly. But, as he advances in this
course, he will find his mind strengthening, his faculties
becoming more manageable, and his resources more ample;
so that after ten, perhaps five, years have elapsed, the two
hours are sufficient for sermonizing, and the three may be
devoted to study. As the clergyman grows into a learned

and systematic thinker, he becomes able to preach with much less immediate preparation. These five hours, every day, are sufficient for literary purposes, provided they are strictly hours of intellectual toil. Let there be in the study no idleness, no reverie, and no reading outside of the prescribed circle. Let the mind begin to work as soon as the door is shut, and let it not cease until the clock strikes the appointed hour; then stop study, and stop composition, and devote the remainder of the day to parochial labours, the amenities of life, and the relaxation of lighter literature.

Again, in order to the prosecution of such a course of study as has been described, it is evident that the clergyman must read no more of second-rate literature, of either the past or the present, than is consistent with these severer studies. He must dare to be ignorant of much of it, in order that he may know the *Dii majorum gentium.* He must purchase very little of it, and none of it at all until he has obtained the standard works. His library, like his culture, should be choice,—a *gem* of a library, and then he will not be tempted by inferior productions to waste his time. And especially must he be upon his guard against the great mass of periodical literature that is coming into existence, and dying as fast as it is born. Periodical literature, as a species, is the direct contrary of standard literature, and its influence upon education is directly antagonistic to that of true study. The nature of this class of mental products is analogous to that of one of the lowest grades of animal existence. The periodical is like a polypus. The polyp propagates itself by sprouting and swelling like a vegetable. Cut a polyp into two halves, and these two halves complete themselves, and become two polypi. Cut each of these two into two, they become four perfect polypi; and so the process goes on *ad infinitum.* And this is the process in periodical literature. A very slender idea or thought is bisected, and these parts are exhibited each as a complete whole, and the entire truth. These, again, are subdivided by another journalist, and re-exhibited. And thus the polyp process goes on, until a single idea, not very solid at the beginning, is made to propagate itself through page after page. One man writes a book, the whole of which does not contain a thousandth part of the truth that is to be found in some standard work. Another writes a review of this book,—unless, perchance, to employ the comparison of Matthias Claudius, the hen reviews her own egg; another writes a review of this review. And so the work goes bravely on, from month to month, and year to year.

The true course for the clergyman, as well as for the student generally, is to devote no more attention to the current and periodical literature of his age than is just sufficient to keep him acquainted with its tendencies and currents of thought and action, devoting himself, in the meanwhile, to those standard products which are for all time, and from which alone he can derive true intellectual aliment and strength.

CHAPTER IV.

THE third topic in Pastoral Theology to be examined, is the *social and professional character* of the clergyman. These terms will be employed in a comprehensive sense, and include all that part of clerical character which has not been considered under the heads of religious and intellectual. The subject of clerical manners naturally constitutes the substance of this chapter. These are two-fold, and may be discussed, in their reference to the *personal* conduct of the clergyman towards individuals, and his *professional* conduct towards his congregation.

1. In respect to the first branch of the subject, it is obvious that the conduct and bearing of a clergyman ought to be appropriate to his profession, and distinguish him, not perhaps from a Christian man generally, but from the world at large. A sanctimonious behaviour, so different from that of a Christian gentleman as to call attention to it and inspire contempt, is to be carefully avoided. A clergyman ought not to advertise himself beforehand, and, by something exquisite and peculiar, give notice that he is more than a Christian layman ; yet he should always maintain such a port and demeanour, that a stranger, while plainly seeing that he is a Christian, would not be surprised to discover that he is also a clergyman.

The clergyman ought to be of *grave* manners,—in the phrase of St. Paul, a man of decorum ($\varkappa\acute{o}\sigma\mu\iota\sigma\varsigma$).[1] His behaviour in society must be serious. He should make the impression that he is a thoughtful person. These terms, gravity, seriousness, and thoughtfulness, imply that his mind is preoccupied with great and good subjects, so that, wherever he goes, and with whomsoever he associates, he cannot stoop to ' foolish talking and jesting,' to frivolity, gaiety, or levity. Gravity, though assumable for the hour, cannot be permanently simulated. The hypocrisy is sooner or later detected. The innate levity of the mind unconsciously breaks out. A single word betrays the secret, and then there is no recalling ; for men reason correctly, that a really light-minded person can temporarily assume seriousness and gravity, and often has a motive to do so, but a really serious and solemn man cannot so readily imitate levity and worldliness, and, what is more, will not, because he has no motive for so doing. Hence the secret of Christian decorum in social intercourse is, to be really and at heart a serious man. Let the clergyman form such a religious and such an intellectual character as we have described, and be absorbed in his calling, and he will spontaneously be grave and dignified in manner.

Secondly, the clergyman should be of *affable* manners. As the etymology denotes (*affari*), it must be easy for him to speak to others, and thus easy for others to speak to him. He ought to be an accessible person in social intercourse. Clerical character is apt to run to extremes. On the one hand, gravity becomes false and excessive, so that

[1] 1 Tim. iii. 2.

it repels address. If this be the case, the clergyman's influence is much diminished. The timid are afraid of him, and the suspicious dislike him; and thus the really good man is avoided by two very large classes of society. By one he is thought to be stern, and by the other he is thought to be proud. On the other hand, affability sometimes becomes excessive, so that the clergyman loses dignity of character and weight of influence. He is too ready to talk. He speaks upon all subjects with the same ease, and the same apparent interest. He opens his mind to every one he meets, without regard to character, and, unlike his Divine Master, 'commits himself' to men.[1] There is not sufficient reserve in his manner. He does not study the characters of men, and consequently does not know men. His conversation is not adapted to the individual he is addressing, because it is adapted to every one alike. The consequence is, that affability degenerates into familiarity, and familiarity breeds contempt. The social manners of the clergyman ought, therefore, to be a just mingling of gravity and affability. The one must temper the other, and prevent an extreme in either direction. The clergyman will then be a dignified and serious man, to that degree which represses frivolity and inspires respect; and he will be an affable man, to that point which wakens confidence and wins regard.

2. We pass now to consider the professional bearing of the clergyman among the people of his charge. The clergyman sustains more intimate and special relations to his parish than he does to general society and the world

[1] John ii. 24.

at large. He is a person of more authority and influence in his own Church than elsewhere; and hence the need of further statements and rules than those that have been given respecting his general social relations.

In the first place, it is the right and the duty of the clergyman to be a man of *decision* in administering the affairs of his parish. The Apostle James, addressing a Christian Church, gives the admonition, 'Be not many masters' (διδάσκαλοι),[1] indicating thereby that the interests of a congregation flourish best under the guidance of a presiding mind. When Church members are disposed, each and every one, to be the teacher, nothing but rivalry among themselves, and the destruction of ministerial authority and respect, can possibly result. The genius of a truly scriptural ecclesiastical polity is undoubtedly republican. Whenever the monarchical spirit has shaped ecclesiastical government, the Church has speedily declined in spirituality and power, as the history of the Papacy, not to speak of other Church organizations, plainly evinces. But republicanism is not a wild and ungoverned democracy. It supposes, indeed, like democracy, that all power is ultimately lodged in the people, but, unlike democracy, it supposes that some of this power has been freely delegated to an individual or individuals who, by virtue of this endowment, possess an authority which, as ordinary members of the community, they would not have. The people of a republic are not compelled to delegate their sovereignty—it is a voluntary procedure on their part; and neither are they compelled to bestow power upon any

---

[1] Jas. iii. 1.

particular man or class of men. But when they have once freely made their choice of officers, and have solemnly invested them with authority and a delegated sovereignty, then they have no option in regard to obeying their rulers. They are bound to respect their own work. They are solemnly obligated to submit themselves to the government which they themselves have established, so long as it is faithful to the trusts that have been committed to it. The difference between a pure democracy and a republic consists not in any difference of opinion respecting the ultimate seat of sovereignty. Both alike claim that it resides in the people. But a pure democracy does not put any of this sovereignty out of its own hands. It never delegates authority. As in Athens, the entire population meet in popular assembly, enact or repeal laws, try causes as a court, and make peace or declare war. The people in this instance are not only the source of authority, but the acting government itself. Republicanism, on the contrary, while adopting the same fundamental principle with democracy, finds it more conducive to a stable and reliable government to lodge power for certain specified purposes in the hands of a few, subject to constitutional checks,—to a recall in case of maladministration, and, in some instances, to a recall after a certain specified time, even though it has been well used. Most Churches in this country claim that the Scriptures enjoin a republican form of polity. Very few are disposed to contend for a purely democratic ecclesiastical organization. The dispute between non-prelatical Churches relates mainly to the grade of republicanism; that is, to the amount of authority that shall be delegated, the number of persons to whom, and the time for which.

We assume therefore, that, under existing ecclesiastical arrangements, the pastor is a man to whom the people have entrusted more or less authority. In the Presbyterian Church, they have formally dispossessed themselves of power,/ to a certain extent, and have made it over to the session, consisting of the pastor and elders. In the Congregational Church, though they have not formally done this, and though they reserve the 'power of the keys' in their own hands, yet they expect their clergyman to be the presiding mind of the body.

The clergyman, then, standing in this leading attitude in his parish, ought to be a man of decision. But this implies that his own mind is settled and established. There is nothing which weakens a leading man—that is, a man who by his position ought to lead—like wavering and indecision. Doubt and uncertainty are a tacit acknowledgment of unfitness to guide and preside. The clergyman must therefore be positive in his theological opinions. Inasmuch as he is called to the work of indoctrination, he ought to be clear in his own mind. It is his vocation to shape the religious views of an entire community, and consequently his own views ought not only to be correct, but firmly established. For how can he say to his auditory, 'This doctrine is false, and fatal to your salvation; but this doctrine is true, and you may rest your eternal welfare upon it,'—how can he say this with any emphasis, unless he knows what he is saying, and is made decided by his knowledge ? The clergyman's communication must not be yea and nay together. King Lear, in his madness, remarks that, ' Ay and no, too, is no good divinity ;' and there is reason, if not method, in his madness.

And so far as the doctrines of Christianity are concerned, why should not the clergyman be a man of decided opinions ? If the gospel were a merely human system, there would be ground for hesitation and doubt; but since it is the revelation of an infallible Mind, what is left for the Christian teacher but to reaffirm the Divine affirmation, with all the positiveness and decision of the original communication itself ? The Scriptures teach but one system of truth, though the ingenuity of the human intellect, under the actuation of particular biases, has succeeded in torturing a variety of conflicting systems out of it, by dislocating its parts instead of contemplating it as a whole. This one evangelical system has been received by the Christian Church in all ages ; and if the clergyman feels the need of aids in getting at it, imbedded as it is in the living, and therefore flexible substance of the Bible, let him study the creeds of the Christian Church. An examination of the doctrinal statements which the orthodox mind has constructed out of the Bible, to counteract and refute those which the heterodox mind has also constructed out of the Bible, will do one thing, at least, for the clergyman, if it does nothing more. It will very plainly show him what system of truth the Scriptures contain, in the opinion of the Church. The Church, it is true, may be mistaken. It is not infallible. Creeds may be erroneous. But after this concession has been made, it still remains true that the symbols of the Christian Church do very clearly and fully display the opinions of the wisest and holiest men, and the closest students of the Scriptures, for sixteen hundred years, in respect to the actual contents of Revelation. The clergyman who adopts the theology embodied in them may possibly be in an error; but if he is, he is in good company, and in a large company. Moreover, that man must have a very exaggerated conception of his own powers, who supposes that he will be more likely to find the real teaching of the Scriptures, upon each and all of the profound subjects respecting which they make revelations, by shutting himself out of all intercourse with other human minds, who have gone through the same investigation. That the Bible must be studied by each one for himself, and that each individual must, in the end, deliberately exercise his own judgment, and form his own opinion as to the system of truth contained in Revelation, is the fundamental distinction between Protestantism and Romanism. But this does not carry with it the still further and really antagonistic position, that the individual should isolate himself from the wise and the good men who have preceded him, or are his cotemporaries, and do his utmost to be uninfluenced by those who have studied the Scriptures for themselves, and have, moreover found themselves coming to the same common result with thousands and millions of their fellow-men. There is, and can be, but one truth, and therefore all men ought to agree. The position that, so far as the nature of the case is concerned, there may be as many minds as there are men, and as many beliefs as there are individual judgments, is untenable. We affirm, then, that the clergyman should make a proper use of the studies and investigations of his brethren in the Church, not merely of the particular Church to which he belongs, and not merely of the particular Churches of the age and generation in which he lives, but of the Church Universal—the holy catholic Church, not in the Roman sense, but in that in which the Scripture employs the term when it denominates the Church 'the pillar and ground of the truth.' And the result of this study and investigation of the Scriptures by the general Christian mind is embodied in the creeds that have formed the doctrinal basis of the various branches of the one body of Christ.

Now the clergyman will be likely to be positive in his doctrinal opinions, in proportion as he perceives that his own views of the meaning and contents of Scripture are corroborated by those of the wise and good of all ages. If, on the contrary, he finds himself unable to agree with his predecessors and cotemporaries in the ministry, we do not see how he can be a decided man in the proper sense of this term. He may be a presumptuous, self-conceited, arrogant man, setting up his individual judgment in opposition to that of the great majority of individual judgments. He may be a kind of private pope, first throwing himself out of the line of historical Christianity and then calling upon the Church Universal to unlearn all that it knows, and forget all that it has learned, insisting that it bend the neck and bow the knee to the new infallibility that has appeared—he may be all this in spirit, if not in form, and still be very far from being established in his own mind. The first serious opposition to him would probably unsettle his views. Yet, even if his convictions should take on a fanatical temper, and carry him like Servetus to the stake, he knows nothing of the true martyr spirit.

The clergyman, again, is obliged to form opinions upon other subjects than doctrinal, and to give expression to them. The social, economical, and political questions of the day will be put to him by society, or else he will feel urged up to an expression of opinion by the condition and wants of his people. He should not, by any means, seek for opportunities of this sort. Blessed is the clergyman who is permitted by the community and his own conscience to devote his whole thinking and utterance to strictly religious themes. Blessed is that parish which seeks first the truth as it is in Jesus, takes most interest in the conviction and conversion of sinners and the edification of Christians, and desires to see the evils of society removed by additions to the Church of such as shall be saved. Still the clergyman will not be permitted to be entirely silent, during his whole ministry, respecting those semi-religious subjects which underlie the various reforms of the age. He should therefore be a decided man in this sphere as well as that of theology. Let him not be in haste to discuss these themes; let him wait for the sober second thought upon his own part, and especially upon the part of the people, before he gives his opinion. ' In reference to the exciting subjects of the day and the hour,' said a wise and judicious minister, ' do as the sportsman does—never fire when the flock is directly over your head, but fire when it has passed a little beyond you, that your shot may be raking.' When, however, the time has evidently come to speak upon these semi-religious themes, the clergyman should do so with decision. Let him make up his mind fully; and when he sees that the interests of his people require it, let him speak out his mind without doubting or wavering.

But in order that the clergyman may be a decided man in respect to such themes as these, he needs to pursue the same course as in reference to strictly religious opinions. He should take counsel of history and of the wisest men of his own generation. If he isolates himself from them, and sets up for a reformer, or associates with those who are so doing, he cannot be a truly determined man. He will be blown about by the popular breeze that is blowing for the hour, and which changes every hour. He will be carried headlong by designing men, who cloak the worst aims under a religious garb. In the present condition of society, there is great need of a power in the clergy to stem currents,—of a decision and determination that are rooted in intelligence, in reason, and in wisdom. But such a settled and constant mental firmness can proceed only from a historic spirit, or, what is the same thing, out of a truly conservative temper. For conservatism, properly defined, is the disposition to be historical, to attach one's self to those opinions which have stood the test of time and experience, rather than to throw them away and invent or adopt new ones. A conservative theologian, for example, is inclined to that system of doctrine which has been slowly forming from age to age ever since the Christian mind began a scientific construction of revealed truth, and is unwilling to make any radical changes in it. He concedes the possibility of a further expansion of existing materials, but is opposed to the addition of new as well as the subtraction of old matter. He does not believe that there are any new dogmas lying concealed in the Scriptures, having utterly escaped the notice of the theologians of the past. Christianity for him is a completed religion. The number of fundamental truths necessary to human salvation is full. The Church of the past needed the same truths in order to its sanctification and perfection that the Church of the present needs, and it possessed each and every one of them. There can be no essential addition, therefore, to the body of Christian doctrine until another and new revelation is bestowed from God.

This historic and conservative spirit is not lifeless and formal, as is frequently charged. It does not tend to petrifaction. For it keeps the individual in communication, not only with the whole long series of individual minds, but with the very best results to which they have come. Conservatism is dead and deadening, only upon the hypothesis that the universal history of man is the realm of death. There was just as much vitality in the past generations as there is in the present, which is soon to become a thing of the past. Furthermore, the steady and strong endeavour to become master of the past stimulates and kindles in the highest degree. For this knowledge does not flow into the individual as a matter of course. It must be toiled after; and the more the student becomes acquainted with the past workings of the human mind, the more conscious is he of his own ignorance as an individual. He finds that there is much more in the past with which he is unacquainted than there is in the present. He discovers that sixty centuries are longer than threescore years and ten. Where one subject has been thoroughly discussed by a cotemporary, one hundred have been by preceding minds. The whole past thus presents an unlimited expanse, over which the choicest intellects have careered; and instead of his being well acquainted with their investigations and conclusions, he finds that life itself is too short for the mastery of all this tried and historic knowledge. The old, therefore, is the new to the individual mind, and as such is as stimulating as the novel product of the day, and more likely to be nutritious and strengthening, because it has stood the test of ages and generations.

By the conservative, rather than the radical method, then, the clergyman should render himself a decided man in his opinions and measures. His mind will then be made up in company with others, and he will not be compelled to stand alone as an isolated atom, or, at most, in connection with a clique, or a clan, or a school, that has nothing of historic permanence in it, and which must vanish away with the thousands of similar associations, and never be even heard of in human history, because history preserves only the tried and the true for all time.

In the second place, the clergyman ought to be a *judicious* man. As it was necessary to mingle affability with gravity, in order to an excellent manner for the clergyman in general society, so decision must be mingled with judgment, in order to an excellent manner for him in his parish. Judiciousness teaches when to modify and temper the resolute and settled determination of the soul.

Y

Some subjects are more important than others.   Some
opinions and measures are vital to the prosperity of religion, and others are not.   The clergyman must be able to
distinguish fundamentals from non-fundamentals, so that
he may proceed accordingly.   It is absurd to be equally
decided upon all points.   A conservatism that conserves
everything with equal care, insisting that one thing is
just as valuable as another, is blind, and therefore false.
It is this spurious species which has brought the true into
disrepute, or, rather, has furnished the enemies of historic
views and a historic spirit with their strongest weapons.

When a fundamental truth is menaced, or a funda-
mentally wrong measure is proposed, the clergyman must
be immoveable.   In the phrase of Ignatius, he should
'stand like an anvil.'   If he does so, he will in the end
spoil the face of the hammers, and wear out the strength
of the hammerers.   But when the matter in controversy is
not of this vital nature, even though it have great importance, judiciousness in the clergyman would dictate more
or less of yielding.   If the clergyman can bring his parish
over to his own views upon every subject, he ought to do
so ; but if he cannot, then he must accomplish the most he
can.   In case the congregation are restless and disposed to
experiments, he will be more likely to prevent radical and
dangerous steps in primary matters and measures, if he
yields his individual judgment to them in secondary
matters.   His people will perceive that he has made a
sacrifice in regard to subjects which he deems to be important though not fundamental, and will feel obligated and
inclined to make one in return, when, with a serious tone

and a solemn manner, he insists that there be no yielding, upon either their part or his own, in matters that are absolutely vital to the interests of Christ's kingdom.

By thus mingling decision with judiciousness, the clergyman will be able to maintain himself as the presiding mind in his parish. It is his duty to be such. He cannot be useful unless he is. We do not hesitate to say, that if, after fair trial of a congregation, a minister discovers that he cannot secure that ascendency in the guidance and management of their religious affairs to which he is entitled, his prospects for permanent influence are too slight to warrant much hope. But a due mingling of intelligent decision and wise judgment generally does, as matter of fact, secure that professional authority and influence in the parish, which are inseparably connected with the prosperity of religion. Under the voluntary system, the clergyman is not much aided by ecclesiastical institutions or arrangements, and the republicanism of the people strips off from the clerical office, as it does from all other offices, the prestige of mere position. The American clergyman, unlike the member of an establishment, derives no authority from the mere fact that he is a clergyman. It is well that it is so. For now he must rely upon solid excellences, upon learning and piety, upon decision and good judgment, in the administration of his office. And if he possesses these qualities, he will be a more truly authoritative and influential man than the member of an establishment can be; because all the authority he has is fairly earned upon his side, and voluntarily conceded upon the people's side.

CHAPTER V.

PASTORAL VISITING.

WE have had occasion, in previous chapters, to remark that the clergyman bears two characters,
and sustains two different relations. He is an orator; that
is, one whose function it is to address public assemblies.
The relation which he sustains to society, by virtue of this
character, is public and formal. It requires the regularly
constructed address, the sacred time, and the sacred place.
It calls for the sermon, the Sabbath, and the sanctuary.
In this capacity, the clergyman is the minister of a public
instruction and a public worship.

But this is not the whole of a minister's character, and
these are not all his functions. He is a pastor; that is, one
whose duty is to go from house to house, and address men
privately and individually upon the subject of religion.
This kind of labour as necessarily forms a part of the
ministerial service as preaching. A perfect clergyman, if
such there were, would combine both the oratorical and
the pastoral character in just proportions and degrees.
The clergyman is liable to be deficient upon one or the
other side of this double character. He is a better preacher
than he is pastor, or else a better pastor than he is preacher.
It should therefore be the aim of the clergyman to perfect
himself in both respects.

It is an error to suppose that these two offices are totally independent of each other, and that the clergyman can secure the highest eminence in one by neglecting the other. Some make this mistake. Supposing themselves to be better fitted by nature to be preachers than pastors, or, what is more commonly the case, having more inclination to address men publicly and in bodies than privately and individually, they devote their whole time and attention to sermonizing and eloquence, with the expectation of thereby becoming more influential and able preachers. They are mistaken in this course. They may indeed, by close study, make themselves popular preachers, while they are neglecting personal intercourse with their hearers; but they would make powerful preachers if their study and composition were vivified by the experience of the pastor. If without that knowledge of men, which comes from direct intercourse with them, in health and in sickness, in prosperity and in adversity, in joy and in sorrow, they are able to construct attractive sermons, with that knowledge interpenetrating their reading and rhetoric, they might compose discourses of eminent or pre-eminent excellence. On the other hand, it sometimes occurs that the clergyman, being naturally of a social turn, and finding it easier to converse with individuals than to address an audience, turns the main current of his activity into the channel of pastoral work to the neglect of his pulpit ministrations. In this instance the same remark holds true as above. Even if by this course he should succeed in becoming a measurably useful pastor (a thing not very likely to occur), by a different course in respect to sermonizing he would be-

come a highly useful one.   The degree of success in both
instances is much increased, by cultivating a complete
clerical talent.   The learning and study of the preacher are
needed to enlighten and guide the zeal and earnestness of
the pastor, and the vitality and directness of the pastor are
needed to animate and enforce the culture of the preacher.
Instead, therefore, of regarding the functions of the preacher
and the pastor as totally independent of each other, and
capable of being carried to perfection, each by itself, the
clergyman must perform them both, and with equal fidelity.
And as he must, from the nature of the case, exert his
chief influence as a pastor, by pastoral visiting, we proceed
to lay down some rules for the performance of this part of
clerical service.

1. First, the clergyman should be *systematic* in pastoral
visiting, regularly performing a certain amount of this labour
every week.   There will be extraordinary seasons, when
he must visit his people for personal religious conversation
with greater frequency.   Times of unusual religious interest
will compel him to abridge his hours of study, and go from
house to house, that he may guide the inquiring, or awaken
the slumbering.   We are not giving a rule for such extraordinary occasions; and we need not, for they will bring
their own rule with them.   But, in the ordinary state of
religion among his congregation, the minister ought to accomplish a certain amount of this parochial work in each
week, not much exceeding or falling short of it.

There are two advantages in this systematic regulation.
In the first place, if the pastor is more inclined to address
men individually and in social intercourse than he is to

address them collectively, and in the regularly constructed sermon, this fixedness of the amount of pastoral visiting will prevent him from neglecting his sermons. Having performed the labour in the homes of the people, he will return to his study and his books. In the second place, if his tendency is in the opposite direction, he will be very much helped by systematizing that part of clerical duty to which he is most disinclined. There is no way so sure to overcome the indisposition of a reserved or a studious man towards direct personal conversation with individuals as working according to a plan. He may enter upon the discharge of the unwelcome service from a sense of duty, but, before long, he begins to work with spontaneity and enjoyment. There is no fact in the Christian experience better established than that the faithful performance of labour, from conscience, ends in its being performed with relish and pleasure. Conscience is finally wrought into the will in a vital synthesis. Law, in the end, becomes an impulse, instead of a commandment.

In systematizing this part of his work, the clergyman should fix a day for its performance. Let it uniformly be done on the same day of the week, and in the same part of the day. Again, he should pass around his entire parish within a certain time. This will make it necessary to visit his people by districts or neighbourhoods ; and unless there be a special reason for it, he should not visit in the same locality again until he has come round to it in his full circuit. This course will compel the parishioner, should there be need of a special visit, as in case of sickness, religious anxiety, or affliction, to send for him, in obedience to the apostolic direction, ' Is any sick among you ? let him call for the elders of the Church.'

In regard to the day of the week to be selected by the pastor for this work, the nearer it is to the middle of it the better. This is the time when his own physical strength is most recruited from the labours of the Sabbath, and when he will be most inclined to leave his study to mingle with his people. It is also the time when the congregation most need to have their attention recalled to spiritualities, as the mid-point between two Sabbaths. With regard to the length of time to be spent, much depends upon the extent of the parish, and the number of the people. In a parish of ordinary size, one afternoon every week, especially if the evening ensuing be devoted to preaching in the district or neighbourhood, is sufficient, provided the pastor makes his visits in the manner which we shall describe under another head. This may seem a short time to devote to parochial visiting ; but if it be systematically and regularly devoted, it is longer than it looks. As in a previous chapter we remarked that even five hours of severe close study will accomplish a great deal in the way of intellectual culture and sermonizing in the course of years, so we shall find that a half day in each week will accomplish much in the way of parochial labour in the lapse of time. The clergyman, like every other man, needs to pay special attention to the particulars of system and uniformity in action. Small spaces of time become ample and great by being regularly and faithfully employed. It is because time is wasted so regularly and uniformly, and not because it is wasted in such large amounts at once, that so much of human life runs to waste. Every one is familiar with the story of the author who composed a voluminous work in the course of his life, by merely devoting to it the five or ten minutes which he found he must *uniformly* wait for his dinner after having been called.

Besides these advantages upon the side of the clergyman in systematic visiting, there are others upon the side of the congregation. They will be pleased with their pastor's business-like method. They will copy his example, and become a more punctual and systematic people, both secularly and religiously. They will notice that their pastor is a man who lays out his work, and, what is more, does it, and, what is still more, does it thoroughly. They will respect him for it. They will not crowd him and urge him, as they will a minister who has no system, and who is therefore always lagging in his work. They will not volunteer advice to him, for they will perceive that he does not need any. And if a parishioner, with more self-confidence than self-knowledge, should take the clergyman to task, and suggest that more pastoral visits would be acceptable, or that fewer would suffice, the systematic pastor can say to him, ' The work is laid out for the year ; the campaign is begun, and going on.'

Again, by this method, the clergyman will avoid all appearance of partiality. One prolific source of difficulty between pastor and people in this age and country, lies in the suspiciousness of a portion of the people. All men are free and equal, but some are more tormented by the consciousness than others. This part of society are afraid that their merits are not sufficiently recognised, and are constantly watching to see if others are not esteemed more highly than themselves. A true republican feeling is dignified and unsuspicious ; but vulgar democracy impliedly acknowledges its desert of neglect, by continually apprehending that it is neglected. This spirit leads to rivalries and jealousies among a people, and the pastor needs great tact and judgment in managing it. There is no better way of dealing with this temper, if it exists, than to visit a parish systematically. Each family then takes its turn. No person is neglected, and no person can claim more than the prearranged and predetermined amount of attention, except for special reasons. The pastor, upon this plan, moves around among his whole people, a faithful, systematic, and impartial man. He is no respecter of persons. He goes to converse with the members of his flock upon the concerns of their soul, each in his turn. He sees no difference between them, except moral and spiritual difference. If he takes a deeper interest, for the time being, in one of his parishioners, than he does in the rest of them, it is only because the one sinner that repents causes more joy than the ninety and nine just persons who need no repentance. The spiritual condition of this person distinguishes him from the thoughtless and indifferent mass, and the pastor would rejoice if his whole parish might become an object of equally distinguished attention, for the same reason.

2. Secondly, the clergyman should visit his congregation *professionally.* The term is employed here in its technical signification. When he performs strictly parochial labour,

let him visit as a clergyman, and go into a house upon a purely and wholly religious errand. Much time is wasted by the pastor in merely secular, social intercourse, even when going the rounds of his parish. Ostensibly, he is about the business of his profession, the care of souls ; but really he is merely acting the part of a courteous and polite gentleman. Even if he gives the subject of religion some attention, it is only at the close of his interview, after secular topics have been discussed. It may be that he shrinks from a direct address to an individual upon the concerns of his soul, and therefore, as he thinks, prepares the way, that he may broach the difficult subject indirectly. He enters into a general and miscellaneous conversation ; and if he comes to the subject of religion at all, it is only late, and after the energy and briskness of the conversation have flagged. Moreover, the person to be addressed is quick to detect this shrinking upon the part of his pastor, and if really unwilling to be spoken to upon the subject of religion, will adroitly lead the conversation away into other directions. The man who is averse to religious con- versation, and who, therefore, specially needs to be directly and plainly addressed, is the last person to be surprised into such a conversation. His eyes are wide open, and the only true way for the pastor, when the proper time for it has come, and the pastoral visit is made, is to look him in the eye, and speak directly and affectionately upon the most momentous of all subjects.

That he may visit in this professional manner, the pastor should have an understanding to this effect with his people. In the very opening of his ministry, let him preach a ser-

mon upon the subject of parochial labour, explaining the
nature and purpose of this part of the clergyman's duty,
and preparing the minds of his people for a strictly professional performance of it.   Then they will expect nothing
but religious conversation when a pastoral visit is made,
and will be ready for it.   Appreciating the fidelity of
their minister, they will be at pains to meet him at their
homes.   A clergyman who is thus systematic and faithful, soon accustoms his congregation to his own good
way of performing duty, so that they not only adjust
themselves to his exact and thorough methods, but come
to like them.

This is by far the most successful mode of reaching the
individual conscience in direct religious conversation.   We
have already alluded to the fact that the endeavour to
introduce the subject of religion indirectly and imperceptibly commonly fails, because of the adroitness of the unwilling person addressed.   He is quick to detect the
shrinking of the clergyman from the performance of the
most difficult part of ministerial duty; and though it may
or may not result from a sensitive nature, he is very apt to
impute it to a false shame.   The consequence is, that the
clergyman loses much of his weight of authority and
influence in the eyes of the parishioner, and never gains
the ascendency over him to which he is entitled by his
profession and calling, because he does not act up to its
privileges and prerogatives.

When, therefore, a parochial call is made, let the pastor
plunge *in medias sacras res.*   Let him not attempt to
bridge over the chasm between secularities and spirituali-

ties, but let him leap over. He has a right to do so, because it is understood between the parties what particular subject it is that has brought him into the household. He courteously concedes a few words to ordinary interests; but when this concession is made, he proceeds to the proper business of the occasion. This method brings the subject of the soul and its needs before the mind of a parishioner with a formal authority, that causes him to realize that it is no merely passing and secondary topic. The clergyman does not admit that religion may be introduced sidewise to his attention. He has come upon purpose to direct his thoughts to this great concern. And this method relieves both parties from embarrassment or constraint. For the parishioner is entirely free in the matter. He is not compelled to be a party to the arrangement which brings the clergyman upon a purely religious errand to himself and to his household. But if he does voluntarily admit him to personal conversation in the capacity of a spiritual adviser, then he is obligated to let him do his work faithfully and well. And even the worldly man is better pleased with this thorough professional dealing than might be supposed at first sight. Even if, owing to the hardness of the heart and the intensity of the worldliness, the pastor makes no other impression, he will show beyond dispute that he is an earnest and sincere watcher for souls, and fisher of men. The parishioner will say to himself, ' My pastor understands his work, and performs it with fidelity; it will not be his fault if I continue irreligious.' It is certain that this spiritual earnestness and love for the human soul, when thus organized into a regular plan of operations, and systematized into regular uniformity, will produce results. Thoughtless men, finding their pastor upon their trail, coming into their families, and to themselves personally, with a plain and affectionate address upon the subject of religion, and nothing else, once in every year or half-year, will begin to think of what it all means. They will find themselves in a network. They will see that they are caught in a process. Their pastor has laid out his work ahead for many long years; and if he lives, and they live, they know that the regular motion of the globe will bring him round to them once in so often. They will come to some conclusion. They will either submit, and subject themselves to these uniform and persistent influences, or else they will get clear of them altogether. In ninty-nine cases out of a hundred they will do the former thing, and thus the pastor will be instrumental, by his determined parochial fidelity, in bringing into the Church a great number who would otherwise go through life almost Christians, and die unregenerate.

We have advised a systematic visitation of the parish by districts or neighbourhoods. In case the clergyman is settled among an agricultural population, widely scattered, he will find this much the easiest and surest way to communicate with the whole body of his people. His parish is his diocese, and he is its bishop. Let him make his visitations through the whole length and breadth of it with the same system and regularity with which the prelatical bishop makes his annual visitation. The pastor should also imitate the method of the prelate in another respect, and preach in these districts in connection with his pastoral calls. If he is settled in a city or town, where the main body of the congregation are within a short distance of the church edifice, his public discourses must be in one place. But if his lot has been cast among an agricultural people, who are scattered (and this is the kind of parish in which the majority of clergymen are appointed to labour), he should preach a free, extemporaneous discourse in the evening of the day of his visitation. Having gone from house to house in the manner that has been described, let him wind up the earnest work of pastoral visiting for the week with a plain and glowing address to the families of the district, assembled at an appointed place. He will find it a most genial and exhilarating service upon his own part, and a most interesting and profitable one upon the part of the people. Enforcing in a common assemblage all that he has said in the families and to the individuals, he will clinch the nails which he has been driving.

Pastoral visiting, conducted in the manner described, is a very efficient aid to the public preaching of the Sabbath and the sanctuary. The parochial call, combined with the free, extemporaneous lecture, corroborates the sermon. The pastor of this true stamp is the complement of the preacher. He supplies and fills out what is lacking, in the strictly public character and functions of the sacred orator. Having, upon the Sabbath, and in the Christian temple, logically and elaborately enunciated the principles of the oracles of God, he comes down from the pulpit, and on the week-day goes into the private house, and applies the truth to the individual. The clergyman is in this way a complete man, and does a complete work.   He is both a preacher and a pastor.

If there were space, it would be natural here to enlarge upon the reciprocal relations and influences of these two clerical functions, particularly with reference to sermonizing.   It is obvious that such a regular and systematic intercourse with his congregation will fill the mind of the clergyman with subjects for sermons, with plans and methods of treating them, and with trains of reflection. Nothing so kindles and enriches the orator's mind as living intercourse with individual persons.   A preacher who is in the habit of conversing with all grades of society, and becomes acquainted with the great varieties in the Christian experience and the sinful experience, will be an exuberant and overflowing sermonizer.   Full of matter, and full of animation, he will vitalize every subject he discusses, no matter how trite it may have become in the minds of others.   Passing through the parched valley of Baca, he will make it a well.   He will rain upon the driest tract, and the rain will fill the pools.

The systematic and professional manner of visiting his congregation recommends itself to the clergyman, upon the ground of its great practical usefulness.   It is a very sure means of producing conversions and revivals.   So far as human agency is concerned, it seems to be the divinely appointed method of bringing the experience of individuals to that crisis which results in actual conversion.   The public preaching of the Sabbath and the sanctuary is formal, logical, and oratorical.   It ought to be so.   Its general purpose, like that of all eloquence, is to instruct

the mind, with a view to move the affections and actuate
the will. But this practical effect of sacred eloquence does
not, commonly, occur immediately, and at the close of the
discourse. It is indeed true that the sermon is sometimes
instrumental in conversion, upon the spot, in the house of
God. But this is a rare case. While the secular orator,
the jurist, or the statesman sees the effect of his eloquence
in the verdict or the vote given immediately, the sacred
orator does not ordinarily see the practical effect of his
eloquence until after many days, it may be months or
years. Hence the need of following up the sermon with
the pastoral visit. Hence the pastor must tread close
upon the heels of the preacher.

Preaching upon the Sabbath, if it is plain and powerful,
produces an impression, which, if it could only be perpetu-
ated, would result in a change of character and conduct.
But, occurring at intervals of a week, the effect of sermons
is too often evanescent, unless it is seconded by other
agencies. Hence the disposition, in some periods and
localities, to protracted sermonizing, to a series of public
addresses to the popular mind,—a method, which, if judi-
ciously employed by the pastor, aided by his ministerial
brethren rather than by an evangelist, is often productive
of great and good results. Without in the least disparaging this mode of promoting conversions and revivals, and
believing that it is perfectly legitimate and safe to employ
it whenever the craving for additional preaching upon the
part of the people renders it necessary, we yet insist that
systematic pastoral visiting is the principal means to be
relied upon by the ministry, in order to bring individual

z

men to a crisis and a decision.   Whenever it has been
faithfully employed, this part of the clergyman's service
has been rich in fruits; and it is an evil day for the
Church when it is neglected, and more public and mechanical means are adopted in the place of it.   Addressing
parishioners in person, inquiring into their state of mind,
telling them plainly and affectionately what their prospects
for eternity really are, and what they need in order to
salvation, entreating them not to stifle convictions, urging
home the truths that have impressed them upon the Sabbath,—doing this work is the surest way to bring matters
to an issue with the impenitent.   If the clergyman would
see what may be accomplished by pastoral work, let him
read Baxter's account of his labours at Kidderminster.
Few ministers have so large a charge as he had, and few
are called to do so much of this service.   But the same
proportionate laboriousness will produce the same proportionate results.   When Baxter first went to Kidderminster, he says, ' There was about one family in a street
that worshipped God, and called on His name ; and when
he came away, there were some streets where there was
not more than one family on the side of a street that did
not do so, and that did not, in professing serious godliness,
give him hopes of their sincerity.'   From his own account,
this was, in a great measure, the consequence of following
his people to their homes, and there enforcing the lessons
of the Sabbath and the sanctuary, catechising the families,
and conversing with individuals.   The pastor can do nothing
more serviceable to his own ministerial power and influence
than to study that account which Baxter gives of his labours

as a pastor,[1] to set up Baxter's zeal and earnestness as a model, to adjust Baxter's plan and method of operations to the state of modern society, and then to make full proof . of this part of his ministry.

[1] Compare also the very interesting narrative given of Chalmers' parochial work at Glasgow.   Hanna, *Life of Chalmers,* vol. ii. ch. vi.

CHAPTER VI.

CATECHISING.

THE catechising of the children and youth in a congregation is a theme that deserves to be discussed with the comprehensiveness and precision of a systematic treatise. In the whole range of topics in Pastoral Theology, there is not one that has stronger claims upon the attention of the clergyman than the doctrinal instruction of the rising generation. Within the half century, catechising has fallen greatly into disuse. Creeds themselves have been more undervalued than, in some periods, they have been over-estimated. The consequence is, that the experience of the Church has outrun its knowledge. There are many undoubtedly experimental Christians who are unable to define the truths of Christianity, either singly or in their connections in the system. They feel more than they reflect, and more than they can state. There is danger in this state of things. The Church cannot advance, it cannot even maintain itself upon its present position, by this theory and method of religious culture. Experimental religion, without doctrinal knowledge, must deteriorate. Religious feeling will become more superficial, religious zeal more insincere, and religious action more fitful and selfish, if the mind of the Church is not obtaining clear and self-existent conceptions of religious truth. A dead orthodoxy is an evil, and so is an ignorant pietism. But there is no necessity for either. Feeling and cognition are not antagonistic, but exist together in the most perfect Being. And only as they co-exist in the renewed mind is there the highest type of Christian life. Without, however, dwelling upon this part of the subject, we proceed to recommend the practice of catechising children and youth, by considering its influence, first upon the *clergyman* himself, and secondly upon the *people*.

1. The habit of imparting catechetical instruction developes the power of lucid and precise statement. The clergyman's theological knowledge is liable to be imperfect in respect to the subtler and sharper distinctions in the Christian system. He apprehends the doctrines in their general scope and drift, but does not draw that thin hair-line which marks them off from each other. Some very bitter controversies have arisen from the fact that the one party distinguished interior differences, used language with scientific exactness, and stuck to terms while the other party recognised no differences but external and obvious ones, and employed a loose phraseology, and even this with no rigorous uniformity.

There is something in the endeavour to convey doctrinal instruction to the human mind, especially when it is in the forming period, that is highly adapted to promote discrimination and clearness. The catechising pastor does not, that is, he should not, confine himself to merely putting the questions and hearing the answers. After the work of reciting is through, he then explains to the body

of youth gathered before him the meaning of the phraseology they have learned, and of the truths they have committed to memory. To do this well and plainly, so that
children and youth may understand, will draw upon the
clergyman's nicest discrimination, the choicest portion of
his vocabulary, and his most pertinent illustrations. It is
often asserted that it is impossible for children to understand the creed,—that the doctrines of justification, sanctification, and election are too strong meat for babes. The
difficulty lies rather in the teacher than in the capacity of
the pupil, or in the intrinsic nature of the doctrine. He
has only a vague and general apprehension of revealed
truth, and has never trained himself to make luminous
and exact statements of it. Any clergyman who is master
of Christian theology, and who thoroughly understands the
creed and catechism, will be able to make the youth of his
congregation understand it also, as others have done before
him. And this endeavour will bring out into clear and
definite forms of statement those great ideas and truths of
Christianity, which lie large but vague in too many minds.
That clergyman who is in the habit of catechising will
know exactly what his own creed is, and can phrase it
in language and illustrations intelligible to children and
youth.

2. A second effect of catechising upon the clergyman, is
to render his views in theology decided. The importance
of decision in theological opinions was remarked upon in
a previous chapter, and it was affirmed that the study of
creeds is one of the best means of acquiring it. He who
is able to adopt a creed cordially because he perceives and

feels its intrinsic truthfulness, will be a positive man. It is plain, therefore, that all this work of teaching a creed tends to determination and firmness of theological character. Catechising is, in reality, the intensely practical study of systematic theology, in the endeavour to transmute the dogmas of religion into the thoughts and feelings of the youthful mind. As man becomes a little child in order to enter the kingdom of truth, so in this process the kingdom of truth becomes a little child. The creed is incarnated in the little children. While imparting this catechetical instruction, therefore, the clergyman becomes more profoundly certain of the truth of Christianity. He finds it more and more impossible to doubt it. He grows more and more positive in his views and affirmations, and gradually acquires that scriptural boldness which causes him to speak with authority. Finding a response to the evangelical system in the heart and mind of childhood and youth, and hearing the testimony of the most sincere and unsophisticated period of human life respecting it, the catechising clergyman matures into the most undoubting and impregnable of men.

3. A third effect of catechising upon the clergyman, is to assure him of the harmony of revelation and reason. It may at first sight seem strange to recommend the doctrinal instruction of children and youth as a means of attaining to the true philosophy of religion. Nothing is more common in the sceptic, than to speak of the creeds of the Christian Church as at the very farthest remove from rationality. He is generally a little more willing to allow that the Scriptures are reconcilable with reason, than that

the theological system which an Augustine or a Calvin derived from them, is.   But he has a design in this.   The Calvinistic creed is definite.   It is impossible to make it teach more than one system.   There is no dispute, except among disingenuous men, in respect to what Calvinism really is.   The Bible, on the other hand, is not a creed or a system, though it contains one.   But what this system actually is, is the point in regard to which Churches and theologians are disputing; and hence the sceptic is more ready to concede the general rationality of the Bible than he is that of a particular system, like the Calvinistic for example, because he can immediately append to his admission respecting the Scriptures the qualifying remark, that it is yet an open question what the Scriptures really teach. This addition is a saving clause for him and his sceptical purposes.   It has, moreover, passed over into the religious world in the form of a feeling; and hence we sometimes hear good men disparaging the creed, even the creed of their own Church, and advising, in a controversy with the infidel, to have as little as possible to do with doctrinal theology.

There never was a greater error than this; for what is a creed but a generalization from the Scriptures ?   The Westminster symbol, for example, is the scientific substance of revelation, in the view of the divines of the Westminster Assembly.   That Assembly was composed of the most learned and reflecting men of the Church of Christ in England at that time.   It embodied the philosophic mind of the Church in that country and century. If there was no scientific talent in the Westminster

Assembly, then there was none in England. And that assembly aimed to give to the Churches that had called them together a systematic statement of the contents of revelation, or, in other words, a philosophical exhibition of the Scriptures in a creed. It was their purpose. to present the fundamental truths of Christianity, not in a popular, oratorical manner, but in a self-consistent and compact form that should commend itself to the reason and judgment of mankind. If, therefore, there be any rationality in the Christian religion, any philosophy of Christianity, it is most natural to seek for it in the carefully constructed symbol; and hence the clergyman, instead of conceding to the infidel that the catechism is indefensible at the bar of reason, ought to refuse the concession instantaneously and always, and to join issue with him and try the point. In so doing, he will certainly have one advantage which we have already hinted at, namely, the distinctness and definiteness of the creed ; and if the position which we have taken to be correct, that the creed is the philosophical analysis of the contents of revelation by the philosophic mind of the Church, he will have the still further advantage of the rationality of the creed.

Hence we affirm, that the habit of studying the catechism, in order to teach it to youthful minds, conduces to the clergyman's perception of the unity of reason and religion.[1] The longer he studies and teaches the creed,

[1] It is a fact of history, that the scientific theology of the Church took its first beginnings in the endeavour to impart an advanced knowledge of Christianity to the more cultivated catechumens at Alexandria. Compare Guericke, *Church History*, § 59.

the more unassailable does his conviction become of its absolute rationality. He finds it commending itself to the frank and unsophisticated reason of the young. He sees the ingenuous mind responding to its statements concerning God and man, with that artless spontaneousness which is the strongest of evidences for the truth. 'It is the most beautiful mark of the excellency of a doctrine,' says Herder, 'that it instructs a child.' That which is welcomed by the open, unbiassed nature of childhood, is certainly true; for if there be any *pure* reason, as Kant phrases it, among mankind, it is in children and youth. During this period in human life, reason shows itself in an instinctive, recipient, and docile form, and responds more immediately and unhesitatingly to the voice of truth than at an after period, when it has become better acquainted with error, and more or less sophisticated and blunted by it. There may be a deeper meaning than appears upon the face of our Saviour's words, 'Except ye receive the kingdom of heaven as little children, ye shall not enter therein.' He may have also taught a lesson to the philosopher, and have meant to say, in addition to what we commonly understand by these words, 'Except ye open your rational nature to the truth with that freedom from prejudice and that docile recipiency which marks the child, ye can never apprehend it.'

1. Passing to the second division of the subject—namely, the influence of catechising upon the congregation—we remark, in the first place, that it results in the indoctrination of the adults. We do not now refer to adults who were once the children and youth of a pastor's charge, but

to such as have more recently come under a clergyman's ministry. In a long pastorate, the adult population becomes indoctrinated, as a matter of course, in case the pastor begins to catechise at the opening of his ministry. But besides this, the practice of catechising tends to the indirect spread of doctrinal knowledge among those who are not the immediate objects of its influence. Uncatechised parents are unconsciously affected by their catechised children. Uncatechised adults imperceptibly learn to set a juster estimate upon the systematic doctrines of Christianity, through their intercourse with catechised youth. The creed of the Church is more respected among the congregation, in case it is taught and explained to the children and youth. The pastor who is faithful in the performance of this' duty, will see adults coming into the catechetical exercise as listeners. Parents whose early religious education was neglected, will accompany their children, not from mere curiosity, but from a desire to obtain a knowledge of the Word of God, which they value in their children, and of which they are conscious of being too destitute themselves. In these and other ways, doctrinal knowledge will radiate from the class of catechumens into the whole body of an adult population whose catechetical education was neglected, both by their parents and their minister.

2. Secondly, catechising the youth of a parish protects them against infidelity and spurious philosophy. A well-indoctrinated person can state the fundamental truths of Christianity in exact phraseology, can specify their connections in a system, and their relations to each other, can quote the texts of Scripture which prove them, and, in

proportion as his pastor has been thorough with him as a catechumen, can maintain and defend them in an argument with an opposer. One thus disciplined is preoccupied, forewarned, and forearmed. The sceptic cannot, as he can and does in case he is arguing with the uninstructed, misstate and caricature the truth. The catechumen will set him right, by citing to him the well-weighed and precise phraseology of the creed; and this rectification in the outset of an incorrect statement always gravels the infidel, whether his misstatement originates in a real or a pretended ignorance. A well-trained youth, in a contest with an ordinary sceptic, soon ceases to act upon the defensive. The unbeliever soon discovers that he is dealing ·with a mind that knows where it is, and what it is about, and is willing to give over a contest which he began, not from any love of the truth, or any desire of finding it, but solely from a mischievous and really malignant wish to undermine the religious belief of an ingenious youth.

Again, there is no preservative against philosophy, falsely so called, so effectual as a doctrinal education. The youth, and especially the reading and literary youth, of a congregation, are liable to be misled by spurious science, because it is pretentious and assuming. They have not yet reached ' the years which bring the philosophic mind,'—to employ the phrase of Wordsworth. The genuine philosophic spirit is a thing of slow growth. The truly scientific mind adopts its philosophy, which is no other than its method of looking at things with great circumspection, judgment, and deliberation. The immature understanding is exposed to great mistakes in the formation and adoption of opinions in philosophy; and hence the great influence which a showy, pretentious, and utterly unscientific scheme sometimes exerts over the young men of a nation or an age. The counterfeit science comes up before the youthful intellect, like Comus to the Lady, with an insolence that is never seen in genuine philosophy, and attempts to carry it by rudely bearing down upon it. It is both confident and contemptuous in its tone, and too often, like the arrogant and impudent adventurer in general society, succeeds in imposing upon the unpractised and untaught.

But he who has received, from the mind of a learned and thoughtful clergyman, a thorough grounding in the principles and truths of Christianity, is the last one to be taken captive by a false system of speculation. He sees through it, and is not deceived by its pretentions. He is not thus to be irresistibly borne down by its imposing appearance. Socrates is represented by Plato as remarking, that nothing so speedily disposes of a showy and sounding system, like that of the Sophists, as a cool and deliberate examination of it. A big bell, he says, booms out a great noise; but place only one single finger *firmly* upon the bell, and the sound which is going out into all the earth will stop. A youth who understands the scheme of Christianity, and has been made deliberative and reflecting by the catechism, will examine a pretentious system before he adopts it, and especially before he surrenders his religious belief for the sake of adopting it.

In the present condition of society, there is great need of catechetical instruction, in order to protect the rising generation from infidelity in the form of false philosophy.

Unbelief does not now adopt the open, and comparatively manly, method of the last century. The English deists did not pretend to be Christians, but attacked Christianity with all their force. The French infidels did the same, only with more virulence and hatred. But the infidel of the present day claims to be only a more philosophic and advanced Christian. Scepticism now represents itself as the refinement and inmost essence of Christianity. The infidel schools in England and America deny the charge of unbelief. They affirm that they are themselves the highest of believers, and have a mission to lift up the general mass of Christians to a higher, even the highest, religious position. Their system does not contain so much truth as that of the English deists, neither is it as consistently constructed, nor as clearly expressed ; but instead of allowing it to pass for what it is, these pantheistic and materializing sceptics attempt to palm it off as the permanent residuum of truth, after the biblical and ecclesiastical elements have been purged out as dross.

The ministry cannot protect the cultivated youth of their care from these artifices of unbelief, by decrying philosophy in the abstract. This only renders them suspicious, and strengthens their doubts, if they have any, respecting the rationality and philosophic necessity of the Christian faith. A clergyman should never vilify a legitimate department of human knowledge; and philosophy is such. His true method is to guide the inquiring mind into the very science of Christianity as it is presented in the creed, and thereby enable it to see, beyond dispute, that the truths of revelation are excellent in themselves and in their influence; that they exhibit worthy views of the divine character,—representations of the holiness, justice, mercy, wisdom, truth, and power of God that are intuitively rational; that in respect to man's character (a point which usually troubles the sceptic, for he is more solicitous about imputations upon man than upon God), the statements in the catechism are questions of fact, and may be verified by every man's consciousness;—let the clergyman, in brief, fill the mind of the catechumen with the conviction that the Christian system, as laid down in the doctrinal standards, is the absolute and ultimate religion for man, and he may then leave him to deal with infidelity and spurious philosophy by himself. Instead of being made ashamed of Christianity, and of his Christian education and belief, by the tone of the scorner, the pastor himself may perhaps have to guard his pupil against a too intense contempt for the shallowness of scepticism, and remind him, that he that thinketh he standeth, must take heed lest he fall. It is certain, that if the rising generation could only receive such a catechetical and doctrinal education as we are describing from the pastorate of the land, infidelity and false philosophy would find it difficult to draw breath in such a pure *intellectual* atmosphere as would exist for the next fifty years, to say nothing of the moral and religious atmosphere that would be generated.

3. A third effect of catechetical instruction upon the congregation, is to promote a better understanding of the Word of God. The youth of this country during the last half century have committed much of the Bible to memory.

The Sabbath-school has made the present generation of both parents and children familiar with the contents of Revelation; but we are inclined to think that this mass of material is somewhat lacking in system and organization. It is not sufficient to learn by rote, independent passages and isolated texts of Scripture; they ought to be made to teach some truth and establish some doctrine, and ultimately be systematized into a body of theology. It is an error to study the Bible without generalizing its teachings, and acquiring some conception of it as a whole. Single unconnected texts are oftentimes dangerous half-truths, or positive untruths. Nothing but the power and impression of isolated passages of Scripture keeps Universalism in existence. The moment that that denomination shall begin to understand and interpret the contents of the Bible as a self-consistent *whole*, it will begin to die. 'Texts of Scripture,' says Donne, 'are like the hairs in a horse's tail. Unite them, and they concur in one root of strength and beauty; but take them separately, and they can be used only as snares and springs to catch woodcocks.'

The pastor should therefore combine catechetical with Sabbath-school instruction. While he enlists the active zeal of his best educated parishioners in the Sabbath-school, he should show his own deep interest in this excellent institution, by personally generalizing its teachings in the catechetical exercise, and thereby putting the crown upon its influence. The pastor who thus completes the work of the Sabbath-school teacher, will raise up a generation of exceedingly intelligent biblical scholars. It was once said of a very learned, and at the same time very logical jurist, that his learning was continually passing from his memory into his judgment. His acquisitions were not merely passively held, but were used for the argumentative purposes of his profession. In like manner, the indoctrination of Sabbath-school scholars causes the contents of the memory to pass over into the reason and the judgment, and makes all the texts and passages that have been learned subservient to an intelligent and self-consistent religious belief. Indeed, to borrow an illustration from the Kantean philosophy, the catechism does with the memorized contents of Scripture, what the understanding, by its categories, does with the passive contents of the sense. It reduces the scattered and manifold elements to compactness and unity, and converts the large and distracting variety of items into distinct forms and clear conceptions, so that the mind can take this great number of particulars all in at once, and feel their single and combined impression. The catechism enables the pupil to feel the force of the whole Bible, and of the Bible as a whole.

4. A fourth effect of catechising is to render the youth of a congregation more intelligent hearers of preaching. One reason why preaching is uninteresting to youth, is the fact that they carry no clue to it in their minds. They do not see any very close connection between the sermon and anything within themselves. No one can be interested in a discourse unless he perceives the drift and bearing of it;[1] and in order to this, he must carry within himself

[1] This supposes, of course, that the sermon has a drift and bearing. In some quarters, however, this unity and self-consistence is thought to be a

some kind of internal correspondent to it. Now, the mental correspondent to an excellent sermon is an excellent scheme of Christian doctrine in the mind of the hearer. When this exists, the sermon has a reference, and an easy reference; and the mind possesses a key that unlocks it— a clue or magic thread which leads it along through the whole performance. This is the reason why clergymen are better auditors, generally, than laymen. They have more of the inward correspondent to the sermon—more knowledge of the Christian system. It is plain, therefore, that just in proportion as the pastor indoctrinates the youth of his charge, he is making good auditors for himself. He will find the youth, who is generally too little interested in preaching, looking up to the pulpit with as keen an eye as any of his hearers, and with a more tender and susceptible heart.

5. A fifth effect of catechising is to induce seriousness among the youthful part of the congregation. There is such a correspondency between truth and the reasonable soul of man, that reflection naturally results in a grave temper. This is seen even in the sphere of secular know-

---

defect in sacred eloquence. For example, a Dogberry, in a recent number of a popular monthly magazine, represents a certain pulpit celebrity as having introduced a new era in sermonizing, by showing how to deliver discourses that 'Edwards and Voltaire, Whitefield and Thomas Paine, would heartily and equally enjoy!' It is impossible, since the invention of printing, and with the freedom and cheapness of the press, to prevent the shoemaker from going beyond his last. But such judgments of a mere *littérateur* upon a subject like pulpit eloquence, which requires scientific training and professional culture, and at least a little faith in the Christian religion, in order to its comprehension, are as worthless as they would be in regard to the calculus itself.

ledge. The men of science—the studious mathematician, the curious and analysing chemist, the gazing astronomer —are seriously disposed. Study casts a shadow. This is still more true in the province of morals and religion. He who meditates upon divine truth may not be so changed by it as to become a new creature in disposition and feeling, but he will be sobered by it. He has no option. His rational mind was created to be influenced by the great truths of God and eternity, and it is true to its construction to the extent of being made serious, though not necessarily to the extent of being made holy. Just so far, consequently, as a pastor brings the doctrines of Christianity to bear upon the youthful mind, does he solemnize it. For they are the most serious of all themes of reflection, and throw a deeper shadow over a frivolous and volatile spirit than all other truths; and this is one reason why the worldly and the gay shun them, as they do the house of mourning and the graveyard. The pastor can take no course so effectual against that giddy levity which so infects the younger portion of society, as to imbue it with evangelical ideas. Such knowledge elevates the mind, and this mental elevation is opposed to the emptiness and littleness of fashionable life. If an intellectual person does not avoid the ballroom from any higher motive, he is very apt to, from the lower motive of self-respect. He is too literary to dance. The same feeling, in kind, that keeps the philosopher and the thoughtful man of science from the rounds of fashionable life, keeps him from them. In this manner, the high religious education which we are recommending makes its power felt through that younger portion of the community

which so often gives tone to society, and prepares the way
for the more decisive and actually converting effects of
divine truth.

6. And this suggests, as the sixth effect of catechising,
that it results in frequent conversions. The Spirit of God
is the Spirit of truth. Hence that mind which is saturated
with the teachings of revelation, contains something with
which the divine energy can work. It is indeed true that
the indoctrinated natural man is as really averse to God
and holiness as the unindoctrinated. The carnal will is
the same, whether within the pale of Christendom or out
of it, and the necessity of divine influences, in order to its
renewal, is as great in one instance as the other. But he
who has acquired a clear theoretical apprehension of the
doctrines of Christianity, is much more likely to be the
subject of special and efficacious grace than is the pagan
or the uninstructed nominal Christian. There may be as
much perversity and obstinacy of will as worldly and sinful affections in the catechised as in the uncatechised
youth, but there is also an amount of truth in the mind of
the former which is not in the latter. This truth is God's
truth. God the Spirit finds his own Word congruous with
his own agency, and therefore acts with it and by it. The
Holy Ghost, like the Redeemer, 'comes to his own,' and
'his own' are the doctrines of revelation. Hence, conversions may be expected with more frequency among an
indoctrinated than among an unindoctrinated population.
God honours his own revelation. The human mind is not
worthy of honour from the Eternal, but the truth lodged
in it is worthy; and God says to the preacher, as He did

to the children of Israel, ' It is not for your sake, but for my truth's sake and my name's sake, that I bestow the blessing.'

7. A seventh and final effect of catechising is, that it results in genuine conversions. Knowledge is favourable to thoroughness in mental exercises generally. The surest way to prevent hypocrisy or self-deception, is to cause the light of truth to shine into the mind. Give a youth or a man correct conceptions of the holiness of God, and the spirituality and extent of the divine law, and you take the most direct means of preventing a spurious religious experience. He may not come to a genuine experience, but he will not be liable to rest in a false one. He may not become a Christian, but neither will he rank himself with Christians. His orthodox head will be likely to keep him out of the visible Church, until he is really fit to join it. But besides this negative effect, catechising tends directly to a deep and wide religious experience. Christian character matures rapidly, when the mind is leavened with evangelical truth ; and it is developed symmetrically, because the fundamental doctrines have been studied in their connections in a system. These co-ordinated truths regulate and shape the experience, so that one grace or quality is not neglected for the sake of another. The Christian character is developed and compacted by that which every doctrine supplies, making increase of the whole in true and beautiful proportions.

These, then, are the principal reasons why the practice of catechising children and youth should be repristinated in the American Churches. It is the hope, and perhaps

somewhat too much the boast, that the American Republic
is called to perform a great work in the evangelization of
the globe. It will not be either inclined or able to do
this, unless it is itself a deeply thoughtful and profoundly
religious nation. It would be a most hopeful indication
if the intense interest which the American feels in politics
could be transferred to theology, and that wide acquaintance
with government which marks him might be equalled and
exceeded by his knowledge of the purposes and plans of
God in redemption. Would that the laws and principles,
the ideas and doctrines, of the Christian religion, might be
for the new power that is rising in the West, what the
civil law and the political constitution were for imperial
Rome in the East! 'The Romans, in their best days, made
every schoolboy learn by heart the Twelve Tables; and the
Twelve Tables were the catechism of Roman public and
private law, of their constitution, and of the proud *jus
Quiritium* that led the Roman citizen to pronounce so
confidently as a *vox et invocatio*, his *civis Romanus sum*, in
the most distant corners of the land, and which the captive
apostle collectedly asserted twice before the provincial
officers. Cicero says that, when he was a boy, he learned
the Twelve Tables *ut carmen necessarium*, like an indispensable formulary, a political breviary, and deplores that
at the time when he was composing his treatise on the
Laws, in which he mentions the fact, the practice was
falling into disuse.'[1] Such ought to be the interest taken
in the Christian faith by a people like the American, the
foundations of whose government were laid in the truths

[1] Lieber, ' Inaugural Discourse before Columbia College.'

of revelation, and all of whose early history was religious. Upon the clergy it mainly depends whether systematic religion or systematic infidelity shall be the future *carmen necessarium* of the multiplying millions on this continent. Sir Joshua Reynolds, in the last of his Lectures before the Royal Academy, thus expresses his sense of the importance of the study of the works and spirit of the mightiest and greatest of artists : ' I should desire that the last words which I should pronounce in this Academy, and from this place, might be the name of Michael Angelo.' In closing these brief chapters upon Pastoral Theology, we feel deeply that there is not a topic of greater importance than this subject of catechising; and the last words we should desire to address to a young clergyman, as he is going forth to his life-long labour, would be an exhortation to make full proof of that part of his ministry to which belongs the indoctrination of the rising generation in the truths and principles of the Christian religion.

THE END.

SGCB Classic Reprints Series

A History of Preaching by Edwin C. Dargan is a two volume set that covers the history of preaching from AD 70 - 1900. A masterful work, it is the standard in its field, and one every pastor, student and teacher should have on the shelf.

The Power of God unto Salvation by B.B. Warfield is the 100th anniversary edition of this rare volume of his sermons. Last published in 1930 it also has a very rare appendix with hymns and religious verse written by Warfield.

Christ in Song: Hymns of Immanuel from All Ages is a remarkable volume compiled by Philip Schaff best known for his "History of the Christian Church." In this volume Schaff has gathered the greatest hymns beginning in the early centuries. Of this rare volume Charles Hodge of Princeton said, *After all, apart from the Bible, the best antidote to all these false theories of the person and work of Christ, is such a book as Dr. Schaff's 'CHRIST IN SONG.'*

First Things by Gardiner Spring is a two volume set that addresses the foundation upon which all life is built, as recorded in the opening chapters of Genesis. Today these chapters are challenged even in so-called evangelical churches and seminaries, but Spring takes us back with absolute assurance that we are reading genuine history. Every page is filled with pure spiritual gold.

The Church Member's Guide by John Angell James was once the most popular book in both the UK and the USA for instructing Christian's in their privileges and responsibilities as members of the body of Christ. It would be a great tool for those who teach New Member's Classes, or Discipleship Training classes, and all seeking to serve in the Church of Jesus Christ.

The Life and Sermons of Dr. Ichabod Spencer is a three volume set that introduces the life and sermons of the author of the remarkable volumes called *A Pastor's Sketches*. The First Volume contains a very helpful sketch of the life of Dr. Spencer written by a dear friend, as well as 20 examples of Spencer's preaching called Practical/Experimental Sermons. Volume Two contains 35 Doctrinal Sermons, and Volume Three has 26 Sacramental Discourses delivered at the Lord's Table. A feast awaits all who love Christ.

The Young Lady's Guide by Harvey Newcomb is a manual intended to train young ladies in the harmonious development of Christian character. Newcomb wrote over 170 volumes in his lifetime, but this was considered the very best. The perfect companion for Ryle's *Thoughts for Young Men*.

The Shorter Catechism Illustrated by John Whitecross is a precious volume for all who love the Shorter Catechism, and desire to explain its riches to the next generation. First published in 1828, this edition is the 1968 Banner of Truth edition. Biography and church history fill every page.

Call us toll free at **1-877-666-9469**
E-mail us at **sgcb@charter.net**
Visit us on the web at **solid-ground-books.com**

Printed in the United States
34843LVS00001B/1-18